Early Childhood
Qualitative Research

Changing Images of Early Childhood

Series Editor: Nicola Yelland

Early Childhood Qualitative Research

Edited by J. Amos Hatch

Routledge
Taylor & Francis Group
New York   London

Routledge is an imprint of the
Taylor & Francis Group, an informa business

Routledge
Taylor & Francis Group
270 Madison Avenue
New York, NY 10016

Routledge
Taylor & Francis Group
2 Park Square
Milton Park, Abingdon
Oxon OX14 4RN

© 2007 by Taylor & Francis Group, LLC
Routledge is an imprint of Taylor & Francis Group, an Informa business

Printed in the United States of America on acid-free paper
10 9 8 7 6 5 4 3 2 1

International Standard Book Number-10: 0-415-95341-3 (Softcover) 0-415-95472-X (Hardcover)
International Standard Book Number-13: 978-0-415-95341-2 (Softcover) 978-0-415-95472-3 (Hardcover)

Library of Congress Cataloging-in-Publication Data

Early childhood qualitative research / edited by J. Amos Hatch.
        p. cm. -- (Changing images of early childhood)
    ISBN 0-415-95340-5 (hardback) -- ISBN 0-415-95341-3 (pbk.)
    1. Early childhood education--Research. 2. Child development--Research. I. Hatch, J. Amos. II. Title. III. Series.

    LB1139.23.E2743 2006
    372.2107'2--dc22   2006014051

Visit the Taylor & Francis Web site at
http://www.taylorandfrancis.com

and the Routledge Web site at
http://www.routledge-ny.com

For Sally

Contents

Series Editor's Introduction

The terrain of educational research has been significantly remodeled since the new millennium emerged. Conservative forces have constructed and implemented an agenda that attempts to reduce educational outcomes to the minutiae of observable outcomes that can be demonstrated in simple tasks that require routine responses rather than consider the educational experience as engagement with people and ideas. What counts as evidence for effective practices for teaching has been brought into question because those in, and aligned with, positions of power have determined that what counts are specifically observable phenomena that are universal and unvarying. The paradox that is education at this point in time, reflects a confusion about the kind of citizens we want to help to mature in the 21st century against a desire to have individuals perform specific tasks that a few consider to be universal indicators of a being a successful student at any given point in time. The former context is complex and messy while the latter is contained and specific. The former requires research that attempts to explore the nature of our existence and challenges our belief systems while the latter reduces performance to specified criteria with observable outcomes and derives generalizations that attempt to describe universal phenomenan that bear resemblance to a limited population of aggregated averages.

The book that Amos Hatch has compiled has come at a particularly relevant time. Hatch himself presents a compelling case for research that enables us to capture the richness of educational experiences as events that defy a reductionist conceptualization of behavior. The authors in this important collection stress the importance of conducting research that is rigorous and allows us to encounter the nuances that are part of our everyday lives. They do not reduce our experiences to the simple and trivial. Rather, they enable us to generate new understandings about those issues and dilemmas that underpin the work that we do every day. In foregrounding the issues under discussion here it becomes apparent that their examination gives voice to a new cohort of participants who have previously been considered as subjects to be studied, rather than as collaborators and agents of change in our shared and intersecting lives.

This book describes research in early childhood educational contexts that is rigorous and diverse. It encapsulates powerful notions of agency and asks questions that are of direct importance to teachers and children's lived experiences. In his powerful first and last chapters Hatch provides a context and rationale for quality early childhood research that is empirically based and relevant to the daily enactment of education for young children. The chapters by the authors that constitute the book live up to the high standards that Hatch has set and illustrate the ways in which we might engage with theory and practice as a profession.

The book enhances the series with its thoughtful interrogation of what constitutes quality research at a time when the conservative agenda has high-jacked the schooling and education debate and successfully infiltrated spaces of influence in order to maintain their belief system as curricula. The changing images of early childhood books challenge and confront educators with a wide range of topics. The compilation of chapters in this book has been carefully considered and highlights three aspects that make them significant. They reflect the *complex* nature of our lives in a postmodern world where issues around globalism and the multifaceted nature of our experiences are not easily resolved. Secondly, they *respect* the participants in the research by giving them voice. Finally, they provide us with *rich* descriptions of classrooms, teachers' experiences and decision making, and conversations around intricate sets of circumstances.

The books in this series were included because we thought that they would enable early childhood professionals to engage with contemporary ideas and practices from alternative perspectives than those that have been traditionally associated with the education of young children and their families. They provide opportunities to critique aspects of the field that many early childhood educators have accepted as being beyond question as well as act as catalysts for contemporary interrogations and investigations. The ideas contained in the books incorporate a wide range of theoretical perspectives that are particularly appropriate to life in the postmodern world. In this way this latest addition is vital since it provides a rationale, exemplars, and a discussion of complex issues and dilemmas that can act as a guide or springboard for those who want to interrogate early childhood education.

The contemporary field of early childhood is no longer solely influenced by the psychological perspective, despite the efforts of conservatives to reduce it to a set of observable behaviors. Early childhood education also benefits from the ideas that have emerged from other disciplines such as anthropology, cultural studies, sociology, and philosophy. This has enriched the capacity of early childhood educators to respond to the new demands of contemporary times with pedagogies and practices that are appropriate to the varying and changing needs and interests of young children and their families. The books in this series consider alternative theoretical perspectives and demonstrate their relevance to everyday practices and in doing so enable us to create learning environments that are underpinned by a respect for all, equity, and social justice. Amos Hatch and his collaborators have compiled a volume of major importance that will be relevant to all those who are considering doing research in the field.

Nicola Yelland
Victoria University, Melbourne

Introduction

J. AMOS HATCH

University of Tennessee

In 1995, I published an edited volume entitled *Qualitative Research in Early Childhood Settings*. The concluding paragraph of the introduction to that book noted that "'state-of-the-art' has a shorter and shorter shelf life in all aspects of our experience, including our own scholarship" (p. xvi). Although the research reports, reviews, and essays in the 1995 book have held up pretty well, changes in the early childhood and qualitative research fields prompted me to put together this entirely new "state-of-the-art" collection.

A variety of changes have had an impact on early childhood education and related disciplines over the past decade. The experience of being a child in the postmodern era is very different from what it was just one or two generations ago, and while many would argue that the mainstream has been dragging its feet, early childhood policy makers, researchers, and practitioners have been forced to respond. The knowledge base in early childhood studies has expanded, and perspectives that were previously on the fringes of the field have moved closer to the center. Accountability concerns have been pushed down into early years schooling, forcing everyone in the field to reconsider what counts as appropriate early childhood education. In addition, globalization and new patterns of immigration have created opportunities and challenges that require early childhood professionals at all levels to think and act in new ways.

Qualitative research and educational research in general have also changed over the past 10 or 12 years. As I argue in chapter 1, what appeared to be an acceptance of qualitative approaches has turned into an attempt to label any kind of inquiry that does not meet the standards of positivism as outside the realm of "scientifically based" research. The field of qualitative research increased its breadth and depth over the past decade, making a place for alternative ontologies and epistemologies and generating studies that moved understandings of social phenomena in school contexts to new levels. At the same time, those in positions of power (within academe and in the world at large) are currently doing all they can to reduce qualitative approaches to "less than normal" status. Since 1995, early childhood qualitative research has made great strides in opening itself to new qualitative paradigms. At the same time, it faces threats from neo-conservative forces that seek to limit what counts as knowledge to that which is generated under the "scientifically based" banner.

This book is designed to provide novice researchers, those who teach and mentor them, and more experienced scholars with a valuable resource for conceptualizing, doing, and evaluating early childhood qualitative research. The book locates early childhood qualitative research in the new millennium, provides descriptions of a variety of research methods, and discusses important issues related to doing early childhood qualitative research in the early 21st century. The book is divided into two sections that focus on "Qualitative Methodologies in Early Childhood Settings" and "Issues in Early Childhood Qualitative Research." Authors of methodology chapters were asked to also address issues specific to their approaches; and issues chapters' authors also wrote about methodological aspects of their work. Authors were invited to contribute chapters based on their track records of producing high-quality work, and they have all grounded their discussions in experiences with real studies. The book includes chapter authors from five continents, and this diversity improves the scope and credibility of its contents, given the global nature of research, early childhood education, and our world.

In chapter 1, "Back to Modernity? Early Childhood Qualitative Research in the 21st Century," I discuss the place of early childhood qualitative studies in the era of "scientifically based" research. I review the reemergence of positivist definitions of science, taking the position that it is part of a larger, politically driven movement away from postmodern thinking—in effect, an orchestrated attempt to go back to modernity. I recall the paradigm wars of the 1980s and '90s, arguing that the apparent rapprochement between quantitative and qualitative types was an illusion. The chapter presents examples of high-quality qualitative studies done during the past decade and contrasts those with studies of similar early childhood phenomena that have been undertaken within the paradigmatic assumptions of positivism. The chapter concludes with a call for resistance to the arbitrary standards of the scientifically based movement and for the production of early childhood qualitative studies that cannot be ignored.

Chapter 2 is entitled "Hermeneutic Text Analysis of Play: Exploring Meaningful Early Childhood Classroom Events." It is the first chapter in the section on Qualitative Methodologies in Early Childhood Settings, and it is authored by Stuart Reifel. Reifel describes hermeneutic text analysis and discusses its application in early childhood research, particularly in the study of children's play. He explores three different approaches to hermeneutic analysis, including his own studies of play, Vivian Paley's reflections on her kindergarten practice, and poststructuralist uses of text for critical exploration. He also identifies some of the challenges associated with hermeneutic text analysis.

"Using Digital Video in Field-Based Research With Children: A Primer" is the title of chapter 3. Daniel J. Walsh is the first author of this chapter, and his co-authors include Nesrin Bakir, Tony Byungho Lee, and Ya-hui Chung, along with Hugo Campuzano, Yu-ting Chen, Kayoun Chung, Yore Kedem,

Wei Liu, Yasin Ozturk, Soyoung Sung, Aysel Tufekci, and Noemi Waight, all of whom were involved with Walsh in a digital video seminar at the University of Illinois at Urbana-Champaign. The chapter aims to provide practical guidance to those interested in applying the advantages of digital technology to field-based studies in early childhood settings. Noting possibilities and challenges, the authors build a solid foundation for generating data, constructing data records, and analyzing data via digital video.

Chapter 4, "The Potential of Focus Groups to Inform Early Childhood Policy and Practice," is written by Sharon Ryan and Carrie Lobman. The chapter gives readers a clear description of ways to effectively utilize focus group strategies to generate research findings that have the potential to influence policy and practice in early childhood education. Using examples from their own research, Ryan and Lobman provide step-by-step procedures for designing focus group studies, facilitating focus groups, and analyzing focus group data. Noting that qualitative research often has difficulty being recognized as useful to policy types, the authors include an extensive discussion of the possibilities of focus group work for informing those who operate in the early childhood policy arena.

Janice A. Jipson's "Wanderings: Doing Historical Research in Early Childhood Education" is chapter 5. This essay is presented in the form of three interwoven narratives that recount Jipson's experience preparing and writing up a history of Elizabeth Peabody, founder of the American kindergarten. One narrative is an artfully written chronology of Jipson's own research journey; a second narrative, told mostly in footnotes, tells the story of Peabody's life in 19th-century New England; and the third tracks Jipson's intellectual processes as she considers methodological and ethical issues related to doing historical research in early childhood education.

Chapter 6, by Frances O'Connell Rust, is entitled "Action Research in Early Childhood Contexts." The chapter addresses action research as a kind of practitioner research and explores qualitative data collection and analysis within the contexts of early childhood teachers studying life in their classrooms and schools. Rust lays out action research processes she has used with her teacher education students and with practicing early childhood teachers, providing examples from her own work and that of others who have produced high-quality qualitative action research projects.

Chapter 7, "Critical Pedagogy and Qualitative Inquiry: Lessons From Working With Refugee Families," is written by Elizabeth P. Quintero. In her chapter, Quintero describes how she utilizes critical theory, critical pedagogy, and critical literacy along with qualitative research methodologies in her courses with graduate students (from the United States) who are working with refugee families in the United Kingdom. After presenting her rationale for guiding students to take a critical stance, Quintero details how the mix of qualitative research approaches, critical epistemologies, and direct experience plays out in research projects that examine the lives of young children and their families who are refugees living in East London.

Chapter 8, the first chapter in the section on Issues in Early Childhood Qualitative Research, is "Surviving a Methodological Crisis: Strategies for Salvaging Your Classroom-Based Research When Things Go Wrong in the Field" by Lisa S. Goldstein. Goldstein draws directly from her recent experience doing a study of U.S. kindergarten teachers' perspectives on managing the complex and often contradictory circumstances of their work lives. Using data from her study, she details two methodological crises that threatened the integrity of her research project. She then describes how these crises were resolved, concluding with a set of strategies for addressing crises in early childhood qualitative research.

Susan Grieshaber takes on another set of difficulties related to early childhood qualitative research in chapter 9, "Never Certain: Research Predicaments in the Everyday World of Schools." Grieshaber reflects on the experience of doing two school-based studies in primary classrooms in Australia, detailing predicaments related to epistemological decision making, gatekeeping, researcher–teacher relationships, and researcher effects in classrooms. Grieshaber tells the story of how she and her co-researchers handled these predicaments and concludes with her own suggestions for early childhood classroom researchers.

Also based in Australia, Glenda MacNaughton, Kylie Smith, and Karina Davis are the authors of chapter 10, "Researching With Children: The Challenges and Possibilities for Building 'Child-Friendly' Research." Based in their research with the Centre for Equity and Innovation in Early Childhood at the University of Melbourne, these authors explore the possibility of framing qualitative research in "child-friendly" ways. They seek to reconceptualize children's participation through a children's rights perspective, in effect disrupting the knowledge–power dynamics that dominate researcher–child relations at present. From their own work, they offer possibilities for giving children opportunities to be active participants in the design and implementation of research that involves them directly.

In chapter 11, Beth Blue Swadener and Kagendo Mutua discuss important issues related to "Decolonizing Research in Cross-Cultural Contexts." Drawing on their experiences doing qualitative research in cross-cultural settings and the work of indigenous scholars from around the globe, Swadener and Mutua describe possibilities for troubling traditional research practices in early childhood and special education. They define decolonizing research in relation to postcolonial scholarship, provide narratives of their own journeys as decolonizing researchers, and present examples of their experiences applying decolonizing principles to their qualitative research.

Chapter 12 is entitled "Who Chooses What Research Methodology?" The author, Jeanette Rhedding-Jones, organizes a discussion of methodological decision making around the experiences of her advanced students in a

Norwegian early childhood graduate program. Rhedding-Jones makes a distinction between methods and methodologies, discusses a variety of research strategies, and describes processes for making research decisions. The chapter relates Rhedding-Jones's analysis of data from seven early childhood graduate students concerning methodological decisions they have made or are making as part of their advanced studies.

In the concluding chapter, I address an issue that is of great interest to producers and consumers of early childhood qualitative research: "Assessing the Quality of Early Childhood Qualitative Research." The chapter aims to provide a set of criteria that can be used to make judgments about the merits of qualitative research that has already been produced and to make sound decisions as qualitative projects are planned and carried out. A set of 10 questions is presented along with explanations for why the questions address important issues in qualitative inquiry and discussions of ways to answer the questions successfully.

I am confident that those who do and those who aspire to do early childhood qualitative research will find much to value in this collection. Neither every methodology nor every issue could possibly be addressed in one volume, but the authors have generated chapters that fairly represent cutting-edge thinking in a scholarly area that continues to change. Each chapter includes extensive citations to important work in a variety of areas that are important to the disciplines of early childhood education and qualitative research. And, each author has located his or her ideas within a framework of experience and research practice that can be instructive to readers at all levels of expertise and experience.

I am grateful for the opportunity to take up this project in the new millennium, and I appreciate the efforts of my colleagues who supported me, especially those who wrote chapters. Authors worked under tight deadlines and were always responsive and civil, even when I asked for third and fourth revisions. Of course, there is no book without their effort and generosity. I also want to thank Nicola Yelland for her help in placing the book in a series that I admire with a publisher I respect. Finally, I want to remember Sally Lubeck, to whom this book is dedicated. I like to think Sally would have agreed to do a chapter (as she did in the 1995 collection) if she were still with us. Anyone who knows anything about early childhood qualitative research knows how important Sally's contributions remain. Anyone who knew Sally knows how much she is missed.

Reference

Hatch, J. A. (Ed.). (1995). *Qualitative research in early childhood settings*. Westport, CT: Praeger.

1
Back to Modernity?
Early Childhood Qualitative Research in the 21st Century

J. AMOS HATCH

University of Tennessee

The purpose of this chapter is to explore the place of early childhood qualitative research in the sociopolitical contexts of the early 21st century. With the evolvement of efforts by conservative forces in the United States to define certain kinds of research as scientific and to label other forms of inquiry as something inferior, many researchers (and practitioners) are concerned about the future of research approaches that do not meet the narrow criteria being raised as the norm. In this chapter, I review the reemergence of the scientifically based standard, arguing that it is evidence of a rejection of postmodern thought and an attempt to return to modern ways of thinking about knowledge, science, and progress. I revisit the paradigm wars that characterized discussions of educational research during the 1980s and '90s, making the case that the apparent détente between quantitative and qualitative researchers was an illusion. Quantitative and qualitative research approaches are grounded in fundamentally different ontological and epistemological assumptions and are therefore based in different research paradigms. I take the position that the paradigm wars are not over and that the positivist paradigm has taken the high ground as part of a larger conservative attack on postmodern thinking. The chapter presents examples of early childhood qualitative research that demonstrate the usefulness of inquiry done within qualitative research paradigms and contrasts those with "scientifically based" approaches to the study of similar phenomena. I conclude the chapter with a call for resistance tempered with patience. Postmodernity will not go away just because conservative political leaders and scholars have risen to positions of power. The best argument for the efficacy of qualitative studies in early childhood is the generation of high-quality qualitative work that reveals the inadequacies of a narrow definition of "scientifically based" approaches.

Scientifically Based Knowledge and the (Re)Turn to Modernity

The neo-conservative political agenda of the early 21st century includes a concerted effort to control schools and what goes on in classrooms, from pre-kindergarten through graduate school (Bracey, 2003). A strategic feature of this effort has been to take charge of defining what constitutes acceptable research on schools and schooling, then mandating that only findings coming from research that meets the definition of those in power can be applied to classrooms funded by government agencies (Davis, 2003; Lather, 2004; Torff, 2004). By defining scientifically based knowledge as that and only that which has been generated based on studies done in the positivist tradition, the political right has effectively elevated a certain kind of inquiry to the status of "real science" and made it possible to dictate policy and pedagogy for schools based on its own narrow definition of scientifically based research.

The visible beginnings of an active attempt to define educational research as scientifically based (or not) can be traced to the work of the National Reading Panel (NRP) formed by the National Institute of Child Health and Human Development. The panel was charged by the United States Congress to review and assess the research on literacy instruction in order to determine the most effective methods for teaching children to read. The panel began by limiting the studies it would consider in its review to those that met standards for research established in experimental psychology and medicine, that is, those designed to assess the effectiveness of "behaviorally based interventions, medications, or medical procedures" (National Reading Panel, 2000, p. 5). Application of the positivist epistemological assumptions of the medical model meant that a preponderance of reading research was ignored because it could not meet the standard (Cunningham, 2002). What remained has been roundly criticized for furthering the political right's efforts to emphasize circumscribed approaches to reading instruction (e.g., Allington, 2002, 2005; Garan, 2005; Krashen, 2005). What is more troublesome to me is that the NRP's position on evidence-based research has been extended to other federally sponsored initiatives, most notably the No Child Left Behind (NCLB) legislation that (at this writing) drives educational policy and practice in the U. S.

The complex education reform plan spelled out in NCLB is rooted in the concept of scientifically based research. Someone who bothered to count found 70 places where the exact term "scientifically based" was used and over 100 places where variations on the term are found in the 670-page law (Giangreco & Taylor, 2003). The rationale for insisting on the use of only scientifically based research is that most educational research done in the past is vapid, it lacks rigor, and it serves to perpetuate vapid instructional approaches that lack rigor in vapid schools that lack rigor. What is needed, it is claimed, are studies that reflect the rigorous research principles of medicine or experimental psychology. The U.S. Department of Education Web site includes sections devoted to extolling the virtues of scientifically based research. In one of these sections, Reyna (n.d.) lays out the connections between the medical research model and what has been legislated for educational researchers:

> The bottom line here is these same rules about what works and how to make inferences about what works, they are exactly the same for educational practice as they would be for medical practice. Same rules, exactly the same logic, whether you are talking about a treatment for cancer or whether you're talking about an intervention to help children learn. (p. 3)

Redefining scientific research in education became a driving force behind neo-conservative attempts to reform the educational landscape of the United States. The U.S. Department of Education invited the National Research Council to take up the issue, and their conclusions, summarized in *Scientific Research in Education* (National Research Council, 2002), continued the pattern of relying on positivist epistemological principles when deciding what constitutes science in education (Erickson, 2005; Erickson & Gutierrez, 2002; Gee, 2005; Moss, 2005; St. Pierre, 2002).

Across the board, the "science" in scientifically based research has been narrowly defined as that which conforms to the assumptions and methods of the positivist research tradition (Cunningham, 2002). Positivists believe that reality exists and is driven by natural laws that are fixed, unchanging, and inflexible. They assume an objective universe that has order independent of human perceptions. Researchers and the objects of their research are assumed to be mutually independent. The product of positivist research is verifiable knowledge in the form of facts and laws. Prediction is the ultimate aim of positivist science—if conditions are controlled, positivist researchers can predict what will happen when certain changes are introduced (Denzin & Lincoln, 1994; Hatch, 2002).

Positivist science is one of the great inventions of modernity. The idea that absolute truth could be uncovered by applying the technology of experimental research changed the ways we think about the world and our place in it. If the truth is knowable, then continuous progress only depends on our ability to reveal that truth, so science is reified as *the* legitimate source for knowledge, and science becomes the engine of progress (Elkind, 1994; Seidman, 1994).

Postmodern thinkers have deconstructed the illusion of progress and the façade of scientific objectivity. They have exposed the inseparable connections between knowledge and power and opened the door to alternative ways of thinking about and doing research. New research paradigms based on different ontological and epistemological assumptions have risen and been recognized as legitimate (Hatch, 2002). During the 1980s and '90s, the great paradigm wars raged at meetings of education research organizations and in the pages of *Educational Researcher* and other important journals. Many of us qualitative research types thought that, although we never really reached the stage of "normal science" (Kuhn, 1970), we were at least accepted as legitimate educational researchers. If the conservative right has its way, and they seem to be doing pretty well near the middle of the first decade of the 21st century, the return to positivism means that research done within any worldview other than the positivist paradigm is not "scientifically based." Cunningham's (2002) critique of the National Reading Panel's capitulation to positivist assumptions should serve as a warning to all educational researchers:

> Like all positivism, the Panel's work reveals a desire for certainty and a willingness to engage in reductionism to achieve it. . . . Practicing scientists of reading should be embarrassed by the simplistic, old-fashioned, and generally discredited verificationism of the National Reading Panel. (p. 56)

I see this return to positivist research as part of a larger movement *back to modernity*. I believe the agenda of the conservative right to be an active, well-orchestrated offensive designed to return the world to the modern comfort of the 1950s. Families will be normal again—a married man and woman with children conceived in wedlock will be the optimum condition. The USA will be a genuine superpower again—other nations will do as we say or suffer our wrath. Americans will be Americans again—those who look, talk, or act differently will be denied, dismissed, or detained. Schools will be standardized—those who know what's best for children will hold teachers accountable for delivering the prescribed goods or else. And, knowledge production will be scientifically based—alternative ways of knowing will be eliminated or marginalized.

Postmodern ideas are tantamount to blasphemy to the zealots who have so much power at the time of this writing. I believe the yen to return to the unquestioned authority of modern discourses drives the political agenda of neo-conservatives in the United States. Three examples of postmodern notions and contemporary conservative reactions to them will help make my case. Postmodern thinkers have deconstructed the modern concept of universal truth, offering in its place the notion of local, conditional, and temporary truths (Sarap, 1993; Hatch, 2000). Neo-conservatives see the rejection of absolute truth as an abomination. In the same ways that natural laws are seen as universal, so are moral laws also thought to be fixed, unchanging, and inflexible. Their approach to issues related to abortion is a good example: abortion is wrong for anyone, at any time, under any circumstance; so we will pack the courts and change the Constitution to ensure that everyone abides by this unquestionable truth.

The promise of progress is another modern discourse that has been discredited by the postmodern critique (Elkind, 1994). Modernity itself depended on the assumption that the human condition was constantly improving because of advances in all realms of endeavor, from parenting to atomic science. By challenging the Western world's taken-for-granted belief in continuous progress, postmodernists made it possible to question the policies and practices of individuals and institutions in terms of the consequences of implementing those policies and practices rather than their claims to "progress." The neo-conservatives have to defend progress as a viable goal; otherwise, invading countries with inferior forms of government or destroying natural habitats in order to drill for oil would be hard to justify.

Uniformity is a third element of modern thought that is under serious scrutiny within the postmodern critique. Postmodern thinkers' expectation that diversity is inevitable and invaluable rubs social conservatives the wrong way. Families that look different from the traditional nuclear family of the 1950s are the postmodern norm by far (Elkind, 1994), and everyone recognizes that the U.S. is becoming more demographically diverse by the day (Washington & Andrews, 1998). Still, conservative forces continue to promulgate policy initiatives that reward traditional family structures and punish those whose family values don't align, and they attempt to legislate cultural uniformity by requiring English-only teaching in schools and building fences along U.S. borders.

Again, I see the push to constrict knowledge production by imposing narrow definitions of scientifically based research as one piece of a larger effort to return to the comfort of modernity. Later in this chapter I build a case for the folly of such an attempt by arguing for the unique contributions of early childhood qualitative research and by exposing some of the weaknesses of studies purported to be scientifically based. I will next briefly revisit the paradigm wars of the past two decades, arguing that the apparent rapprochement between qualitative and quantitative researchers was a façade that has recently been stripped away.

From Disdain to Détente and Back

Over 20 years ago, I used a biological metaphor to show that qualitative researchers ("smooshes") and quantitative researchers ("quantoids") were from different species and, therefore, could not interbreed (Hatch, 1985). I built my argument on Kuhn's (1970) notion of scientific paradigms. Kuhn's premise was that schools of scientific thought reach the status of paradigms when they have firm answers to the following questions: What are the fundamental entities of which the universe is composed? How do these interact with each other and with the senses? What questions can legitimately be asked about such entities and what techniques employed in seeking solutions? Answers to these questions reveal different ontological and epistemological assumptions that form the basis for different and competing belief systems about how the world is ordered (or not), what we may know, and how we may know it. Kuhn argued that once you are thinking inside the belief system of your paradigm, logic is necessarily circular—that is, it makes sense only to those who share your metaphysical assumptions.

In 1985, I portrayed quantoids and smooshes as competing paradigmatic species that could not comfortably join together as simply different forms of educational research. Following Kuhn, I noted the contrasting assumptions at the core of what I then labeled positivist and constructivist paradigms and made the case that rapprochement was impossible—if you adopted the world-view of the quantoids, then the logic of the smooshes made no sense, and vice versa. But almost no one agreed that quantitative and qualitative paradigms were mutually exclusive. The overwhelming sentiment of the day favored détente between educational researchers of different stripes (Rist, 1977). There seemed to be room for differences, and much of the research community seemed to accept the idea that findings generated from different scholarly approaches had value and deserved respect. I say "seemed" because the current push to elevate positivist approaches to the status of "normal science" and to relegate other approaches to the less-than-normal category exposes the thin veneer of acceptance that is summarily being stripped away.

As will be evident below, I have enlarged my conceptualization to include four different qualitative paradigms (Hatch, 2002). Each has its own internal integrity and each stands in contrast to the other qualitative paradigms and to the positivist paradigm. Research generated within the assumptions of none of these qualitative paradigms would qualify as "scientifically based." The apparent acceptance of alternative forms of scientific inquiry has been legislated away by forces on the political right and welcomed by those who stand to profit from the reemergence of the positivist paradigm. The disdain that characterized early reactions to qualitative research in education settings 30 years ago has been raised to the level of policy in the early 21st century. Kuhn's (1970) project was to trace the history of scientific revolutions, the rise and fall of competing scientific paradigms. According to his thesis, relevant scientific communities made the determination of what constituted normal science. But the battleground has shifted. In the postmodern world that emerged over the past few decades, multiple ways of thinking about and doing scholarly inquiry were generally seen as possible and valuable. What changed is that the relevant community's apparent acceptance of these alternative approaches was trumped by those in power, with the support of those in the research community who relished the opportunity to reestablish quantoids as kings of the educational research mountain.

Studies in Contrast

The next part of the chapter is an attempt to show what is lost when different types of early childhood qualitative work are devalued in favor of positivist work related to the same topic. In my 2002 qualitative methods book, I identify four qualitative research paradigms based on different sets of assumptions about how the world is ordered and how we may come to understand it. I labeled those qualitative paradigms: postpositivist, constructivist, critical/feminist, and poststructuralist. Very briefly, postpositivists believe that while there is inherent order in the universe, that order can never be known completely; therefore, reality can be approximated but never fully apprehended. Grounded theory (Glaser & Strauss, 1967) is a prominent example of a postpositivist approach. Constructivists assume that absolute realities are unknowable, and the objects of inquiry ought to be individual perspectives that are taken to be constructions of reality. Naturalistic inquiry (Lincoln & Guba, 1985) is an application of constructivist assumptions. The critical/feminist paradigm is based on the assumption that the material world is made up of historically situated structures that are perceived to be real, and their perceived realness leads to differential treatment based on race, gender, and social class. Critical/feminist qualitative researchers usually engage in research that is openly political and intentionally transformative in nature (Carr, 1995). Poststructuralists argue that order is created in the minds of individuals in an attempt to give meaning to an inherently meaningless existence; thus, there are multiple realities, each with its own claims to coherence, and none can be logically privileged over another. Poststructuralist researchers often approach their work as deconstructionists after Derrida (1981), as genealogists following Foucault (1980), or as the producers of multi-vocal texts (Tobin, Wu, & Davidson, 1989).

A colleague and I recently completed a review of early childhood qualitative research published over the past decade (Hatch & Barclay-McLaughlin, 2006). We organized our review based on the four qualitative paradigms outlined above, and I have selected high-quality studies from that review as examples for this chapter. Dyson's (2003) postpositivist study of children's literacy development in the context of school and popular culture is contrasted with "scientific" research on literacy learning. Lubeck and Post's (2000) constructivist examination of local meanings and issues in Head Start is contrasted with current approaches to evaluating Head Start effectiveness. Barclay-McLaughlin's critical/feminist inquiry describing the decline of communal systems in neighborhoods characterized by poverty is contrasted with ways positivist researchers deal with poverty in their work. And Tobin's (2000) poststructuralist analysis of how children think and talk about media representations of violence, race, gender, and class will be compared with "cause and effect" approaches to studying media's influence on young children. The qualitative examples are used to argue the case that carefully done qualitative studies provide understandings and insights that are impossible to find in work that fits current criteria for scientifically based research.

Dyson's (2003) study details how literacy development is imbedded in the complex social worlds of two 6-year-old girls and a small circle of friends (the "brothers and sisters") in an urban K–5 school. Dyson's work examines the interplay of children's actions as writers, peers, community members, and consumers of popular culture. Her data were collected through participant observation in classrooms and on playgrounds; formal and informal interviews with children, teachers, parents, and community members; artifact collection, especially samples of children's writing; audio recording of children's talk, especially during peer discussion sessions; and analyses of commercial media referred to by children. Dyson focused on children's literacy development in the contexts of child and school cultures and the broader influences of popular media. She selected particular children in a particular primary school setting and carefully documented their writing accomplishments within the complexities of their everyday worlds. Dyson explored the ways popular culture was expressed in children's communicative practices, the ways nonacademic practices and materials were utilized by children in school literacy activities (and vice versa), and the consequences of reconceptualizing nonacademic material for individual and classroom learning. Dyson's work seeks to place childhoods themselves and children's localized symbols and practices at the center of literacy research. She uses the voices of children throughout her report to illustrate the connections between popular culture and literacy learning in school. Dyson takes the reader into the worlds in which literacy learning happens in a real school. I will contrast her approach to a study of literacy learning that was part of the National Reading Panel synthesis.

I was amazed when I went to the National Reading Panel's Web site and pulled down the list of research reports that the panel counted as worthy of being included in their analysis. Their goal was to synthesize what "science" had to tell us about how to teach children to read. As I looked through their lists for a study that seemed to be addressing the same phenomena as Dyson, I was surprised at what made the cut. In order to meet the criteria for experimental control, many of these studies were so tightly focused that their findings seemed pointless.

The study I picked is not pointless, but it shows the differences in knowledge produced in comparison with the Dyson study of similar kids in similar settings. This study divided second grade children into two groups. All the students were given a reading comprehension test, and those scoring at or above the 25th percentile participated in the study. One group received instruction in whole language classrooms and the other in phonics and skill-based classrooms. At the end of the second grade year, three kinds of word recognition tasks were given to all the students. Although one measure showed a significant difference that favored the whole language classrooms, there were no other significant differences in word recognition between the two instructional practices. The authors concluded that for these students, instructional approach had little effect on word recognition.

If you buy into the positivist assumption that the world can be known by breaking it down into its components, studying those components independently, then putting them back together, this study may be valuable. In fact, that there were no significant differences in word recognition across the classes may be seen as a victory for whole language advocates. But consider how little we know: Scores on two out of three instruments purported to measure word recognition ability were virtually the same for children who had a year of whole language or phonics and skills-based instruction. And think about how much we assume: Scores on a comprehension test are assumed to provide a valid basis for matching experimental and control groups. Word recognition is assumed to be a distinct and measurable component of reading. Instructional practices are assumed to cause changes in word recognition performance. Whole language and phonics and skills-based classrooms are assumed to be distinct and mutually independent. The tasks given at the end of the treatments are assumed to measure word recognition. What if just one of these assumptions turns out to be wrong?

This was judged to be a scientifically based study by the National Reading Panel, and I am willing to acknowledge that if you are standing inside the positivist paradigm, this may be a valuable contribution to the knowledge base in reading. But, is the Dyson study inferior and unworthy of inclusion in attempts to understand how literacy is acquired in early childhood classrooms? The point I am trying to make by highlighting the four qualitative studies in this chapter is that too much is lost when one way of thinking about and doing research is raised to the status of science, while excluding other legitimate, rigorous, empirical research approaches.

Lubeck and Post (2000) describe an alternative approach to thinking about research and program improvement in Head Start. These scholars designed a constructivist research and program improvement project alongside Head Start teachers. The researchers made careful records of the evolvement of a community of practice in a Head Start program over a 2-year period. Meetings were recorded and tapes transcribed, observers acted as active participants in classrooms, and formal and informal interviews were conducted with teachers and administrators. Lubeck and Post documented how the program improvement efforts of Head Start took shape in the light of community needs and resources, local cultural understandings, and established institutional practices. Researchers and teachers developed a "mutual mentoring project" (p. 41) that involved collaboration between university and Head Start educators and among the teachers themselves. University personnel worked in classrooms as assistants to assistants, teachers visited each other's classrooms, and university and Head Start educators met together to share practical teaching approaches. Lubeck and Post's analysis revealed the processes through which teachers constructed knowledge together—"to think in conjunction with others, to play off, add, invert, transform, and link information" (p. 53). They presented their study as an example of what is possible when subjective experiences in real settings, group learning dynamics, and an emphasis on local and contextualized meanings are brought to the foreground. Current government efforts to bring accountability to Head Start program evaluation will be used as a counterpoint to Lubeck and Post's research.

In 2003, the Bush administration implemented the Head Start National Reporting System (NRS), which requires every 4-year-old in the Head Start program to be tested twice each year. At the beginning and end of the year, children are given standardized achievement tests in Comprehension of Spoken English, Vocabulary, Letter Naming, and Early Math. According to the government's Head Start Web site, the tests are designed to strengthen Head Start effectiveness by providing child outcome data that can be used to supplement local program self-assessment efforts and results, plan future training and technical assistance efforts, and inform program monitoring reviews (Head Start Bureau, 2003). Critics argue that the NRS is nothing more than high-stakes testing shoved down into early childhood programs (e.g., Meisels & Atkins-Burnett, 2004), but the expressed goals of NRS are similar in spirit to those of Lubeck and Post in terms of improving the delivery of services to Head Start children. What is vastly different are the ways that data are used to accomplish those ends.

NRS data are "scientific" in the sense that they are collected on large groups of individuals using valid measurement instruments administered in a standardized manner. Trained test administrators present the exact items in exactly the same ways to every eligible child in every Head Start program. Scores from five subtests are reported so that statistical analyses can be used to assess annual effectiveness by program, region, subtest, and so on. The model suggests that once areas of weakness are exposed, programs will be informed, and training and technical assistance designed to eliminate those weaknesses will be forthcoming. So the data are test scores, and the consequences of low scores are likely to include the provision of training focused on giving teachers tools for improving their scores.

Lubeck and Post take a completely different approach to data collection and program improvement. Their constructivist paradigmatic assumptions lead them to work side by side with Head Start teachers and assistants in order to co-construct a shared understanding of ways to improve the experiences of children and families in a single Head Start program. Their data, gathered over a 2-year period, were rich, varied, and contextualized. Their findings were nuanced, complex, and deeply imbedded in the local understandings of their participants. The program improvement dimension was impossible to distinguish from the research elements of the project, so participants on both sides became engaged in a concentrated effort to get better at what they were doing. Again, even if I acknowledge the potential value of an accountability system based on positivist principles, I have to ask why qualitative studies such as the one Lubeck and Post produced are seen to be outside the realm of scientifically based research and therefore not to be considered as decisions are made concerning Head Start or other governmentally funded activities.

Barclay-McLaughlin (2000) conducted a critical/feminist study in one of the largest public housing developments in the United States. The research was an attempt to increase understandings of poverty and its influence on parenting and child development. Data from this study were collected primarily through interviews in the homes of twenty-five residents of this urban neighborhood. Participants in the study were parents recruited from an early intervention program serving children from the prenatal stage of development through age 5 and their families. Each informant was interviewed at least twice for approximately 90 minutes per session using a set of guiding questions. Themes that emerged from the analysis framed what participants described as a growing deterioration of the neighborhood. Analysis revealed a pattern of decline of a communal system of support that no longer served as a resource for sustaining a healthy existence for children and their families. Residents who once shared so much in common began to withdraw from each other and from opportunities to provide traditional support, guidance, direction, and tangible resources for children. Increasingly, children were left alone to face challenging periods and situations and to form and pursue their goals without adequate guidance. The stories shared showed how families once created a viable community of neighbors who socialized together, parented each other's children, and provided role models, resources, and support for each other's aspirations. But their stories also showed how the community support residents once cherished may never be revived, given the pervasive influences of contemporary urban poverty. The way poverty is represented in most statistically driven studies is a stark contrast to Barclay-McLaughlin's rich description.

Because they fairly represent what's being published in terms of early childhood research and because they were sitting on a shelf in my office, I examined the articles in three issues of the 2004 volume of *Early Childhood Research Quarterly*. Among the 22 articles I counted as reports of research, one was a qualitative study and one other utilized mixed methods. I searched each article that was presented as a research report based on some kind of quantitative data analysis in an effort to determine if and how considerations of poverty were taken into account. My quick analysis of this small selection of articles revealed three basic patterns in the ways poverty was represented.

In some research reports, authors used family income ranges as part of other demographic information to describe their research samples. These income data were usually taken from self-reports by adult research subjects or from official records collected by school personnel. In this type of study, either homogeneous or heterogeneous groups of subjects were identified, and the income data were only used, along with other factors, to describe the sample.

Another common pattern was to use eligibility for federally or state-funded projects targeted to young children and families in poverty as a way to provide boundaries for the study. These were studies of Head Start programs or "low socioeconomic status schools" that were intentionally limited in their scope to examining factors within the context of schools and communities characterized by poverty. Eligibility for Head Start, identification as Title I school zones, qualification for state-subsidized preschools, and percentages of families eligible for free or reduced lunch were the typical criteria for inclusion in such studies. In these studies, poverty was taken as a given, so other factors were treated as variables and findings were specific to settings with similarly depressed economic circumstances.

A third way poverty was represented in the studies examined was to utilize a variety of means for quantifying socioeconomic status so that such measures could be used as variables in complex statistical analyses. In these studies, ratios were often computed based on subjects' self-reports of income compared to government generated definitions of poverty thresholds, or "risk indexes" were calculated using factors such as income, education levels, and employment. The ratios or index scores were then treated as "family selection covariates" or "background variables" in multivariate multiple regressions or other analyses designed to show relationships among complex sets of factors.

I respect the editors of *Early Childhood Research Quarterly* and the authors whose work I examined. The emphasis of the journal makes sense within the current politics of science outlined above, and the ways poverty was represented make sense within the paradigmatic assumptions of the research that was published. What makes no sense to me is that the voices of individuals who live poverty every day are effectively silenced when qualitative studies such as Barclay-McLaughlin's are marginalized to less-than-normal status because they do not meet the arbitrary standards of scientifically based research. It is not absurd to ask what is lost, hidden, or missing when the complex lives of individuals at the bottom of the socioeconomic hierarchy are reduced to factors, ratios, or covariates. Surely, well-planned, carefully executed, and artfully written qualitative studies of social phenomena such as poverty have an important place in the knowledge base of early childhood education.

Tobin's (2000) poststructuralist study of how children think and talk about media representations of violence, gender, race, and class was conducted in an elementary school in Hawaii. Tobin and his research associates utilized focus group data collection strategies to generate children's talk about movies. Tobin's approach was to show film clips to groups of children, then record their conversations, thus producing multi-vocal texts from which an analysis of how children understand popular media could be made. Thirty-two focus groups were conducted, during which a video clip of the Disney movie, *Swiss*

Family Robinson, was shown. Children were videotaped while they viewed the clip and throughout the group interviews that followed. Utilizing analysis frameworks adapted from literary and poststructural critique, Tobin revealed children's ways of thinking about how gender, race, colonialism, and class were represented in media. Instead of focusing on data excerpts that made sense, Tobin's approach was to look closely at moments in transcripts that were "odd, incoherent, and uncanny" (p. 138). His interpretive readings of these "richly ambiguous texts" (p. 139) led him to conclude that children are not the unwitting victims of media effects that they are usually portrayed to be. Children are capable of making insightful, sometimes resistant, interpretations. Tobin noted that different children bring different understandings to their interpretations of media messages and concluded that those differences are connected to local meanings that are constructed in local community discourses and counterdiscourses. A research synthesis published by the office of the Surgeon General of the United States will be contrasted with Tobin's work.

Youth Violence: A Report of the Surgeon General (2001) is a summary of research on many aspects of youth violence and features a chapter entitled "Violence in the Media and Its Effects on Youth Violence." Experimental studies that examined whether children exposed to violent behavior on film or television behaved more aggressively immediately afterward, and whether such viewing had immediate effects on aggressive thoughts or emotions, were reviewed. A meta-analysis of laboratory and field experiments designed to assess short-term effects of viewing media violence on children's aggressive behavior was also included. The authors of the chapter concluded that the empirical studies cited indicate clearly that "exposure to violent dramatic presentations on television or in films causes short-term increases in the aggressive behavior of youths, including physically aggressive behavior." To their credit, the authors acknowledge some of the limitations of the experimental work reviewed, explaining: "Because experiments are narrowly focused on testing specific causal hypotheses, they do not examine the effects of all factors that might be present in more realistic situations." Although I would resist using "factors" as a descriptor, this statement captures the essence of why studies can be at the same time "scientifically-based" and almost useless.

The standards of rigor that are being applied to define scientifically based research necessarily set up conditions that ignore or distort the real-world contexts in which human behavior takes place. No statistical design can be complex enough or elegant enough to "examine the effects of all factors that might be present in more realistic situations." Who knows how the children in the media effects studies were making sense of the violent media presentations or what was going on for them as they experienced the data collection processes of the studies? These are just the kinds of questions Tobin was asking, and I think the answers generated from his qualitative analyses give us a rich, nuanced understanding of children and violence that is impossible to find in the media effects literature based on positivist research assumptions. Qualitative research approaches are not perfect for exploring social phenomena as they are imbedded within the real-world experiences of young children, their families, and those who work with them; but early childhood qualitative researchers make a systematic effort to do just that.

In Sum

This chapter addresses an issue at the core of research in the field of early childhood education and education in general. What is to be the place, if any, of alternatives to what those currently in power have decreed to be normal science? This chapter lays the groundwork for renewing the debate and makes the case that qualitative paradigms offer special ways of generating knowledge that are essential to the future of the field. Producing high-quality qualitative studies that reveal dimensions of early childhood impossible to capture quantitatively ought to be our primary defensive strategy. But let us also "do our best to offend those who would impose their modern notions of science on us by exposing the flaws in what they call scientifically-based research" (Hatch, 2006, p. 405). As a society, we cannot go back to modernity. As a community of scholars, we must not capitulate to those who would go back to modern conceptualizations of what constitutes acceptable research.

References

Allington, R. L. (Ed.). (2002). *Big brother and the national reading curriculum: How ideology trumped evidence*. Portsmouth, NH: Heinemann.

Allington, R. L. (2005). Ideology still trumping evidence. *Phi Delta Kappan, 86*, 462–468.

Barclay-McLaughlin, G. (2000). Communal isolation: Narrowing the pathways to goal attainment and work. In S. Danziger & A. C. Lin (Eds.), *Coping with poverty: The social contexts of neighborhood, work, and family in the African-American community* (pp. 52–75). Ann Arbor: University of Michigan Press.

Bracey, G. W. (2003). *On the death of childhood and the destruction of public schools*. Portsmouth, NH: Heinemann.

Carr, W. (1995). *For education: Towards critical educational inquiry*. Buckingham, England: Open University Press.

Cunningham, J. W. (2002). The national reading panel report: A review. In R. L. Allington (Ed.), *Big brother and the national reading curriculum: How ideology trumped evidence* (pp. 49–74). Portsmouth, NH: Heinemann.

Davis, O. L. (2003). New policies and new directions: Be aware of the footprints! Notice the nightmares! *Journal of Curriculum and Supervision, 18*, 103–109.

Denzin, N. K., & Lincoln, Y. S. (1994). Introduction: Entering the field of qualitative research. In N. K. Denzin & Y. S. Lincoln (Eds.), *Handbook of qualitative research* (pp. 1–18). Thousand Oaks, CA: Sage.

Derrida, J. (1981). *Dissemination*. Chicago: University of Chicago Press.

Dyson, A. H. (2003). *The brothers and sisters learn to write: Popular literacies in childhood and school cultures*. New York: Teachers College Press.

Elkind, D. (1994). *Ties that stress: The new family imbalance*. Cambridge, MA: Harvard University Press.

Erickson, F. (2005). Arts, humanities, and sciences in educational research and social engineering in federal education policy. *Teachers College Record, 107*, 4–9.

Erickson, F., & Gutierrez, K. (2002). Culture, rigor, and science in educational research. *Educational Researcher, 31*, 21–24.

Foucault, M. (1980). *Power/knowledge: Selected interviews and other writings, 1972–1977.* New York: Pantheon.

Garan, E. M. (2005). Murder your darlings: A scientific response to The Voice of Evidence in Reading Research. *Phi Delta Kappan, 86*, 438–443.

Gee, J. P. (2005). It's theories all the way down: A response to Scientific Research in Education. *Teachers College Record, 107*, 10–18.

Giangreco, M. F., & Taylor, S. J. (2003). Scientifically based research and qualitative inquiry. *Research and Practice for Persons With Severe Disabilities, 28*, 133–137.

Glaser, B. G., & Strauss, A. L. (1967). *The discovery of grounded theory: Strategies for qualitative research.* Mill Valley, CA: Sociology Press.

Hatch, J. A. (1985). The quantoids versus the smooshes: Struggling with methodological rapprochement. *Issues in Education, 3*, 158–167.

Hatch, J. A. (2000). Introducing postmodern thought in a thoroughly modern university. In L. D. Soto (Ed.), *The politics of early childhood education* (pp. 179–195). New York: Peter Lang.

Hatch, J. A. (2002). *Doing qualitative research in education settings.* Albany: State University of New York Press.

Hatch, J. A. (2006). Qualitative studies in the era of scientifically-based research: Musings of a former QSE editor. *Qualitative Studies in Education, 19*, 401–405.

Hatch, J. A., & Barclay-McLaughlin, G. (2006). Qualitative research: Paradigms and possibilities. In B. Spodek & O. N. Saracho (Eds.), *The handbook of research on the education of young children* (2nd ed., pp. 497–514). Mahwah, NJ: Erlbaum.

Head Start Bureau. (2003). 2003 Head Start Information Memorandum. United States Department of Health and Human Services Web site, http://www.headstartinfo.org/publications/im03_07.htm

Krashen, S. (2005). Is in-school free reading good for children? Why the National Reading Panel is (still) wrong. *Phi Delta Kappan, 86*, 444–447.

Kuhn, T. S. (1970). *The structure of scientific revolutions.* Chicago: University of Chicago Press.

Lather, P. (2004). This is your father's paradigm: Government intrusion in education. *Qualitative Inquiry, 10*, 15–34.

Lincoln, Y. S., & Guba, E. G. (1985). *Naturalistic inquiry.* Beverly Hills, CA: Sage.

Lubeck, S., & Post, J. (2000). Creating a Head Start community of practice. In L. D. Soto (Ed.), *The politics of early childhood education* (pp. 33–57). New York: Peter Lang.

Meisels, S. J., & Atkins-Burnett, S. (2004). The National Head Start Reporting System: A critique. *Young Children, 59*, 64–66.

Moss, P. A. (2005). Toward epistemic reflexivity in educational research: A response to Scientific Research in Education. *Teachers College Record, 107*, 19–29.

National Reading Panel. (2000). *Report from the National Reading Panel.* Washington, DC: National Institute for Child Health and Human Development.

National Research Council. (2002). *Scientific research in education.* Washington, DC: National Academy Press.

Reyna, V. (n.d.). What is scientifically based evidence? What is its logic? United States Department of Education Web site, http://www.ed.gov/nclb/methods/whatworks/research/page_pg3.html

Rist, R. (1977). On the relations among educational research paradigms: From distain to détente. *Anthropology and Education Quarterly, 8*, 42–49.

Sarap, M. (1993). *An introductory guide to poststructuralism and postmodernism.* Athens: University of Georgia Press.

Seidman, S. (1994). Introduction. In S. Seidman (Ed.), *The postmodern turn: New perspectives on social theory.* Cambridge, England: Cambridge University Press.

St. Pierre, E. A. (2002). "Science" rejects postmodernism. *Educational Researcher, 31*, 25–27.

Surgeon General. (2001). Youth violence: A report of the Surgeon General. United States Department of Health and Human Services Web site, http://www.surgeongeneral.gov/library/youthviolence/youvoireport.htm

Tobin, J. (2000). *Good guys don't wear hats: Children's talk about the media.* New York: Teachers College Press.

Tobin, J. J., Wu, D. Y., & Davidson, D. H. (1989). *Preschool in three cultures: Japan, China, and the United States.* New Haven, CT: Yale University Press.

Torff, B. (2004). No research left behind. *Educational Researcher, 33*, 27–31.

Washington, V., & Andrews, J. D. (Eds.). (1998). *Children of 2010*. Washington, DC: National Association for the Education of Young Children.

I

Qualitative Methodologies in Early Childhood Settings

2

Hermeneutic Text Analysis of Play
Exploring Meaningful Early Childhood Classroom Events

STUART REIFEL

The University of Texas at Austin

As the two children tussle about in the sand, Francois continues to address Greg in a kind of rhythmic song-like manner, saying: "Oh, I'm gonna catch you." Sand is by now flying about. The teacher begins to monitor more closely. As the children begin to throw sand at each other, the teacher moves to intervene. The sand throwing, though a prohibited activity, is well coordinated, and is not in itself a transition point. However, as a prohibited activity the teacher cannot permit it. A transition that disrupts this interaction occurs when the teacher is required to enter. (Scales, 1996, p. 251)

Early childhood education has a long history of description of classroom activity (e.g., Hall, 1888; Hartley, Frank, & Goldenson, 1952; Paley, 1979, 1984, 2004). Both researchers and practitioners generate descriptions of observed classroom activity, including children's play, in order to illustrate and explain the meanings of early education for children and their teachers. In the opening example, Barbara Scales describes the classroom play of an African-American preschooler who is making progress toward engaging in playful social relationships. Scales uses this section of text as evidence within a longer narrative that describes how this boy uses play communications to become a member of the classroom group. Researchers such as Scales draw on texts generated by observations to make their points about the meanings of classroom activity in terms of children's culture (e.g., Corsaro, 1985; Fernie, Kantor, & Whaley, 1995), learning, cognition, or social development (Fein, 1989), and theory (Reifel & Yeatman, 1993).

Such observations and the texts that emerge from them may amuse readers, or they may be taken as trivial. For some educators, they may serve to provide a touchstone with reality, while for others they may be rejected as fanciful. They may be treated as data, or they may be seen as meaningless. They might persuade some readers with their authenticity, helping create meaningful connections with larger narratives such as theory or visions of educational purpose. Others might see them as part of the messiness of educational practice, background noise from which we ought to distinguish our real work. In any case, such texts often appear within larger narratives about teaching and early education. They mean something within a narrative (or as a narrative) that is intended to convey larger meanings about practice, science related to practice, or other forms of scholarship (ethnography, critique, postmodern analysis) related to practice. They often appear as examples of qualitative research, in the sense that they are based in natural settings, include (to some degree) the perspectives of participants, involve the researcher (in a range of ways) as research instrument, require extended engagement, aim at the centrality of meaning, acknowledge complexity and subjectivity, require flexibility in design, and reflect the reflexivity of those who conduct analyses (Hatch & Barclay-McLaughlin, 2006).

This chapter will present hermeneutic approaches to data collection and analysis related to early childhood classrooms (Reifel, Hoke, Pape, & Wisneski, 2004; VanderVen, 2004). Starting from a philosophical rather than scientific stance, the purpose is to place the meaning of texts (broadly identified) in their most illuminative narrative contexts. Traditional case materials (in this case, observations of classroom play activity) will serve as examples of texts for analysis that are located in a perspective, studied within that perspective, and critically evaluated in terms of meanings that result. Traditional case materials, such as narrative descriptions of children's play actions and play dialogues, are often collected with standard observational running records and transcribed into written texts. A hermeneutic approach requires that any narrative case be considered critically within larger theoretical contexts, including the conditions that contribute to creating the text; only then will such texts become more meaningful. Such narrative analysis will be contrasted with standard developmental views of play and its progress (Sutton-Smith, 1997, 1999), including Developmentally Appropriate Practice (Bredekamp & Copple, 1997), and with grounded theory, naturalistic inquiry, and other qualitative approaches that may also rely on observation and creation of texts based on observation.

The chapter provides a brief background on hermeneutic analysis and what it might mean for our methods of inquiry in early education. From that, we will explore three different approaches to generating and analyzing classroom texts: Vivian Paley's reflections on practice, my own work (necessarily done with collaborators) on theorizing classroom play, and poststructuralist uses of text for critical exploration. We will find methodological guidance for textual data collection and analysis from each of these approaches. How we think about texts based in classroom experience is often limited by theory, discipline, or ideology. Hermeneutics demands that we consider placing texts in multiple narratives, reflecting the multiple perspectives of participants. We will also identify some of the challenges and difficulties associated with hermeneutic analysis.

My own history with children's classroom play as text reflects some of the professional, disciplinary, ideological, and theoretical contexts that frame early childhood research. With an A.B. in anthropology and a minor in psychology from Stanford University, I was directed toward the symbolic meanings of cultural actions, using both theory and critique to interpret observations and narratives. In particular, Michelle Rosaldo's anthropology seminar on structuralism, George Spindler's educational anthropology, and Mark Lepper's work on intrinsic motivation (for which I gathered data in the nursery school) were important experiences that formed my thinking and eventual work with children. I remained at Stanford to work at Bing Nursery School and complete my A.M. under the supervision of Edith Dowley, who directed the school. The play-based curriculum at Bing was engaging, and the demands of observing and relating to the children within that frame were stimulating, with developmental texts (e.g., Erikson, 1950; Piaget, 1962) serving as guides for interpreting children's actions. After three additional years of teaching, I began doctoral study at UCLA, where Norma Feshbach (from a clinical perspective), Ruby Takanishi, and Deborah Stipek offered developmentalism as a frame for understanding children and families. Patricia Greenfield also served as a mentor and provided a social-cognitive perspective, while Louise Tyler supervised my dissertation. Tyler's influence is important for me. She was a student of Ralph Tyler at the University of Chicago, but did postdoctoral work with Bruno Bettelheim and other psychoanalysts. She offered seminars that involved analytic evaluation on literature, and drew on Erikson for theoretical meaning. From professional, empirical, and theoretical perspectives, I have been drawn to studying child action in meaningful contexts.

Why bother with hermeneutics? How does the search for meaning by means of text analysis differ from other qualitative methods of inquiry? Most qualitative approaches involve creation of narrative in some form, and in many cases there is great concern for creating an authentic text that reflects participant perspectives (e.g., Tierney, 2000; Zou & Trueba, 2002). Context and careful documentation of action or language, affirmed by confirmation with participants, is built into several qualitative approaches (e.g., Glaser & Strauss, 1967; Glesne & Peshkin, 1992; Lincoln & Guba, 1985; Strauss & Corbin, 1990). Reflection on data is essential (e.g., Eisner, 1998). Interpretation occurs in all cases. So why consider hermeneutics?

While other methodologies help us find or confirm theory, still others find patterns or themes that assist our interpretation (Hatch, 1995; Hatch & Barclay-McLaughlin, 2006). Hermeneutics forces us to seek meanings in textual data that reveal its complexities. That methodological search requires reflection, theory, exploration of social context, further data collection, and perhaps soul searching about values. Pieces of this process appear in other methodologies, but they come together uniquely in the search for meaning in text analysis. Because many of the texts that interest early childhood teachers and researchers are descriptions of play, with strong imaginary or "as if" elements, some argue that hermeneutics may be necessary to deal with the multiple meanings associated with what is "happening" (Henricks, 2001; VanderVen, 2004)—situated actions and words, what those actions and words refer to, the contexts that contribute to the situation (including multiple meanings for different participants), and professional lenses that guide adult observers (Reifel, Hoke, Pape, & Wisneski, 2004).

But meaning is a messy thing. And meaning that involves the "as if," as so much of young children's activity does, presents challenges that need to be addressed from multiple perspectives. Some approaches have been moored to modernity, in the sense that theory has been a guide. But data challenge theory, professional practice has become more conceptually complex over the past third of a century, and scholarship has evolved. Reading in new areas is necessary to create new opportunities for how we conduct inquiry and understand what we see in classrooms. Hermeneutics takes us in this direction.

Hermeneutics: Interpreting Classroom Texts

Barbara Scales introduced me to Packer and Addison (1989). She was using some of their ideas for interpreting children's art and related play (Scales, 2005). As we discussed her analysis (reported in 2005), I was led to Gadamer (1975), Steinholt and Traasdahl (2002), and Mallery, Hurwitz, and Duffy (1987), who provided me with a picture of text analysis that seemed to be helpful for understanding classroom play as it had not been understood before. VanderVen (2004) brought together many of these ideas related to early childhood practice, in particular, play. The following discussion reflects these influences.

First, in contemporary use, the term *texts* can be used to describe any number of productions: written words, oral discourse (a conversation, an interview), performances (staged, informal, impromptu), or works of art (language based or otherwise). Traditional views of hermeneutics were more limited, typically to written religious texts. Now we can view any number of cultural productions as amenable to, and in need of, a search for meaning. Key here is the identification of text, then finding its meaning(s) as a cultural production. What makes a text meaningful? The answer to this is not proof or science; it is interpretation.

VanderVen (2004) points to a number of perspectives about text analysis that reflect different philosophical emphases. Gadamer (1975) gives weight to the role of language for understanding our relationships in the world; spoken and written text therefore can be seen as one way of documenting and interpreting meaning. Habermas (Habermas & Dews, 2001) points to communications and community, where text is negotiated socially; a critical look at social context and its symbols becomes an important source of meaning. And Ricouer (1984–1988) situates texts in their cultural and generational context; deconstruction of text is a source of meaning. These philosophical distinctions have implications for the weight given to language and action in our data collection and analysis, although in all cases meanings of texts are to be interpreted within social and cultural contexts. Traditional hermeneutics may have led to a preferred reading of a text, but current views allow for "intimations, labyrinths of meaning that we explore" (Henricks, 2001, p. 65). VanderVen (2004) places these philosophies within the early childhood reconceptualizing movement.

While cultural views have a pronounced emphasis within hermeneutic text analysis, developmental views are not rejected (VanderVen, 2004). As part of cultural thought, developmental theory and concepts can have a place in how texts are given meaning. To understand a text, there must be a systematic effort that "reconstructs the world in which the text was produced and places the text in that world" (Mallery et al., 1987, p. 1). Whatever tools are needed to accomplish this analysis of meaning should be used. Earlier theorists, such as Piaget and Erikson, identified texts of child action, but they used their texts to create and affirm their own theoretical agendas, not to understand the texts as they were meaningful for the children. Piaget described symbolic play to build his structuralist view of cognitive development, and Erikson used play to illustrate his psychoanalytic views. Within hermeneutics, texts do not serve as facts to make a point; they serve as complicated phenomena that require contextual analysis. At times that context might lead to structuralist or psychoanalytic meanings, but theories alone should not be guiding interpretation.

Given the imaginary worlds of children's pretend, some have argued that hermeneutics is a way to explore playful meaning. The nature of play, its quality as a "happening" within Gadamer's philosophy, can be understood as independent of the players; therefore, "the play itself is the subject and not the playing child" (Steinholt & Traasdahl, 2002, p. 84). Play events may require a unique text analysis, to disentangle their complex playful meanings.

Schools as cultural institutions and children acting within schools become phenomena in need of interpretive analysis. In fact, some researchers have been doing this sort of thing, although they may not have been calling it hermeneutics. What does being in school mean for children and adults? What texts do they create in schools? How do those texts have meaning(s) for children, teachers, parents, researchers? Contemporary hermeneutics does not tell us how to locate texts, but it does tell us that texts may be performed actions such as play, videotapes of performed actions, written observations of performed actions, verbal descriptions of performed actions, tape recordings of actions, transcripts of any of the above, and written reflections about events.

Interpretation within hermeneutic methods requires selection of frameworks for interpretation, including an audience for findings, contextualizing one's position toward evidence as researcher and teacher, and identifying meaningful frameworks that inform us about play contexts for young children. The final phase of analysis is interpretation, including evaluation and critical reflection on the texts and how they are situated. Text, as a description of classroom activity, is played with in order to interpret its meaning as experience. The recursive process means that there can be multiple interpretations. Among possible frameworks for classroom play's meaning is the teacher's own story of becoming more knowledgeable about play as a lens for understanding children. Play texts may tell us about how teachers view children, how their views change over time, and how they may use play to explore broader understandings of children relating to one another and to teachers in classrooms. Other stories about children and their growth (or difficulties) may be the result.

Three Approaches to Classroom Text Analysis

In addition to my own efforts to find and read meaningful classroom texts, others have also engaged in efforts to find and interpret activities (mostly classroom play activities) that are meant to enlighten us about early childhood education. From a thoughtful, practitioner perspective, Vivian Paley (e.g., 1981, 1990, 1997, 2004) has provided numerous readings of classroom life, often but not always based on her kindergarteners' play (e.g., *Wally's Stories*, *The Boy Who Would Be a Helicopter*). With a number of students I have attempted to derive contextual theoretical elements that can help us to understand the meanings of classroom play (Lin & Reifel, 1999; Neves & Reifel, 2002; Reifel et al., 2004; Reifel & Yeatman, 1991, 1993; Suito & Reifel, 1993; Yeatman & Reifel, 1992, 1997). From a postmodern perspective, Glenda MacNaughton and her collaborators have explored equity and justice by means of analyses of princess games, Barbie play, and other child-created classroom activities (e.g., Campbell, MacNaughton, Page, & Rolfe, 2004; Hughes & MacNaughton, 2000). What follows is a presentation of the methods used for each of these approaches, including described strategies for data collection and data analysis. These methods and the problems they address tend to fall within constructivist, critical/feminist, and poststructuralist paradigms (Hatch & Barclay-McLaughlin, 2006).

A Teacher Reflects: Paley on Her Practice

"Pretend I'm a big sister just like you," said a little girl, climbing out of a doll-corner crib. "I'm not a baby anymore. I'm you!"

"No! Don't pretend that!" cautioned her playmate, suddenly remorseful, stepping out of her role. "Don't be like me! Because I'm really bad!"

"Like the wolf?"

"Oh, wait, now it's okay. I'm a good sister now." (Paley, 2004, p. 17)

Paley never claims to be doing research, from a hermeneutic perspective or any other. In her most recent book (Paley, 2004), she states, "my purpose is to examine their curriculum in its natural form" (p. 3). She, as a thoughtful teacher and observer of young children, is interested in how teachers can use children's language (often from fantasy play) to teach more meaningfully toward literacy (including morals, character, story) as she sees it. Paley is one of our most noted practitioners of thoughtful observation and description, creating rich narratives within which observations raise questions about the complexity of practice. She uses text to make points about our more abstract intentions for children, as in the above quote where she draws parallels between classroom social relationships, children's emerging awareness of who they are, and in this case family relationships as represented by, for example, Eugene O'Neill in *Long Day's Journey Into Night*. Although Paley's work is not presented as research and does not often draw on theory, practitioners and scholars appreciate it as a way to look deeply into children's learning (Wiltz & Fein, 1996; Lindfors, 1999). I believe it can be argued that Paley's work is a version of hermeneutic text analysis.

In *A Child's Work*, Paley (2004) summarizes much of her earlier writing and adds reflections about how her thought and approach have changed over the decades. She remains an advocate for developmental practice and play, as she revisits the details of how she gathered her data about children and reflected on them. It seems relevant to note that she sees her work both in terms of how children have learned in their classroom, as well as how she as a reflective teacher learned from her work. She acknowledges that the texts she analyzes are both the children's (what they said and did, how they learned over time) and her own (how her methods changed, how her thinking evolved). There are parallels with what VanderVen (2004) calls philosophical hermeneutics, wherein both the children's text and its interpretation are in dialogue. Both child insight and teacher insight are Paley's concern. Stories, whether literature or fantasy play, are seen by her to help "interpret and explain our feelings about reality" (Paley, 2004, p. 29).

How does Paley gather her classroom data? She offers both general and specific accounts of this work, building on how she was taught a half century ago to observe play. Recording "anecdotes, samples of conversation, sketches of block constructions, and drippy paintings" (Paley, 2004, p. 2) is one step in revealing the children, but, "We will need to go beyond watching, listening, and remembering" (p. 3). Having a focus matters, and she makes her focus the fantasy themes, characters, and plots that children develop. Data collection might include overhearing children's conversations (possibly tape-recording them), participating in conversations with them, transcribing children's dictated stories, documenting how they enact their stories, and entering children's stories into her journal. As we shall see, these last forms of data collection might be recursive, used to clarify what had come before.

To analyze the texts that she collects, Paley calls "play the work of teachers as well" (2004, p. 3). She was trained to see that "children were inventing stories" (p. 16) as they played. One way, she reflected, was by analogy, comparing children's texts to, for example, literary themes. How were children's fantasy relationships like Charlotte and Wilbur's, or like Jamie and Edmond's in *Long Day's Journey Into Night*? Finding parallels between what children say in class and what exists in literature gives this teacher tools for relating to the children, for probing what is motivating them and what they want to understand.

Analogy is not the only analytic tool that Paley describes. She also points to classroom debate as a source of additional data that she needed to clarify children's meanings. During play or group time, children in Paley's classroom argue about the details of what they played. Through their debates, she could hear fantasy plot and character revised and clarified. If clarity does not come from debate, Paley might interview a parent to clarify a point. She might also interview children, during story dictation or group times. As storybook reading was an ongoing event in her classroom, she could also use discussion of books to elicit children's understandings of plot and character.

As Sutterby (2005) notes, Paley analyzes spoken or dictated data by listening three times to what is said—when it is first dictated, when acted out, and when transcribed from a tape recording. Multiple "hearings" appear to contribute to how she makes sense of fantasy.

Cited theory appears fleetingly in Paley's work; she notes Vygotsky (1978) to highlight children's growth in thought through play, and Egan (1989) to point to the presence of story in classroom life. Perhaps most important for her is to be "the bestower of place and belonging, of custom and curriculum" (2004, p. 19) so that children can expand their play meanings. Offering children ample play time is necessary to allow effective play. The meanings that Paley generates through her data collection serve her ability to create a classroom context that serves children's continuing needs to become literate. The texts she presents in her books are part of a cultural narrative of developmental education, wherein fantasy play is a set of meanings that the teacher must disentangle.

Contextual Texts and Theory: Our Work

"Why do all your stories have to do with fighting?" I asked a group of my kindergarten boys in the spring of the year. "It seems you are always chasing and killing and fighting."

One child named Sam gives me an incredulous look, as if to wonder if I could really be so stupid. He explains slowly for me, "we're not fighting. We are *saving* in our stories." The other children nod their heads in agreement. (Reifel et al., 2004, p. 215)

With our history in the belief that play has an essential place in early childhood practice, a number of graduate students and I have conducted research with the intent of challenging long-standing theoretical interpretations of what play means in classrooms (Bredekamp & Copple, 1997). Reading Piaget, Erikson, or other accepted developmental scholars took us only so far; their work could provide some insights into the sorts of things we see in classrooms, but their work itself was not done in classrooms. What makes classrooms unique settings for play, and what theories might help us make sense of classroom practice? Our questions differed from some researchers who studied play in classrooms, such as Corsaro (1985) and Schwartzman (1978) who were interested in answering sociological and anthropological questions. We wanted to know more about the classroom's construction of meaning for players. The fighting stories that the children told in the text above were related by the boy players not just to "saving" girls (with a sexist presumption of power), but to how boys might grow up to save girls in the campus dormitories that the children saw on their way to school (with that different, if related, presumption of power).

In a series of studies with Yeatman, we took multiple analytic views of classroom and, in some cases, home texts (Yeatman & Reifel, 1992) to argue for the relative merit of a situated theoretical perspective that included elements of Vygotsky (1966, 1978) and Bateson (2000). Rather than seeing play psychologically as a type of behavior with influential component elements (Howes, 1992; Kavanaugh, 2006), we wanted to see how pretend connected to the contexts where it was occurring. We read play actions and talk in terms of culture, curriculum, social relations, ideas, and materials. This approach was telling within our culture (Hoke, 2004; Neves & Reifel, 2002; Reifel et al., 2004) and in other countries (Lin & Reifel, 1999; Suito & Reifel, 1993). For example, Hoke (2004) found that children began to play with nurturance (e.g., taking care of babies) by pretending dangerous or threatening events (such as floods or tornadoes) that created opportunities for tending to the vulnerable; without seemingly violent pretend texts, there was no basis for gentle nurturing. Eventually, we came to see a recursive process of cultural meaning making in context, requiring a hermeneutic approach (Reifel et al., 2004).

From the earliest of these studies, we explicitly argue for including both play actions and language as part of the narratives that we present as text (Reifel & Yeatman, 1991). Theory and professional experience demanded that our data collection include both insider observations and tape recordings. Often, but not always, these data were collected simultaneously. This required that a member of the classroom context (either the teacher or a participant observer who knew the culture) be part of the study. Without this insider knowledge, we believed that classroom and cultural meanings would be missed. Without both observations and child language, we would miss the multiple possibilities of meanings for the "as if" actions and speech of children in play. Our texts reflect both.

Interpretation was more complicated, from both a theoretical and a practical perspective. It was apparent from most of our data that there were multiple narratives associated with many of the texts that we identified, and that those narratives altered in their meanings over time. A story of an individual might become a story of a friendship or of adapting to a classroom; a story of classroom community might become a story about a long-term play "happening," a story of a teacher's growing understanding or of needed theoretical abstraction. Most of the texts revealed not just multi-subjectivities, but layers of meaning related to materials, curriculum, peer relations, customs, and the theories needed to understand them. Interpretation, as a recursive, multi-theoretical effort, is necessary for understanding what was seen and heard. Interviews with teachers, parents, and children were part of the effort to interpret or clarify texts. While Paley documents the simultaneous growth in both children's and teacher's understandings of what happens in the classroom, we focused more on the adequacy of theories for contributing to meaningful interpretation. Bateson (2000) and Vygotsky (1978) proved essential for identifying frames of meaningful reference and the processes of creating meaning in context. Breaking some of the code of "as if" play (Bateson's "map") as it relates to the classroom and children's lives (Bateson's "terrain" on which play maps) has been our goal.

The complications of interpretive analysis exist even when someone else has created the text. When Lisa Cary and I analyzed *Goodbye, Mr. Chips* (Cary & Reifel, 2005), we worked with a written narrative that had been prepared by others, in this case a screenplay that was based on a novel. We actually began with multiple viewings of a video of the film, so that our reading of the novel and the written screenplay was heavily influenced by the performance on film. How we selected to interpret the screenplay, in terms of teaching and teacher–student relationships, was based on what we brought (theoretically and emotionally) to a range of narrative events that made sense on a number of levels: teaching career, curriculum, play and playful relationships, duty, privilege. Our interpretation acknowledged that the text was created (by others) as entertainment and art. Beyond that, we selected a small number of interpretations related to professional practice that seemed to make the film meaningful both theoretically (from our points of view) and in human terms. Part of the complication was selecting texts within the film for interpretation. Part was interpreting the meanings of those texts, including tying those meanings to professional literature. Another complication was resisting the urge to reduce the film to a number of meanings that fail to do justice to its rich narrative.

Traditional developmental tools for understanding and valuing children's classroom play have not been adequate to our purposes, to do justice to play's rich narratives. Interpretation of classroom activities such as play requires additional tools, but those tools can be used only in relationship to the contexts where players create play texts. This perspective seems to be consistent with hermeneutic philosophy (VanderVen, 2004), and our analyses seem to support this view. While these studies focus more on conceptions related to texts,

> We acknowledge that children and teachers have perspectives to bring to a text. Having done so, we need to say that a legitimate inquiry about play text narrative can be a teacher's narrative or children's narrative(s). We want to know what play means to children, how their texts are contributing to whom they are. It is also legitimate to know about how the play text is contributing to the teacher's growing world of reflection about children and play; how does a play text help teachers think more meaningfully about play. (Reifel, Pape, Hoke, & Wisneski, 2004, p. 216)

Multiple perspectives and context are necessary for understanding play. Reflexive thinking about play, rather than categorizing it based on noncontextual theories, seems to be productive, as Paley and we have documented. These analyses point to preparing teachers to "read" and think about play in multiple ways that have particular meanings in each classroom.

Postmodernism's Texts: Probing the Power Reflected in Play Texts

Anne: Gayle? … Can you tell me why you don't ask Mick to play your (princess) games?

Gayle: Because he—I like Barry.

Anne: Yeah and that's okay, but why is it that you choose not to play with Mick?

Gayle: Because I don't, I don't [like] people that are black I—only white people. (Campbell et al., 2004, p. 58)

Classroom play is problematic from any number of perspectives. Parents, teachers, administrators, and researchers value it in different ways, if at all. A growing body of early childhood research is showing how social problems, power relationships, and the ideologies and values that are associated with them, can be understood through textual analysis of classroom play. As Campbell and her colleagues show in the text presented above, racism can show its face in the pretend play of young children. From their scholarly perspective, "We argue that using multiple theoretical perspectives to analyze teaching and learning can generate and drive critical reflection on equity praxis more effectively than using a single perspective that presents a single truth about teaching and learning moments" (Campbell et al., 2004, p. 55). This view seems to reflect both the philosophical foundations of hermeneutics, as well as its analytic methods. As will be seen, their approach to data collection also seems to be consistent with this view.

A growing number of studies are locating classroom play texts as a way of identifying power relationships and working with teachers to confront these matters (e.g., Blaise, 2005; Campbell et al., 2004; Hughes & MacNaughton, 2000; Scales, 1996). Whether from a critical/feminist or a poststructuralist perspective, there appears to be an effort to use a classroom text typically based on observation and/or tape-recorded play to explore issues of gender, race, or other sources of inequity. How any of these matters might have something to say about a text becomes a matter for interpretation, from multiple perspectives and within any number of theoretical frameworks. The purpose is not to provide an answer for a problem, but to generate interpretations and a basis for discourse that will allow fresh thinking about an issue.

Data collection in postmodern studies, as with the other approaches discussed above, relies heavily on observations and tape-recording. Teacher or researcher perspectives and children's dialogue are translated into written text and serve as a basis for analysis. Observers who work in this paradigm must be attuned to matters of inequity (for example), so that they can find texts that merit analysis. How they become attuned is not made clear, although acknowledging researcher history and bias is a commonly recognized aspect of reflection and analysis (e.g., Blaise, 2005). Adults bring their motives to locating text, then they find in the seeming innocence of pretend a way of connecting children's play texts to larger social issues. That connection is crafted as the researcher generates field notes, taped recordings, video recordings, teacher and student interviews, or artifacts such as student pictures or constructions.

As with all hermeneutic approaches, it seems that locating an initial text for subsequent analysis is easier done than described. The reasons why text ought to be analyzed are explicated, but how to spot the action or dialogue that might be analyzed is seldom made clear. In our own work, we looked at preliminary transcriptions, based on days of tape recordings and observations, until an interesting text presented itself. This may be analogous to Paley's finding a "focus." It seems in all cases that a pretend theme, or a conversation about one (for example, who can play what), serves to trigger interest. But, hermeneutic play researchers do not indicate how to find that trigger.

When issues such as gender or ethnicity become an interest for analysis, it appears that both self-reflexivity and reflexivity with children become important data-gathering approaches. Recognizing that what children are playing is connected to power issues has implications for data collection, with reciprocity and its related dialogical process becoming necessary. Blaise (2005, pp. 45–48) described her reflexivity and reciprocity in terms of the dialogues she has in research talks with the classroom teacher, reflective interviews with children, and data sharing with the teacher. In this sense, data analysis contributes to further data collection. This process seems to parallel Paley's long-term work with her children, making sense over time of their play and discussing with them how to make sense of it.

Analysis of data related to power issues contributes to data collection, but consistent with hermeneutic philosophy, it relies on analytic treatment of language (e.g., transcripts of play dialogues, transcripts of teacher interviews, written journals) and of actions (e.g., social context of dialogues and actions). MacNaughton (1998) calls for critical discourse analysis to assist our understanding of texts. Blaise and others make use of critical discourse analysis, along with narrative description of the context of language, social texts themselves (narratives of social interactions), patterns of meanings (including inconsistencies and contradictions in participants' accounts), and recognition that any text may not logically make sense in relationship to others.

Again, as with all the approaches that have been presented, the end result of inquiry is a complex interpretation of text that has been identified from classroom practice. Blaise (2005) found multiple interconnected texts related to kindergarteners' agency in constructing gender in the classroom, often in their play activities; and feminist, queer, and other theories help her interpret the texts she identifies. Campbell et al. (2004) offer multiple interpretations of what a race-linked playmate choice means for teachers and a classroom community; and socio-developmental, critical studies, and feminist poststructuralist perspectives contribute to the interpretation of the text (see chapter opening). Interpretation points to the multiple, complex meanings that any pretend classroom text might reflect. Connections between these inquiries and hermeneutic philosophy and methodology are clear.

Summary, Implications, and Conclusions

This chapter explores hermeneutic analysis of classroom play in early childhood education. The principles of hermeneutic analysis are a philosophically necessary way to understand classroom activity such as pretend or fantasy play, with a method that provides additional meanings for observation and reflection about classroom play. Steps in the methodology of conducting such analysis from three different approaches to classroom inquiry show how textual materials are collected and analyzed to produce complex, meaningful interpretations. Building on debates about early childhood theory and practice (see Grieshaber & Cannella, 2001; Reifel & Brown, 2001, 2004), this perspective is situated within the reconceptualist tradition (VanderVen, 2004). By using a hermeneutic approach, seeing play or descriptions of play as text that is in need of explication, we discover meanings of play from the multiple points of view of the players and observers. Some of the text analysis research described here was not conducted explicitly as hermeneutic, or even as research; the argument is that the kinds of things that are observed and documented, and the complex interpretations that are created for texts that are offered, create a family of inquiry that fits within hermeneutic traditions.

There are a number of implications from this argument. First, philosophically and theoretically, Gadamer (1975) and VanderVen (2004) tell us that play is unique among human activities for how it can be understood. Analyses of classroom fantasy and pretend are inherently complex and meaningful, and they require interpretation that reflects at least the interplay of the subjective, intersubjective, temporal (developmental, historical), material (play objects, play partners, intruders), and conceptual (curricular, power relational). Second, methodologically, the contributions of knowledgeable, reflective participants in the classroom community are necessary for the collection of meaningful data and for contributing meaningfully to analysis. We cannot interpret what these classroom events mean without a guide who can serve as interpreter. Third, data collection and interpretation are recursive and reflexive. A classroom event is a constructed text, whose construction may alter as it is being described, and whose meaning may transform during analysis. Researchers need to address the degree to which interpretation is done about the event, about the researcher's transformation, or some combination of the two. Fourth, analysis of classroom play texts requires broad reading from fields that may appear to have nothing to do with early education. What our classroom language and actions reflect can be fruitfully interpreted in light of a variety of scholarly and artistic literatures, as well as the disciplines we are more attuned to.

As any of us read texts, it is important to remember how difficult it is to construct texts. None of the approaches to text analysis that are discussed above includes all of the methodological steps that contributed to the writings that we read. In particular, it seems important to mention the difficulties and work that are associated with turning a transcription or observation into a written text. Campbell et al. (2004) and Blaise (2005) make a point of affirming that their participants can verify what they have conveyed through their writing, but how many drafts had been prepared before participants were invited to view them, and how many alterations were made in light of those viewings? Paley (2004) refers to her work with her publishing editor, but there is no guidance on how many drafts she prepared to clarify the texts that she wanted to convey. Our own experience has been that it can take up to eight drafts to depict an episode in written form. My co-authors and I have spent as many as six and seven draftings of written texts, traded amongst us with some revisions made face-to-face; and that was before external reviewers asked questions that required additional changes. Is Sam's incredulous look (Reifel et al., 2004; presented above) really wondering if Wisneski can be so stupid, or is that just how she feels? Or is it both? The weight given to what words convey in the construction of a text needs to be carefully balanced and revisited from many perspectives. My experience has been that many think that their written texts speak for themselves, obviously conveying all that the preparer means.

Hermeneutics challenges that notion and points to the importance of careful text preparation and interpretation.

What merits are there to bringing hermeneutic analysis to classroom activity such as play? First of all, we all should have an interest in the meaning(s) of events that pertain to professional practice. From our various worldviews, we strive to participate in our profession's discourse. We know that the profession is complex, although we have different epistemologies that help us make sense of complexity. Hermeneutics asks that we read in different ways, both as creators and as consumers of text. The quote that introduces this chapter is part of an inquiry that asks us to read what could be seen as an annoying, disruptive event that requires teacher attention as a step in a child's growing participation in the social life of the preschool. Paley's text on good and bad sisters may seem like little kids not being clear about what they are doing, but Paley shows its complexity by interpreting it in terms of the growth of literacy. Hermeneutic treatment of classroom activity as text recognizes the complexity of events, denies that they should be seen as trivial, and provides methods for "reading" events as texts by placing those texts in larger interpretive narratives. Our purposes, as teachers and researchers, are merged with the meanings and interests of the children with whom we work.

Part of that analysis forces us, as scholars, to read more broadly. Academic pressure to produce often leads to narrow specialization and narrow reading. Interpreting for meaning in a systematic manner involves approaching the unfamiliar, if it will help us understand the texts that puzzle us. Work like this may not be ideal for those who are beginning their careers; a lack of narrow specialization could torpedo a young career, and time spent exploring the unfamiliar may better be spent getting an article done. But creating understandings that enhance interpretation means exploring out of the narrow. In the late 1970s after attending a day's sessions at AERA, Louise Tyler spoke (perhaps muttered) with disgust to me: "More and more about less and less." The call for more complexity was clear.

Where does hermeneutics intersect with other qualitative methods? Can someone be doing hermeneutics without knowing it? Given the growth in qualitative methodology over the past decades (Hatch & Barclay-McLaughlin, 2006), it is entirely possible that studies have created and analyzed texts without calling it hermeneutics. The argument in this chapter is that approaches to hermeneutics exist, and that they provide methodological guidance for understanding early childhood classrooms. Those of us in the field who have done interpretive work from different approaches might benefit from exploring other forms of interpretation. Others who explore meanings as part of ethnography or discourse analysis may have an interest in text creation and interpretation. But using texts as examples, whether to generate naturalistic theory or to illustrate principles, is not hermeneutic. Making a point is not the same as exploring an event. We must learn to approach our texts with our research purposes and limitations clearly in mind.

Practice may be messy, but meaning making can be just as messy. Hermeneutics is one way of dealing with messiness. Conceptually it forces us to explore context, ideology, theory, discourse(s), and whatever else might assist with multiple interpretations of text. When we allow both language and actions to be content for our analyses, theory may give us some of the language we need to describe and interpret; but the language of theory is meaningful only within that rhetorical world (Sutton-Smith, 1997; VanderVen, 2004). Theories can serve as lenses for understanding activities such as play (Frost, Wortham, & Reifel, 2005), but hermeneutic interpretation asks that we move to an integrative level where multiple perspectives may need to be woven together. And when the interpretation of actions is part of interpretation (especially "as if" or virtual actions), the conceptual task is daunting. What actions constitute a social warrant during play? What cultural customs enter classroom social relationships? What role does dialect play in "as if" signals? How does object manipulation signal pretend story? The messiness of interpretation of such matters is a scholarly challenge.

The examples offered here may provide some guidance for thinking about how texts can be identified and interpreted. If our concern is meaning, then situating researcher perspective within context is essential. Having ways of exploring the meanings of events in context, through knowledgeable informants, is part of the process of deciding what events can be created as text and how to do so. Creation of written text is a translation of experience that must be inspected many times. Interpretation is ongoing, and it is challenging because of the multiple perspectives that may need to be reflected, as well as values and theories that may have something to contribute. All of this activity recognizes the philosophically based argument that early childhood classroom activities are phenomena that require interpretive scholarship.

References

Bateson, G. (2000). *Steps to an ecology of mind*. Chicago: University of Chicago Press.

Blaise, M. (2005). *Playing it straight: Uncovering gender discourses in the early childhood classroom*. New York: Routledge.

Bredekamp, S., & Copple, C. (Eds.). (1997). *Developmentally appropriate practice in early childhood programs*. Washington, DC: National Association for the Education of Young Children.

Campbell, S., MacNaughton, G., Page, J., & Rolfe, S. (2004). Beyond quality, advancing social justice and equity: Interdisciplinary explorations of working for equity and social justice in early childhood education. In S. Reifel & M. Brown (Eds.), *Social contexts of early education, and reconceptualizing play (II): Advances in early education and day care* (Vol. 13, pp. 55–91). Oxford, England: Elsevier.

Cary, L. J., & Reifel, S. (2005). Cinematic landscapes of teaching: Lessons from a narrative of classic film. *Action in Teacher Education, 27*(3), 95–109.

Corsaro, W. A. (1985). *Friendship and peer culture in the early years*. Norwood, NJ: Ablex.

Egan, K. (1989). *Teaching as story telling*. Chicago: University of Chicago Press.

Eisner, E. (1998). *The enlightened eye: Qualitative inquiry and the enhancement of educational practice*. Upper Saddle River, NJ: Merrill.

Erikson, E. H. (1950). *Childhood and society*. New York: Norton.
Fein, G. G. (1989). Mind, meaning and affect: Proposals for a theory of pretense. *Developmental Review, 9*, 345–363.
Fernie, D. E., Kantor, R., & Whaley, K. L. (1995). Learning from classroom ethnographies: Same places, different times. In J. A. Hatch (Ed.), *Qualitative research in early childhood settings* (pp. 155–172). Westport, CT: Praeger.
Frost, J. L., Wortham, S., & Reifel, S. (2005). *Play and child development* (2nd ed.). Upper Saddle River, NJ: Merrill and Prentice Hall.
Gadamer, H.-G. (1975). *Truth and method*. New York: Seabury Press.
Glaser, B. G., & Strauss, A. L. (1967). *The discovery of grounded theory: Strategies for qualitative research*. Hawthorne, NY: Aldine de Gruyter.
Glesne, C., & Peshkin, A. (1992). *Becoming qualitative researchers: An introduction*. White Plains, NY: Longman.
Grieshaber, S., & Cannella, G. S. (Eds.). (2001). *Embracing identities in early childhood education: Diversity and possibilities*. New York: Teachers College Press.
Habermas, J., & Dews, P. (2001). *The liberating power of symbols: Philosophical essays*. Cambridge, MA: MIT Press.
Hall, G. S. (1888). The story of a sand-pile. *Scribner's Magazine, 3*, January-June.
Hartley, R.E., Franks, L. K.,& Goldenson, R. M. (1952). *Understanding Children's Play*. New York: Columbia University Press.
Hatch, J. A. (Ed.). (1995). *Qualitative research in early childhood settings*. Westport, CT: Praeger.
Hatch, J. A., & Barclay-McLaughlin, G. (2006). Qualitative research: Paradigms and possibilities. In B. Spodek & O. N. Saracho (Eds.), *Handbook of research on the education of young children* (2nd ed., pp. 497–514). Mahwah, NJ: Erlbaum.
Henricks, T. S. (2001). Play and postmodernism. In S. Reifel (Ed.), *Theory in context and out: Play and culture studies* (Vol. 3, pp. 51–71). Westport, CT: Ablex.
Hoke, P. A. (2004). *Tapestries of nurturance in children's role play: A case study of children's expressions of nurturing in a preschool classroom*. Unpublished doctoral dissertation, University of Texas, Austin.
Howes, C. (1992). *The collaborative construction of pretend: Social pretend play functions*. Albany: State University of New York Press.
Hughes, P., & MacNaughton, G. (2000). Identity-formation and popular culture: Learning lessons from Barbie. *Journal of Curriculum Theorizing, 16*, 57–67.
Kavanaugh, R. D. (2006). Pretend play. In B. Spodek & O. N. Saracho (Eds.), *Handbook of research on the education of young children* (2nd ed., pp. 269–278). Mahwah, NJ: Erlbaum.
Lin, S.-H., & Reifel, S. (1999). Context and meanings in Taiwanese kindergarten play. In S. Reifel (Ed.), *Play contexts revisited: Play and culture studies* (Vol. 2, pp. 151–176). Stamford, CT: Ablex.
Lincoln, Y., & Guba, E. (1985). *Naturalistic inquiry*. Newbury Park, CA: Sage.
Lindfors, J. W. (1999). *Children's inquiry: Using language to make sense of the world*. New York: Teachers College Press.
MacNaughton, G. (1998). Improving our gender equity tools: A case for discourse analysis. In N. Yelland (Ed.), *Gender in early childhood*. London: Routledge.
Mallery, J.C., Hurwitz, R., & Duffy, G. (1987). Hermeneutics: From textual explication to computer understanding. In S.C. Shapiro (Ed.), *Encyclopedia of artificial intelligence*. New York: Wiley.
Neves, P., & Reifel, S. (2002). The play of early writing. In J. L. Roopnarine (Ed.), *Conceptual, social-cognitive, and contextual issues in the fields of play: Play and culture studies* (Vol. 4, pp. 149–164). Westport, CT: Ablex.
Packer, M.J., & Addison, R.B. (Eds.). (1989). *Entering the circle: Hermeneutic investigation in psychology*. Albany: State University of New York Press.
Paley, V.G. (1979). *White teacher*. Cambridge, MA: Harvard University Press.
Paley, V. G. (1981). *Wally's stories*. Cambridge, MA: Harvard University Press.
Paley, V. G. (1984). *Boys and girls: Superheroes in the doll corner*. Chicago: University of Chicago Press.
Paley, V. G. (1990). *The boy who would be a helicopter: The uses of storytelling in the classroom*. Cambridge, MA: Harvard University Press.
Paley, V. G. (1997). *The girl with the brown crayon*. Cambridge, MA: Harvard University Press.
Paley, V. G. (2004). *A child's work: The importance of fantasy play*. Chicago: University of Chicago Press.

Piaget, J. (1962). *Play, dreams and imitation in childhood.* New York: Norton.

Reifel, S., & Brown, M. (Eds.). (2001). *Early education and care, and reconceptualizing play (I): Advances in early education and day care* (Vol. 11). Oxford, England: Elsevier.

Reifel, S., & Brown, M. (Eds.). (2004). *Social contexts of early education, and reconceptualizing play (II): Advances in early education and day care* (Vol. 13). Oxford, England: Elsevier.

Reifel, S., Hoke, P., Pape, D., & Wisneski, D. (2004). From context to texts: DAP, hermeneutics, and reading classroom play. In S. Reifel & M. Brown (Eds.), *Social contexts of early education, and reconceptualizing play (II): Advances in early education and day care* (Vol. 13, pp. 209–220). Oxford, England: Elsevier.

Reifel, S., & Yeatman, J. (1991). Action, talk, and thought in block play. In B. Scales, M. Almy, A. Nicolopoulou, & S. Ervin-Tripp (Eds.), *Play and the social context of development in early care and education* (pp. 156–172). New York: Teachers College Press.

Reifel, S., & Yeatman, J. (1993). From category to context: Reconsidering classroom play. *Early Childhood Research Quarterly, 8,* 347–367.

Ricouer, P. (1984–1988). *Time and narrative* (Vols. 1, 2, 3). Chicago: University of Chicago Press.

Scales, B. (1996). Researching the hidden curriculum. In J. Chafel & S. Reifel (Eds.), *Theory and practice in early childhood teaching: Advances in early education and day care* (Vol. 8, pp. 237–259). Greenwich, CT: JAI Press.

Scales, B. (2005, February). *Using technology to track developing play themes and the social integration of one child.* Paper presented at the annual meeting of The Association for the Study of Play, Santa Fe, NM.

Schwartzman, H. B. (1978). *Transformations: The anthropology of children's play.* New York: Plenum Press.

Steinholt, K., & Traasdahl, E. (2002). The concept of play in Hans-Georg Gadamer's hermeneutics: An educational approach. In S. Reifel (Ed.), *Theory in context and out (Play and Culture Studies)*(Vol. 3, pp. 73–96). Westport, CT: Ablex.

Strauss, A. L., & Corbin, J. (1990). *Basics of qualitative research.* Newbury Park, CA: Sage.

Suito, N., & Reifel, S. (1993). Aspects of gender role in American and Japanese play. *Journal of Play Theory & Research, 1,* 26–54.

Sutterby, J. (2005, December). *An analysis of play and story in Vivian Paley's* The Boy Who Would Be a Helicopter. Paper presented at the annual meeting of the National Association for the Education of Young Children, Washington, DC.

Sutton-Smith, B. (1997). *The ambiguity of play.* Cambridge, MA: Harvard University Press.

Sutton-Smith, B. (1999). The rhetorics of adult and child play theories. In S. Reifel (Ed.), *Foundations, adult dynamics, and teacher education and play: Advances in Early Education and Day Care* (Vol. 10, pp. 149–161). Stamford, CT: JAI Press.

Tierney, W. G. (2000). Undaunted courage: Life history and the postmodern challenge. In N. Denzin & Y. Lincoln (Eds.), *Handbook of qualitative research* (2nd ed.). Thousand Oaks, CA: Sage.

VanderVen, K. (2004). Beyond fun and games towards a meaningful theory of play: Can a hermeneutic perspective contribute? In S. Reifel & M. Brown (Eds.), *Social contexts of early education, and reconceptualizing play (II): Advances in early education and day care* (Vol. 13, pp. 167–208). Oxford, England: Elsevier.

Vygotsky, L. S. (1966). Play and its role in the mental development of the child. *Soviet Psychology, 12*(6), 62–76.

Vygotsky, L. S. (1978). *Mind in society: The development of higher psychological processes.* Cambridge, MA: Harvard University Press.

Wiltz, N., & Fein, G. G. (1996). Evolution of a narrative curriculum: The contributions of Vivian Gussin Paley. *Young Children, 51*(3), 61–68.

Yeatman, J., & Reifel, S. (1992). Siblings playing and learning. *Play & Culture, 5,* 141–158.

Yeatman, J., & Reifel, S. (1997). Conflict and power in classroom play. *International Journal of Early Childhood Education, 2,* 77–93.

Zou, Y., & Trueba, E. (2002). *Ethnography and schools: Qualitative approaches to the study of education.* Lanham, MD: Rowman and Littlefield.

3
Using Digital Video in Field-Based Research With Children
A Primer

DANIEL J. WALSH, NESRIN BAKIR, TONY BYUNGHO LEE,
YA-HUI CHUNG, KAYOUN CHUNG, AND COLLEAGUES*

University of Illinois at Urbana-Champaign

This chapter builds on the long tradition of using film and video in field-based research with children (e.g., Spindler & Spindler, 1992; Tobin, Wu, & Davidson, 1989; Walsh, 2002). We intend this chapter to be a practical primer for researchers familiar with field-based research but with limited experience using digital video in the field. The goal is a solid foundation for (a) generating data, (b) constructing data records, and (c) analyzing data.

Field-based refers to research that is done in the contexts within which children spend their lives, that is, in the field. Erickson and Wilson observed that field-based research "gives us a detailed view of events that are naturally occurring at a particular place and time" (1982, p. 39). They list five questions that field-based (they use *fieldwork*) research can answer well:

1. What is happening, specifically, in the social action and interaction in a particular place?
2. What do the actions mean to the actors?
3. How are happenings organized in the patterns of social organization and learned cultural principles for the conduct of everyday life?
4. How is what is happening related to other system levels outside and inside the setting?
5. How do the ways everyday life is organized in this place compare with other ways of organizing social life in other places and times? (p. 40)

---

* Hugo Campuzano, Yu-ting Chen, Yore Kedem, Wei Liu, Yasin Ozturk, Soyoung Sung, Aysel Tufekci, and Noemi Waight were involved with the lead authors of this chapter in a seminar at the University of Illinois at Urbana-Champaign. In the seminar, they developed a Web page and workshop on using digital video. This chapter is based on these workshops.

We speak of *data generation* rather than the more common *data collection* to emphasize the active nature of research: "Acquiring data is a very active, creative, improvisational process. Data must be generated before they can be collected" (Graue & Walsh, 1998, p. 91). The same principles that govern fieldwork in general apply to fieldwork with a camcorder. Readers seeking a more solid base in field-based research in general are directed to Erickson (1986). Graue and Walsh (1998) address field-based research with children.

Digital video holds great promise for field-based research because of (a) its ability to generate data, (b) the ease of transforming raw data into a data record, and (c) the availability of software that facilitates analysis. We begin with a brief history of video in field-based research. We then explore possibilities and challenges of digital video. Practical instruction on generating data, for example, camera placement, framing, using microphones, and so on, follows. We then discuss analyzing digital video data. The chapter concludes with some resources.

A Brief History of Film and Video in Fieldwork

Our brief treatment of the history of film and video draws heavily on the work of the National Research Council (2001). The use of film/video images in social science research, particularly anthropology, has a long history. *Nanook of the North*'s (released in 1922) compelling images of an Eskimo family remain riveting today. Mead and Bateson used images of children and families in their classic *Character Formation in Different Cultures* series, filmed from 1936 to 1938. The Spindlers used 8mm film for their Schoenhausen, Germany, and Roseville, Wisconsin, study (1977–1985). Tobin, Wu, and Davidson's (1989) video-based *Preschool in Three Cultures* was a watershed study on early schooling. The Spindlers and Tobin et al. used film and video not only to record data but also to stimulate responses, a creative advance in data generation.

From the beginning, the size, weight, and general obtrusiveness of film cameras and camcorders challenged researchers. Smaller film—Eastman Kodak introduced 16mm film in 1923 (de Brigard, 1975)—brought smaller, more manageable cameras. Eight millimeter film (1932) reduced camera size further, but it also reduced quality. Super-8 film (1965) offered greater brightness and a larger projected picture without increasing camera size.

Film provided remarkable power in generating data. Regnault, arguably the first to use film in research, stated that research film "preserves forever all human behaviors for the needs of our studies" (1931, p. 306, as cited in de Brigard, 1975, p. 15). Regnault was overly sanguine, but film does preserve records of human behavior in a way that written description does not. Film, however, remained a clumsy medium. Sensitive to light and heat, it required processing before it could be viewed. Nevertheless, fieldworkers persevered. Bateson and Mead, in response to charges of "soft" and unverifiable data, shot

22,000 feet of 16mm film and 25,000 stills in their fieldwork in Bali (for *Balinese Character,* 1942; de Brigard, 1975).

Videotape technology dates from the 1950s. By the late 1960s, videotape was used for television recording and transmission. Home VCRs arrived in the mid 1970s, in two competing formats, Beta (1975) and VHS (1976). Home video camcorders arrived in the mid '80s (Katz, 1994, p. 1413). Although camcorders were large, video images could be viewed immediately, both by the researcher and by the research participants. Eight millimeter videotape (1983) and HI8 (1989) brought small camcorders. Educational research using video became increasingly widespread, for example, Erickson (1982), Erickson and Schultz (1977), and Tobin, Wu, and Davidson (1989). Beginning in the 1970s, sociolinguists and educational anthropologists developed "micro-ethnography" (discussed below), using film and video to generate rich data from small samples (e.g., Erickson, 1982; Erickson & Schultz, 1977). The TIMSS study (discussed below) in the 1980s "sought to integrate the qualitative richness of small-scale video studies with the representative sampling of large-scale quantitative approaches in cross-national studies" (National Research Council, 2001, p. 6).

Analog video, for all its advantages over film, has drawbacks. Copying analog video results in loss of quality. Videotape fades over time and from repeated viewings. Tape can break, get caught in a VCR, and so on. Digital video appeared in the late 1980s. The first versions, D-1 and D-2, were 19mm-wide. In 1990, the D-3 format, with a half-inch tape, brought compact camcorders (Brown, 1992, p. 154). With Mini-DV tape (1996) came the small camcorder, reasonably unobtrusive, with small, long-life, quickly rechargeable batteries. Digital video marked a significant improvement over analog video in terms of storage, manipulation, and copying.

Possibilities and Challenges

Video has many strengths as a research tool. Our discussion draws heavily from Erickson, who has theorized well the use of video in research. We discuss strengths first, then turn to cautions.

Strengths

Detail. Video can reveal the unnoticed details of daily life (Erickson, 1992). Even the most perceptive observers can miss details recording by hand. Most places where researchers study children are fast moving and complex. Trying to catch and record everything is impossible. Anyone working with video knows the frustration of wanting to see what is happening off-camera. Nevertheless, the recorded details can be viewed repeatedly, they can be viewed in slow motion, the video can be paused, and so on.

Video can capture finely shaded details of everyday life, subtleties difficult to describe in fieldnotes. Small differences in patterns of social interactions in daily life have implications for big differences in unconscious levels and qualitative characteristics of social relations in a setting (Erickson & Wilson, 1982). Simple interaction patterns, such as how people shake hands, or how children greet each other and adults, will differ subtly depending on the situation and the other actors involved.

Rare events. Erickson (1992) noted audiovisual record's ability to capture rare events. The focus on counting events in quantitative analysis ignores the reality that the most salient events, which may have the most impact on what happens then and later, may occur rarely, or even once. Traumatic events do not have to occur regularly to affect people. The toughest kids in the class may rarely get in fights—often once is enough to convince other kids not to challenge them. Video does not guarantee being in the right place at the right time with the camcorder pointed at a rare but salient event, but, if captured, it can be viewed closely and repeatedly.

Revisiting data in real time. The most carefully recorded fieldnotes do not allow one to revisit the field in real time. Fieldnotes describing an hour on a playground can be read in a fraction of that time. Video puts the researcher in direct contact with real-time data that can be revisited in various times and ways (Erickson & Wilson, 1982; Erickson, 1992). Written descriptions often give the illusion that more is occurring than, in fact, is. Daily life, even daily life in a classroom, can be repetitious and tedious. Video records force the researcher to remain aware of that reality and not to present only the most interesting and compelling episodes.

Completeness of analysis. Video data help reduce "the dependence of the observer on premature interpretation" and "the dependence of the observer on frequently occurring events as the best source of data" (Erickson, 1992, p. 210). Video allows the researcher to view events and interactions repeatedly. Often, one does not begin to see critical aspects of an event until after repeated viewings. With video, one begins to see beneath the surface by viewing repeated versions of an event, for example, circle time in a preschool. The more times one views circle time, the more detailed one's fieldnotes become and the more focused one becomes on aspects not apparent initially. Viewing the same event repeatedly and viewing different versions of the same event are not the same. As Erickson (1992) points out, in order to view different versions of an event repeatedly, one becomes dependent on "frequently occurring events." Video allows one to look closely and repeatedly at events that may not occur frequently and to look closely at a subsample of frequently occurring events.

Coding in separate passes. Viewing a video repeatedly allows researchers to code for specific actions or interactions in different analytic passes. One can, for example, first view verbal interactions. As we discuss below, analysis software can facilitate this process. One can recode. One can go back to the video as many times as needed. Often later analysis will modify earlier analysis.

Stigler, Gonzales, Kawanaka, Knoll, and Serrano (1999) described how they coded data from the TIMSS study (described later) in multiple passes:

> On the first pass, for example, we coded the organization of the lesson; on the second, the use of the instructional materials; and on the third, the patterns of discourse that characterize the classrooms of each country. It would have been impossible for a live observer to code all these simultaneously. Not only can coding be done in passes but it can also be done in slow motion. With video, for example, it is possible to watch the same sample of behavior multiple times, enabling coders to describe behaviors in great detail. This makes it possible to conduct far more sophisticated analyses than would be possible with live observers. (p. 4)

Collaborative analysis. Rarely in fieldwork can groups of researchers view the same events. Three or four people observing the same circle time and writing furiously, unless they are behind one-way mirrors, are highly obtrusive. Video allows researchers to view the same events or interactions individually and in groups and to discuss them. Group viewing provides opportunity for communication among researchers—particularly helpful for cross-cultural study because the image can show subtle differences and help identify cultural assumptions (National Research Council, 2001).

Weaknesses

Exaggerated sense of confidence. The power of images allows researchers to believe that what they capture in the video is what is happening in a setting all the time, or that they have captured all that is happening (National Research Council, 2001). Tobin described how the video made to accompany *Preschool in Three Cultures* had the unintended consequence that once people viewed the video they saw little need to read the book (personal communication). We have heard people talk confidently and apparently knowledgeably about early schooling in Japan based on a single viewing of one part of the tape. D'Amato wrote of the video that became the basis for his research on the Kamehameha School in Hawaii (e.g., 1986, 1988):

> Here's something to think about. My account of this lesson is rich because I spent a lot of time looking at the tape and I knew a lot about the kids. But you know what? The first time I looked at it, I thought, "This was it? What did they get so excited about?" … The fullness of the moment lies in the sensuality of the experience of the here-and-now. That feeling is missing when you are looking at a tape or a transcript because your ongoing experience is not of the here-and-now of the interactional record but of your own context. Making the record come alive is a creative act. It requires engaging the document as though it were the here-and-now, building up a stream of thought within the record

itself. Yes? So: if your students have been disappointed at the thinness of their experience of their own records, they shouldn't expect anything different with this tape—the problem doesn't lie in the record. (personal communication, 1990)

Lack of contextual information. Video gives the illusion of, to use Geertz's (1988) phrase, *being there.* A video record is limited by the camera frame. The elements of presence and interaction with the event are absent to the analyst, particularly one not present during the data generation. This lack of direct participation leads to a loss of contextual information not easily deciphered from film or videotape (Erickson, 1992). Lewis, in a workshop sponsored by the Board of International Comparative Studies in Education, argued that video presents "a danger of overattributing causality to the classroom, because it is easily grasped and memorable, in contrast to other systemic factors [e.g., standards, working conditions, management practices], which may be murky yet causative" (National Research Council, 2001, p. 12).

Video requires decisions about what to record and what not to record—when, where, whom, and so on. The researcher must decide where to point the camcorder and when to turn it on and off. The camcorder captures what is occurring within the frame. It may record sound occurring outside the visual frame, giving some context, but an incomplete and often confusing one. Erickson (1992) emphasized, "Any audiovisual record is an incomplete document of what actually happened, even though a continuously shot film or tape is a more complete record than the observer's fieldnotes. Decisions about what to record and how to record it, then, are not neutral. They are research decisions that should be informed by the overall conduct of participant observation in the study" (p. 207).

Light and other challenges. Video is neither as sensitive nor as sophisticated as the human eye. For example, writing on a chalkboard or paper cannot be seen without zooming in, which excludes the larger activity. Video tolerates a limited range of brightness and has a narrower field of vision and less depth of field than the human eye (Roschelle, 2000, p. 721). Video reproduces sight and sound, but it cannot reproduce other aspects of an event, for example, the smells, the temperature, and so on. Jordan and Henderson (1995) observed,

> Whereas human beings have available to them their full sensory capacities (color, full resolution, peripheral vision, etc.) standard video [does not]. ... More subtly, what for a human observer may be at the periphery of attention but still appreciable, may be altogether off screen in a video recording. ... [T]he record will always be impoverished in some way or other, and it is important for the analyst to be aware of that. (p. 54)

Confidentiality. Video records contain faces and places. Written records can protect confidentiality with pseudonyms and adjusted descriptions. One can blur faces in video, but facial expressions are lost. An awareness of participants' concern about the embarrassment that visual records can produce is critical. At times, one must simply turn the camcorder off. Certain events do not need to be recorded, events that could cause embarrassment or worse. Video requires a heightened awareness of the need to decrease risk for participants (Erickson, 1992). Researchers must control who will see the tapes and under what circumstances. Teachers, for example, will be reluctant to participate if supervisors will view the video.

Getting approval. Ironically, as digital video equipment and software for creating data records and doing analysis becomes more sophisticated and easy to use, getting permission to use video in research in schools and institutions becomes more difficult. Using video can lengthen considerably the process of getting approval from the Institutional Review Board (IRB). Permission can usually be gained from participants by specifying exactly who can view the video and under what circumstances. Erickson (1986) pointed out that participants are generally less concerned about what happens in academic conferences in faraway cities than about being viewed by people who know them or people they work with, particularly people who are above them in the workplace hierarchy.

We recently made video recordings of a local preschool for a cross-cultural research project involving researchers in the U.S., Japan, and Germany (e.g., Kadota, Walsh, & Noguchi, 2004; Walsh, Kadota, Ashida, & Lee, 2005). The videos are being shown to teachers in the three countries to elicit their perspectives on activities that facilitate and hinder children's development. We gained permission by agreeing not to show the video to teachers within 90 miles of where the video was shot.

Ideally video will allow researchers in the future to view data records constructed many years earlier. For example, looking at Bateson and Mead's films brings one into their research in ways that written reports cannot. The National Research Council (2001) noted that "in some extreme cases, in the interest of confidentiality, IRBs might require that videos be destroyed rather than archived" (p. 20). The council noted further that issues surrounding confidentiality are

> very complex and require continuing attention from educators and ethicists, as well as researchers who have used video technology for a variety of purposes, to develop guidelines for the research community. Issues of confidentiality are further complicated in the case of international video because of the cross-cultural differences in perceptions of privacy and teaching, as well as the potential power of international video to reach and affect large and disparate audiences. (p. 20)

Why Digital Video?

Digital video marks a watershed improvement over analog video. In this section we discuss the possibilities and advantages of digital video.

Advantages

Ease of storage. Analog tape, like all things physical, deteriorates. We have begun to digitalize a collection of research videos from as far back as the 1970s, but we began the process too late. The tapes have already begun to fade. Digital tape also deteriorates. Mini-DV tape is fragile because of its small size. Storing digital images on hard drives, CDs, or DVDs, however, is straightforward. Images thus stored are easily catalogued and retrieved. We have some concern about the formats the images are stored in becoming obsolete, making stored video inaccessible.

No loss of quality in copying. Copying is necessary because one should not work with the original tape. Should the tape become damaged, the data record is gone. When an analog tape is copied, the quality is reduced. As copies are copied, the quality loss continues. Copying digital images does not reduce quality. Images can be copied indefinitely, and each copy is true to the original. Ideally, researchers generations from now will be able to view digital-video data records at the same level of quality that the original researchers saw.

Analysis. There are considerable advantages to using digital video for data analysis. We discuss those advantages in a later section.

Concerns

Inaccessibility in the future. A legitimate concern is that stored digital images may not be accessible in the future as formats, players, and hardware become obsolete. As technology changes, some things get left behind.

Trustworthiness. Digital images can be readily manipulated. Anyone with minimal computer skills and Photoshop can create seamless images that contain people and things not in the original. Manipulating digital video takes more sophisticated skills but is doable. Image manipulation is not new; it dates from photography's inception (Winston, 1998). For example, Andrew Gardner, who photographed the battlefield within 48 hours of the end of the Battle of Gettysburg, "was lugging a body around with him, recostuming it as he went and even, some suggest, turning the head despite rigor mortis" (p. 62). Winston gives another provocative example, quoting Andrew Bennett, a member of the British House of Commons, of the partial truth of images, "Perhaps there sits on the mantlepiece a photograph of Uncle Albert with a broad grin on his face, yet we know that, except for that one picture, he almost never grinned in his whole life" (p. 61).

Not all manipulation is wrong. Enhancing digital images by changing the light, for example, is easily done, and we do not believe that doing so is unethical. Manipulating images in more dramatic ways, for example, inserting people into an image or combining images without telling the reader or observer, is certainly skulduggery.

As we pointed out at the beginning, the principles underlying data generation remain the same regardless of how data are generated. Digital images can be manipulated, but so can written records. The ethical challenge is a perennial one. Digital video simply allows for more sophisticated forms of fraud.

Generating Data

The guiding rule for shooting video is *simplicity*. Keep the camera still. Get as many people as possible in the frame. Shoot interactions continuously. Erickson (1992) summed it up eloquently, "For use as a primary research document, a video record needs only three things: (1) visual framing that is consistent across time (not zooming in and out or panning from side to side for narrative emphasis), (2) a clear picture, and (3) a clear sound" (pp. 214–215).

A second rule is to think carefully about what to shoot and how long. Shooting video can be enjoyable. Viewing hours of video can be tedious. Ratcliff (2003) pointed out that "video contains an incredible amount of information; one can spend hours describing a 10-minute segment of video if the goal is to include as much detail as possible. For example, an exhaustive account … may require several pages of description for even a few seconds of video" (pp. 116–117). One does not have to provide an exhaustive account of all the video one takes, but one should keep in mind how long even viewing and logging (described below) tape takes.

Classrooms

Videotaping in classrooms, or in any closed space, presents challenges. One cannot video the entire room, and getting the audio one wants can be difficult. We reproduce here some suggestions from TIMSS, "the largest cross-national study of educational achievement ever conducted. Forty-one countries participated in the TIMSS, which included mathematics and science achievement testing of 4th, 8th, and 12th grade students" (Stigler, Gallimore, & Hiebert, 2000, p. 91), and the follow-up TIMSS-R studies (Stigler, Gonzales, Kawanaka, Knoll, & Serrano, 1999). These studies made extensive use of video. The suggestions below are based on shooting video of formal lessons. Their applicability to the more free-form early childhood classroom is not perfect, but the suggestions are useful for thinking about how and what to video.

1. Start before the instruction begins and end after instruction ends. This lessens the risk of missing something important because the camera is not on. An underlying premise here is simply that it is easier to discard data that one does not need or use than it is to acquire data that one failed to generate.
2. Document the perspective of an ideal student. Focus on the important activity and the learning tasks assigned by the teacher. The goal is to capture the lesson as it unfolds from the students' point of view.
3. Document the teacher. Regardless of what the ideal student does, the teacher should be followed at all times to document exactly what he or she does in order to teach the class.

In deciding what to shoot, one should proceed as in any fieldwork, that is, begin by looking generally, then focus in on specifics: "Overall, the strategy is to be increasingly selective as the research progresses in deciding what to record, while still controlling carefully the degree of selectivity at any given point" (Erickson & Wilson, 1982). Stigler et al. (1999, p.19) produced a list of possible flaws as they evaluated the videographers' camera work for TIMSS. Many involved zooming or panning and can be avoided by limiting severely the amount of zooming and panning that one does. The flaws included the following:

- Cropping shots too tightly (e.g., cutting off part of someone's head)
- Cropping shots too widely (e.g., too much head room)
- Zooming in and out and then having to reframe the shot
- Zooming in and out and then having to refocus the shot
- Panning while zoomed in tightly
- Jerky or awkward camera movement during zooms or pans
- Losing from the frame the object that is being tracked

Roschelle (2000) provided a useful checklist of things to do before the day of the shoot, things to do before recording, more things to do before recording, and things to do while recording (pp. 730–731). The list is too long to reproduce here, and most of the directives appear in this chapter. We recommend copying the list and referring to it often.

General Hints

Good research of any kind requires much planning and preparation. Spend time in the field before beginning to video. Let people get used to your presence. Find good places to situate yourself and from which to video. Experiment with tripod placement when no one is around. Experiment with the audio, finding the best locations for microphones and cords. Most important, think hard about how much video to shoot. Logging video (described below) takes much time; transcribing interviews takes even more.

Take care of the little things. Make sure that the camcorder battery is fully charged; bring a spare. If using a battery-driven microphone, check the batteries, and have spares. Have extra videotapes. Use the long-play option to reduce changing tapes. Label the videotapes immediately. Begin each taping with an announcement of the time, date, and place. Always have the time stamp on when shooting. Start shooting before the activity begins, and continue shooting after it ends. Keep the camera as still as possible. You will rue the tendency to pan and to zoom in and out when you begin coding.

Take fieldnotes. Videotapes need context. Without concurrent fieldnotes, contextualizing video becomes difficult. Video records behaviors. It does not record intentions—what Erickson (1986) termed *action*, that is, the behavior and the meaning behind it. A week or a month later, the reasons something occurred, which were obvious at the time, no longer are.

Obtrusiveness

Children find camcorders fascinating. They like to mug for the camcorder or get their face right up to the lens. They want to see themselves on the LCD panel. In time, kids become used to the camcorder, to some extent at least, or they find more interesting things to do. Still, the camcorder and the researcher never become invisible. Ratcliff (2003) "found that children made faces, grinned, used exaggerated movements, made obscene gestures, and even enacted drama for the camera. Although this was obvious in the early weeks of the study, some reactive effects were noted throughout the duration of the four-month study" (p. 115). Ting (1998) provides a salient example. In a preschool, she aimed a camcorder on a tripod at the block area. She turned it on, then moved away. After many weeks, she assumed that the kids had forgotten about it. One day three boys were playing in the block area. Suddenly, the three, who had been playing with their backs to the camcorder, turned in synch, pulled down the front of their pants, and waved their penises at the camcorder. They pulled their pants back up, turned back around, and continued to play. The episode, which took less than 4 seconds, went unnoticed by the adults in the classroom. The kids are always aware you and the camcorder are there.

A camcorder operated by someone is more noticeable than one left unattended. If possible, put the camcorder on a tripod or on a shelf, and move away from it. Once you start the camcorder, make sure it is running, then do not check it again. If you cannot leave the camcorder unattended, close the LCD screen and learn to shoot by aiming the camcorder, that is, without looking through the viewfinder. We have found that kids pay less attention to a camcorder if the LCD screen is closed. A closed LCD and not using the viewfinder makes zooming impractical, which, as noted above, is not necessarily bad.

Equipment

We recommend a high-quality small camcorder. Studio-quality camcorders are available. They are relatively expensive, and they are also comparatively large and obtrusive. For research purposes, studio quality is not required, and the performance of high-quality camcorders is excellent, even in less than ideal light. The most important accessory is a wide-angle lens. Wide-angle lenses are relatively inexpensive and screw onto the regular lens. A wide-angle lens increases the frame size dramatically, making video-recording within a room much easier. One can capture much of what is going on without continually panning.

Microphones. Roschelle (2000) stressed the importance of audio: "Without top-quality audio, research videos will usually be useless. Good quality microphones and an audio mixer [if more than one mic is used] are excellent investments. In audiorecording, as in real estate, the three most important rules are 'location, location, location'" (p. 716). We strongly suggest an external microphone. The camcorder microphone is usually binaural, recording 270 degrees, that is, not only what one is shooting, but much of the surrounding sounds as well. *Power zone microphones (PZM) microphones* work exceptionally well in recording an activity occurring in one place, for example, circle time or a group gathered around a table. *PZMs* are nondirectional. They lie flat and require a flat hard surface, such as a table top or floor. They can be mounted on a wall using double-sided foam tape, but be cautious because removing foam tape can also remove paint or even plaster. *PZMs* do not look like microphones. They don't tempt young kids to imitate their favorite singers or to talk directly into them. They are quite sensitive and can be placed to the side of an activity. They are monaural and, on camcorders with a stereo microphone, will record on one side of the stereo spectrum.

For directional microphones, a *zoom microphone* is an improvement on the *shotgun mic.* Attached to the camera, it zooms in synch with the camera's zoom lens. The *zoom microphone* is directional, that is, it records only in the direction that it is pointing. Zoom microphones work well when one wants to record the individual child speaking.

Wireless microphones are most useful when recording one person, for example, the teacher or a target child. The most common type is a lapel mic, attached to clothing. These mics can be sewn into clothing, for example, a vest that a target child wears. One must take care that the mic is not rubbing against fabric when the person moves, or this rubbing sound will dominate. Wireless mics record clearly the person wearing them, but in dialogue between the wearer and others, others' voices may be lost.

Microphones can be frustrating. Some sounds, often unwanted, record more readily than others, for example, sharp sounds such as a pencil dropping or fingernails drumming on a table top. On playgrounds, wind noise can mask what people are saying. Windscreens help somewhat. Playground and classroom noise can drown out speech. The best advice is to experiment with different microphones and placement and have different kinds of microphones ready.

Videotaping Interviews

Video the interview at eye level. Do not place the interviewee's face too close to the edge of the screen, which makes the viewer feel uncomfortable. Allow plenty of space, especially if the person is moving. Do not shoot a person or object straight on. Find a location that reinforces the story and informs the viewer about the speaker (e.g., office, classroom, playground). If interviewing outside, seek consistent lighting, for example, an overcast day or consistent sunshine. The intensity and inconsistency of sunlight make it preferable to shoot the interview in the shade, avoiding backgrounds in the full brightness of the sun.

A common mistake is to center the subject in the frame, then to zoom in keeping the subject the same distance from all 4 sides of the frame. The effect is that the frame visually implodes on the subject. Instead, keep one or two sides of the frame at the same distance from the subject for the zoom, allowing the other two or three sides of the frame to change their relative position to the subject. When a subject is looking out of the frame, for example, to the side, give the subject looking room, that is, additional space in the direction of gaze; similarly, when the subject is walking across the frame, give more space in front than behind (Musberger, 1993).

Analysis

Before analysis comes planning—how one intends to generate video data, how these data will fit into the larger research plan, and how analysis will be done. Video is but one part of the data record, one form of evidence. Lesh and Lehrer (2000, p. 684) argue that an interpretive framework will be enhanced by decisions made before generating video data about the following:

- The primary function of the videotape
- Likely targets of the video, for example, small groups or individuals
- Methods for triangulation, that is, using other sources of evidence
- How the research team will conduct analysis

Good analysis requires interacting with video as it is shot. Waiting weeks or months removes one from the immediacy of the event. The first step to constructing a data record is to log the tape. The log should be made as soon as possible while the events are still fresh in one's mind. A log is basically a table of contents for the tape referenced to the time stamp.

[Logs] consist of a heading that gives identifying information, followed by a rough summary listing of the events as they occur on the tape. The level of detail is determined by the interests of the researcher and the available time. No attempt is made at this stage to provide either consistency or evenness in coverage. Content listings are useful for providing a quick overview of the data corpus, for locating particular sequences and issues, and as a basis for doing full transcripts for particularly interesting segments. (Jordan & Henderson, 1995, p. 43)

Analysis of a video data record proceeds the same way as analysis of any data record constructed from field-based research. The most important rule is to begin analysis early and to continue analysis as data are generated. Erickson's (1986) discussion of data analysis and reporting is useful and complete. We focus here on analysis issues peculiar to video data records.

Analysis begins with systematic and repetitive viewing of the video. Erickson (1992, pp. 217–222) listed five stages:

1. Review the whole event at regular speed, without stopping
2. Identify the major constituent parts of the event
3. Identify aspects of organization within major parts of the event, focusing on the relationships of mutual influence among participants
4. Focus on actions of individuals
5. Compare instances across one's data record

Jordan and Henderson noted that "events of any duration are always segmented in some way. They have an internal structure that is recognized and maintained by participants" (1995, p. 59).

Video supports simultaneous bottom-up and top-down analyses. In the TIMSS study, Stigler, Gallimore, and Hiebert (2000) discussed the tension between top-down, that is, beginning with "global, theoretically driven questions," and bottom-up, that is, "coding of individual units, letting the bigger questions suggest themselves as analysis proceeds" (p. 96). They concluded that doing both simultaneously brought a much richer understanding than either approach alone. Jordan and Henderson (1995) attended to the "'C-issues': cooperation, conflict, conviviality, competition, collaboration, commitment, caution, control, coercion, coordination, co-optation, combat, and so on" (p. 69), a useful beginning point.

Video's ability to preserve detail gave rise to *microethnography*, which Erickson and Wilson (1982) described as follows:

The microethnographic approach is concerned ... with reporting the *what* of face to face interaction in key scenes in people's everyday lives. In addition, the microethnographic approach is concerned with the detailed analysis of *how* people do what they do interactionally. ... [It] depends upon a combination of participant observation (direct, continuous observation and reflection, recorded in running fieldnotes) and microanalysis of films and videotapes of everyday happenings in schools. For such analysis, high quality audiovisual records are necessary. (p. 43)

Microethnography, which focuses on detail, requires awareness of and attention to the larger contexts for analysis. Erickson (1992) described how microethnographic analysis proceeds.

Notice that even when analytic focus is at its narrowest and most precise—in the transcription of the actions of individuals in fine grained behavioral detail—this approach emphasizes the social and cultural ecology of meaning just as does more general ethnography. This is not "micro" study in isolation from macrosocial processes, nor is it behaviorist in orientation despite its close attention to details of interactional behavior. ... Fundamentally, such analysis is not "micro" at all, but "macro" in its interests. ... (pp. 222–223)

Analysis Software

Digital-video data analysis software can facilitate analysis tremendously. As yet, we have not discovered the ideal software. The major shortcoming of existing software is that it works well for either verbal interactions or physical actions, but not both. A second limitation is that programs run either on PCs or on Macs. A third is that they do not support all video formats. In transferring digital video from tape, one must choose a format supported by the software. Nevertheless, the software programs we describe, *Transana, Transtool, The Observer,* and *GameBreaker,* have many strengths.

The major advantages of analysis software are *consistency* and *speed.* Analysis software makes it easy to assign codes. One can quickly search for all the places a given code was applied and easily review all the data assigned to a given code. One can search and re-search the data, quickly re-sort a database, redefine codes, and reassign chunks of video whenever necessary. Once digital video has been copied off the tape, one does not have to wait for tape to reach a given segment. One can move to different segments almost instantaneously or view the same segment repeatedly without rewinding.

Transana. Transana is a Windows-based open-source analysis software developed at the University of Wisconsin–Madison. *Transana* supports MPEG1 and MPEG2. It can:

- Create transcripts of videos
- Navigate through videos using several different mechanisms, including a precise waveform image
- Link places in the transcript to frames in the video

- Automatically highlight the relevant portion of the transcript while the video plays
- Organize analytically selected interesting portions of video into meaningful groups
- Attach keywords to relevant portions of video
- Search keywords and locate video clips to which they have been applied

Transana is free and can be downloaded from http://www.transana.org. *Transana* is well supported, and workshops are offered regularly at conferences and at the University of Wisconsin. It is reasonably easy to use. Developed for coding speech, it is, unfortunately, not useful for coding action.

Transtool. *Transtool* is a Windows-based analysis software for transcribing and coding digital-video data developed at the University of Illinois. Like *Transana*, it is free. It supports *Real Media* (RM). Transtool can:

- Transcribe digital video with accurate time-stamping
- Synchronize existing transcripts with video files
- Define and mark codes
- Rapidly cue to points of interest
- Create SMIL files of the video, transcript, and codes, which can be played back on any platform
- Extract clips of interest for playback as a single presentation
- Export time-stamps and codes as tables of data for use in other applications

We have found *Transtool* easier to learn and use than *Transana*. Like *Transana,* it was developed for coding speech rather than action. A disadvantage to *Transtool* is that the developers have moved on, and it is no longer being updated or supported.

The Observer. *The Observer* is a Windows-based analysis software for generating and analyzing digital-video data on behavior (i.e., what people do as opposed to what they say). *The Observer* supports MPEG 1 and MPEG 2 and AVI. It enables the user to (a) code video data and log events, (b) analyze data using descriptive statistics on frequencies and durations, and (c) structure the process or the occurrence of events. We have used *The Observer* on a trial basis and found it most impressive, but also difficult to learn. It is not free, costing, at this writing, about $6,000.

GameBreaker. *GameBreaker* is a Macintosh-based digital-video analysis system by *Sportstec*. Originally designed for analyzing continuous-play sports, for example, basketball, rugby, or soccer, *GameBreaker* supports QuickTime (MOV). It can:

- Record performance as it happens
- Access any part of video instantly
- Edit material on the spot

- Select and replay individual video frames
- Create a chronological record
- Produce individual movies and presentations

Gamebreaker is less expensive than *The Observer*, about $2,000 at this writing. It is also quite easy to learn and use. We have used it extensively and like working with it. It can be installed on different machines, but it can only be used if a "dongle," which comes with the program, is inserted into the USB slot. This allows one to work on data on different machines, for example, at home and in the office.

Coding with *GameBreaker* is intuitively straightforward. One can generate color codes and code using keys or the mouse. The coding system is easily learned and applied. Once a video is coded, one can make a video that shows only the episodes with the same code. For example, if interested in conflicts, one can in a few seconds make a video that includes only conflict episodes. We find this most useful for comparing similar events.

We first became aware of *GameBreaker* when we realized that early childhood classrooms have much in common with continuous-play sports. It is most useful for coding actions, what people do, rather than what they say. *SportsCode* has a new product, *StudioCode*, which we were told can code both action and speech. It is quite expensive, about $10,000, although site licenses are available. We have not, at this point, used it. Both *GameBreaker* and *The Observer* do descriptive statistical analyses based on frequency of events and duration.

Conclusion

The goal of research with young children is to deepen our understanding of them and of their contemporary realities. This understanding requires what Erickson (1986) called a strong "evidentiary record." Research consists of drawing inferences from observations (King, Keohane, & Verba, 1994). The inferences drawn can never be stronger than the data record on which they are based. Digital video, used well and thoughtfully, can strengthen a data record immensely.

The power of digital video in field-based research with young children is in the detail of the record. Interviewing young children is challenging. It can be done and done well, but one cannot depend on it the way one can with older children or adults (Graue & Walsh, 1998). Deep understanding of young children and their contemporary realities will come from close observation of children in the contexts within which they lead their daily lives and, most important, from the records of those observations. Understanding young children requires close attention to what they are doing and to what they are saying as they are doing it. Quite simply, video can record their actions and interactions better than written records can.

Our group has been using digital video extensively in our research. At this point, we are still exploring the possibilities. For example, Chung and Walsh (in press) studied young children using computers to develop writing skills. An initial frustration was that when Chung videoed the pairs of children working at the computer, she could record the screen or the pair but not both. Using *Camtasia*, a computer screen–tracking program, which records the computer screen from within the computer, she was able to record both the children and the screen. She was then able to synchronize the two and run them side by side, allowing her to see both what the children were doing and saying and what they were writing and drawing on the screen. Walsh's (2002, 2004) study of Japanese preschools focused on the space, both literal and figurative, afforded children and on their physical development. His analysis depended on a fine-grained view of interactions made possible by video. Sung's (2005) study of young children's emotional development in preschools recorded teachers' interactions with young children in fine detail by using a wireless microphone and video. Being able to hear exactly what the teacher and child were saying and to look carefully at their interactions helped immensely in understanding the dynamics of these interactions.

Digital video holds great promise for field-based research with young children. It has become for us an essential tool of the trade. Digital video will not make one a better researcher. But a good, thoughtful researcher will find that digital video opens up new possibilities for doing research on young children and their worlds.

Resources

Editors of *Computer Videomaker Magazine*. (2004). *The Videomaker guide to digital video and DVD production* (2nd ed.). Boston: Elsevier. A collection of short chapters that cover everything from streaming to putting video on DVD to framing good shots to microphones. Invaluable and practical.

Erickson, F., & Wilson, J. (1982). *Sights and sounds of life in schools: A resource guide to film and videotape for research and education*. East Lansing: Institute for Research on Teaching, Michigan State University. A dated but extremely useful resource for anyone doing video research in schools. Long out of print, it may be available in libraries.

Goldman-Segall, R. (1998). *Points of viewing children's thinking: A digital ethnographer's journey*. Mahwah, NJ: Erlbaum. Personal story from someone who has done much video research with children.

Heritage, J. (1984). Conversation analysis. In *Garfinkle and ethnomethodology*. Boston: Polity Press. A thorough discussion of conversation analysis with useful examples.

Jordan, B., & Henderson, A. (1995). Interaction analysis: Foundations and practice. *Journal of the Learning Sciences, 4*, 39–103. A useful discussion of "an interdisciplinary method for the empirical investigation of the interaction of human beings with each other and the objects in their environment ... [using] [v]ideo technology ..." (p. 39). A thorough and rich resource.

Musberger, Robert B. (1993). *Single-camera video production*. Boston: Focal Press. Explains how to plan, shoot, and edit most field and studio video productions, providing clear explanations, details, and visuals.

National Research Council. (2001). *The power of video technology in international comparative research in education*. Washington, DC: National Academy Press. Provides a good overview and history of using video in educational research.

Stigler, J., Gonzales, P., Kawanaka, T., Knoll, S., & Serrano, A. (1999). *The TIMSS videotape classroom study: Methods and findings from an exploratory research project on eighth-grade mathematics instruction in Germany, Japan, and the United States.* Washington, DC: National Center for Educational Statistics. A detailed and practical description of the largest cross-national study ever undertaken. Useful discussions of shooting video in a classroom and of coding.

References

Bateson, G., & Mead, M. (1942). *Balinese character.* New York: Academy of Science.

Brown, L. (1992). *Encyclopedia of television.* New York: Gale Research.

Chung, Y-h., & Walsh, D. J. (in press). Constructing a joint story-writing space: The dynamics of young children's collaboration at computers. *Early Education and Development.*

D'Amato, J. (1986). *"We cool, tha's why": A study of personhood and place in Hawaiian second graders.* Unpublished doctoral dissertation, University of Hawaii.

D'Amato, J. (1988). "Acting": Hawaiian children's resistance to teachers. *Elementary School Journal, 88,* 529–544.

De Brigard, E. (1975). The history of ethnographic film. In P. Hockings (Ed.), *Principles of visual anthropology* (pp. 13–43). Paris: Mouton.

Erickson, F. (1982). Audiovisual records as a primary data source. In A. Grimshaw (Ed.), *Sound-image records in social interaction research* [Special issue]. *Journal of Sociological Methods and Research, 11,* 213–232.

Erickson, F. (1986). Qualitative methods in research on teaching. In M. C. Wittrock (Ed.), *Handbook of research on teaching* (3rd ed., pp. 119–161). New York: Macmillan.

Erickson, F. (1992). Ethnographic micronanalysis of interaction. In M. LeCompte, W. Millroy, & J. Preissle (Eds.), *The handbook of qualitative research in education* (pp. 201–225). New York: Academic Press.

Erickson, F., & Schultz, J. (1977). When is a context? Some issues and methods in the analysis of social competence. *Quarterly Newsletter of the Institute for Comparative Human Development, 1,* 5–10.

Erickson, F., & Wilson, J. (1982). *Sights and sounds of life in schools: A resource guide to film and videotape for research and education.* East Lansing: Institute for Research on Teaching, Michigan State University.

Geertz, C. (1988). *Works and lives: The anthropologist as author.* Palo Alto, CA: Stanford University Press.

Graue, M. E., & Walsh, D. J. (1998). *Studying children in context: Theories, methods, and ethics.* Newbury Park, CA: Sage.

Jordan, B., & Henderson, A. (1995). Interaction analysis: Foundations and practice. *Journal of the Learning Sciences, 4,* 39–103.

Kadota, R., Walsh, D., & Noguchi, T. (2004, April). *Can images of children's intellectual development be shared?* Paper presented at the annual meeting of the American Educational Research Association, San Diego, CA.

Katz, E. (Ed.). (1994). *The film encyclopedia.* New York: HarperCollins.

King, G., Keohane, R. O., & Verba, S. (1994). *Designing social inquiry: Scientific inference in qualitative research.* Princeton, NJ: Princeton University Press.

Lesh, R. A., & Lehrer, R. (2000). Iterative refinement cycles for videotape analyses of conceptual change. In A. E. Kelly & R. A. Lesh (Eds.), *Handbook of research design in mathematics and science education* (pp. 665–708). Mahwah, NJ: Erlbaum.

Musburger, R. B. (1993). *Single-camera video production.* Boston: Focal Press.

National Research Council. (2001). *The power of video technology in international comparative research in education.* Washington, DC: National Academy Press.

Ratcliff, D. (2003). Video methods in qualitative research. In P. M. Camic, J. E. Rhodes, & L. Yardley (Eds.), *Qualitative research in psychology: Expanding perspectives in methodology and design* (pp. 113–129). Washington, DC: American Psychological Association.

Regnault, F-L. (1931). E role du cinema en ethnographie. *La Nature, 59,* 304–306.

Roschelle, J. (2000). Choosing and using video equipment for data collection. In A. E. Kelly & R. A. Lesh (Eds.), *Handbook of research design in mathematics and science education* (pp. 708–731). Mahwah, NJ: Erlbaum.

Spindler, G., & Spindler, L. (1992). Cultural process and ethnography: An anthropological perspective. In M. LeCompte, W. Millroy, & J. Preissle (Eds.), *The handbook of qualitative research in education* (pp. 53–92). New York: Academic Press.

Stigler, J. W., Gallimore, R., & Hiebert, J. (2000). Using video surveys to compare classrooms and teaching across cultures: Examples and lessons from the TIMSS video studies. *Educational Psychologist, 35,* 87–100.

Stigler, J., Gonzales, P., Kawanaka, T., Knoll, S., & Serrano, A. (1999). *The TIMSS videotape classroom study: Methods and findings from an exploratory research project on eighth-grade mathematics instruction in Germany, Japan, and the United States.* Washington, DC: National Center for Educational Statistics.

Sung, S. (2005). *Emotional development in preschool.* Unpublished doctoral dissertation, University of Illinois at Urbana-Champaign.

Ting, H-y. (1998). Getting into the peer social worlds of young children. In M. E. Graue & D. J. Walsh (Eds.), *Studying children in context: Theories, methods, and ethics* (pp. 146–157). Newbury Park, CA: Sage.

Tobin, J., Wu, D., & Davidson, D. (1989). *Preschool in three cultures: Japan, China, and the United States.* New Haven, CT: Yale University Press.

Walsh, D. J. (2002). The development of self in Japanese preschools: Negotiating space. In L. Bresler & A. Ardichvili (Eds.), *Research in international education: Experience, theory, & practice* (pp. 213–245). New York: Peter Lang.

Walsh, D. J. (2004). Frog boy and the American monkey. In L. Bresler (Ed.), *Knowing bodies, feeling minds* (pp. 97–109). Amsterdam: Kluwer.

Walsh, D. J., Kadota, R., Ashida, H., & Lee, T. B. (2005, April). *The culture of community of practices: U.S. preschool teachers' views of children's development.* Paper presented at the annual meeting of the American Educational Research Association, San Francisco.

Winston, B. (1998). "The camera never lies": The partiality of photographic evidence. In J. Prosser (Ed.), *Image-based research: A source book for qualitative researchers* (pp. 60–68). London: Falmer Press.

4

The Potential of Focus Groups to Inform Early Childhood Policy and Practice

SHARON RYAN AND CARRIE LOBMAN

Rutgers, the State University of New Jersey

Those of us who conduct research in early childhood settings in the United States are living in unusual times. While the possibilities for research design continue to expand in response to the multiplicity of theoretical positions and the increasing diversity of populations being served in programs, policy makers seem to be committed to standardizing what counts as valid inquiry. The Institute for Educational Sciences, the research arm of the United States Department of Education, for example, will not fund studies that are qualitative in nature unless they are part of a larger experimental design of some kind. Policy makers want to be able to disseminate evidence-based approaches that will lead to improved teaching and student outcomes. From their perspective, qualitative research, with its focus on the particularities of context and the meanings individuals give to experience, is not up to the task of providing insights on problems of practice that can be applied on a large scale across a number of educational sites. Unfortunately, this view precludes policy makers from seeing the potential of focus group methodology as one qualitative means that can help them to not only capture the perspectives of a large number of constituents but also gain deeper insights into the effectiveness of policies in practice.

A focus group is a group interview structured around a series of questions designed to elicit participants' perspectives on a particular topic (Morgan, 1997). As with other forms of qualitative interviewing, focus groups seek participants' thoughts, experiences, and emotions about a particular issue through the use of a semistructured or nonstandardized interview format (Patton, 1990). However, the data gathered from a focus group interview are framed not only by individual experience but also by the social nature and dynamics of the group. That is, the group interaction created through a focus group interview produces data that might not be available through one-on-one interviews (Morgan, 1997). Because this methodology is group oriented and primarily based on interviews and not other forms of data (e.g., observations), focus groups permit the researcher to sample larger numbers of participants who can be selected as representatives of a particular educational context (e.g., Head Start, public schools, child care), location (state, district), or position within a system (teacher, parent, principal, student). As a consequence, the data gathered through focus groups can be policy capturing in that the findings from these studies can shed light on the ways policies are being implemented and experienced in a number of sites.

Conducting focus groups, however, is not a simple undertaking. In this chapter, we use our experiences studying the implementation of a new state system of teacher education and professional development to illustrate some of the methodological considerations needed to ensure that the data collected can be informative for both policy and practice. After elaborating on designing and implementing a focus group study, the chapter concludes with a discussion of some of the possibilities and challenges of using focus groups in early childhood research.

Designing a Focus Group Study

Like any other qualitative research project, a focus group study needs to be carefully conceptualized and prepared for. As Krueger and Casey (2000) point out, a focus group is not simply about bringing people together in a room to talk. Rather, a "focus group is a special type of group in terms of purpose, size, composition, and procedures" (p. 4). Researchers must consider not only why this methodology is best suited to their purposes; focus groups also require a different kind of attention to sampling and the processes of collecting and analyzing data, as well as the writing up of findings. Each of these practical concerns is discussed next in relation to the decisions and actions we took as researchers employing this methodology for the first time.

Why Use Focus Groups?

As focus groups rely on the emotions, thoughts, and experiences of a group of individuals, they are a methodology best suited to answer questions that seek different perspectives on an issue and to illuminate some of the factors that may be contributing to these differences. Moreover, a group interview format is also relevant if the researcher is trying to get at an issue that may not be apparent to informants when asked individually. Early childhood settings are political spaces, and teaching for the most part is an isolated activity. Being in a focus group may help participants speak about topics that are often left unaddressed.

Each of these concerns catalyzed our interest in using focus groups as part of our study of the early childhood teacher preparation and professional development system in New Jersey. At the time of our study, New Jersey provided a unique context in which to examine the professional preparation and development of preschool teachers. Through a series of Supreme Court decisions (*Abbott v. Burke V*, 1998; *Abbott v. Burke VI*, 2000), 30 *Abbott* districts were required to create systems of high-quality preschool for all 3- and 4-year-old children beginning in the 1999–2000 school year. High-quality programs were defined as those having a class size of no more than 15 students with a certified teacher and teacher assistant for each classroom. As a way of transitioning this policy into practice, most districts chose to collaborate with existing Head Start programs and private child care settings that were already offering preschool in their communities. Prior to the Court's preschool decision, however, the credential required for "teachers" in New Jersey's private preschool centers and Head Start programs was a minimum of a Child Development Associate (CDA) credential (Division of Youth and Family Services, 1998). To ensure quality in these programs, the Court also mandated that all teachers in *Abbott* preschools—unless they already held the Nursery or Kindergarten through Grade 8 certificate and had 2 years of experience working with preschool-aged children—must obtain a minimum of a bachelor's degree with Preschool–Grade 3 (P–3) certification by September 2004.

As there had not been a specialized early childhood teaching certificate in the state, New Jersey's institutions of higher education created specialized P–3 certification programs, utilizing both alternate and traditional approaches to teacher preparation. Several funding sources (Quality and Capacity Grants, Teacher Effectiveness and Teacher Preparation Grants) were also provided by the state government through the Commission for Higher Education to help institutions of higher education expand their early childhood faculties. Further, as school districts were to collaborate with existing Head Start and private child care programs already offering preschool in their communities, and many of these teachers had to obtain a P–3, a state-funded scholarship program was also initiated to pay for teachers' tuition as they upgraded their qualifications.

At the same time this P–3 preparation system was being created, school districts embarked on a series of initiatives to meet the professional development needs of preschool teachers. These initiatives included the employment of master teachers to provide technical assistance and in-classroom support with implementing developmentally appropriate curriculum models. Early childhood supervisors were also employed to oversee and implement ongoing professional development experiences for the district's preschool teachers. Thus, a new teacher preparation and professional development system was developed in a short period of time.

The creation of this system impacted all levels of the early childhood field in New Jersey, from policy makers, to higher education, to district administrators, as well as the teaching staff working within various auspices. As we were interested in examining how this system was being implemented and experienced across the state—particularly from the perspectives of those who had to enact the mandate—a focus group study seemed to be a perfect fit. Focus groups made it possible for us to talk with key stakeholders at all levels of the system while also helping us to understand how the system worked from these different vantage points. Moreover, as teacher educators, it was important to us that the teacher's voice be foregrounded in the study and focus groups seemed to be a helpful way to get teachers from a range of settings to begin to talk about their experiences in the new P–3 teacher development system.

In determining whether to use focus group methodology, researchers must also consider whether the focus groups are to be the primary source of data, or to supplement other data collected as part of a mixed methods study (Morgan, 1997). This decision also depends on the questions being asked by the researchers and whether they are more likely to identify themselves as qualitative or quantitative scholars. In our case, we were both primarily qualitative researchers who had received funding to conduct a survey study of this new system through the perspectives of teachers and the agencies providing professional preparation (see Lobman, Ryan, & McLaughlin, 2005a; Ryan & Ackerman, 2005). As we designed the study, we also knew we wanted to get a deeper picture of what was going on as people responded to this new policy. Therefore, we chose to implement focus groups as the third phase of our study so that it would be possible to revisit our understanding of some of the topics examined in the surveys.

A second purpose in utilizing focus groups at the end of the study was the opportunity they provided to elicit the different perspectives of stakeholders in order to identify some of the barriers to change and perhaps encourage the generation of novel solutions. However, it might also have been useful to have begun with focus groups, as talking with stakeholders before developing our survey instruments could have informed the content and form of the questionnaires that were employed. Clearly, if this method is to be used to gather supplementary data to be used with other qualitative or quantitative datasets, then the researcher must consider for which purposes this supplementary data are to be collected and therefore when and where focus groups might best be employed.

Choosing Participants

As focus groups rely solely on the input of interviewees, sampling is one of the most crucial sets of decisions researchers must make. Krueger and Casey (2000) argue that sampling decisions must be made on two levels. First, "information-rich" participants or cases (Patton, 1990) must be identified and recruited for the study. Here, the researcher should ask what characteristics of participants will help to shed light on the phenomenon being studied. For example, if the purpose of our study had been to elicit teachers' experiences of trying to meet the *Abbott* court mandate to obtain a P–3 teaching certificate, then most of our sampling would have focused on recruiting teachers to represent a range of demographic characteristics as well as experience levels, qualifications (e.g., CDA, AA), and auspice (Head Start, child care, public school). However, because we sought to understand how the *Abbott* policy of qualified teachers had been interpreted, enacted, and experienced at all levels of the newly created teacher preparation and professional development system, we had to find participants who could represent the various levels of the system as well as the different roles and responsibilities within this system. A final sampling criterion that also had to be met was geographic location within the state, as this study was concerned with a statewide policy. Thus, as with other qualitative projects, when determining the sample for a focus group study, it is necessary to aim for maximum variation (Creswell, 1997). But if the researcher is interested in informing policy, then attention must also be given to identifying informants who not only have experience with the policy but are also in locations where the policy is supposed to be having an impact.

The second level of sampling decisions according to Krueger and Casey (2000) concerns number, not only in terms of the total number of participants but also the number of focus groups to be convened. Krueger and Casey recommend that researchers plan on between three and four focus groups by participant type to ensure that there are enough data from each group to conduct comparisons. To ensure that a rich conversation is generated, it is also necessary to keep the composition of focus groups to between six and eight participants. The number issue, however, is also influenced by resources and how much personnel, time, and money are available to conduct the study. In addition, some target samples may not be large to begin with, and therefore, it may not be possible to conduct more than one group interview. In this case, the researcher has to decide if a focus group interview is the best method to use. Sampling decisions, therefore, require a give and take between these two levels of decision making. The aim is to obtain maximum variation in participant characteristics, some kind of representation in terms of the reach of the policy being investigated, and an adequate number of focus groups to achieve some level of data "saturation" (Strauss & Corbin, 1998).

In our own study, for example, resources, availability of participants, and the number of individuals who could be identified at each level interacted to determine the final sample. This selection process varied for each category of stakeholder. Policy makers at the state level were already a small and discrete group. Preschool teachers, professional development providers, and representatives of 2- and 4-year colleges involved in P–3 certification programs were selected based on their responses to survey questions in the larger study.

From this initial listing, we then used a second level of criteria to determine the final participants representing each stakeholder group. As we wanted to get at the experiences of teachers who spanned the spectrum of educational background and levels of experience, the final criteria guiding selection of preschool teachers were location in the state (i.e., north, central, or southern region), level of experience, and education qualifications. Professional development providers were chosen to represent the diversity of agencies providing training to preschool teachers and included representatives from resource and referral agencies, master teachers, child care administrators, district staff developers, and school principals. Equal numbers of representatives from 2- and 4-year institutions of higher education were selected because of the programs offered by their institutions (dual certification programs, alternate route programs, etc.) and the partnerships they had with other training agencies (e.g., articulation agreements).

This selection process generated a list of 69 potential participants, but after contacting everyone, we ended up with a final sample of 38 individuals (16 teachers, 5 higher education representatives, 11 professional development providers, and 6 policy makers) who we organized into eight focus groups (three with teachers, two with higher education representatives, two with professional development providers, and one with state policy makers).

Conducting Focus Group Interviews

One of the advantages of using focus groups is that they are a relatively efficient data collection strategy. While each focus group interview will take several hours, once conducted, the researcher has a complete dataset from a large number of participants. At the same time, as it may not be possible to bring a particular grouping of people together again, it is imperative that the content and form of the interviews are carefully designed so that relevant information on the phenomenon being investigated is gathered. Therefore, the interview protocol and the role of the interviewer are crucial.

Interview protocol. As the aim of a focus group is to get people talking about a particular phenomenon in depth, the interview protocol has to be open enough to facilitate conversation but structured in a way so that the group conversation remains focused on the topic of study. It is also important to begin the interview with some kind of introductory question or set of questions that will enable everyone to be introduced to each other and build a sense of connection (Krueger & Casey, 2000). Opening questions are just as important for the researcher or facilitator as they provide the person conducting the interview with a better sense of the people in the room, and who might be a good person to target to respond to the first question; they also help with identification of respondents during the analysis phase. For example, in our protocol, we began by introducing ourselves and providing an overview of the purposes of the study. We then gave participants a sense of how the time would be used before stating, "Let's begin by going around the table and asking each person to introduce him/herself with your full name, and what you do in the field of early childhood education." In addition to opening questions to help build this group connectivity, it is always also useful to have some refreshments available. Whether it is a light breakfast, lunch, or a snack, the gesture helps make participants feel welcome and encourages them to begin to engage with each other prior to the start of the formal part of the interview session.

Following the opening section of the interview, the main part of the protocol is structured around key questions (Krueger & Casey, 2000) related to the phenomenon being studied. Like any other interview, it is important that the questions are open-ended and clearly stated so that participants are not confused and can readily respond. We found it helpful to begin with more concrete and experience-based questions before moving on to larger questions concerning the system and what was and was not working. The protocol used, therefore, was structured in three parts. First, participants were asked to identify the kinds of knowledge and skills preschool teachers needed to know and be able to do, and what kinds of training contribute to their development. In this section we asked participants, whether they were recipients or providers of that training, to detail their own experiences. The second part of the protocol was comprised of questions about the system of teacher preparation and professional development, and, depending on the stakeholder group, touched on such things as scholarships, partnerships between institutions, and outreach efforts. Just as every interview has a set of opening or orienting questions, there also needs to be space to conclude the discussion (Krueger & Casey, 2000; Patton, 1990). We chose to bring the focus group discussion to closure by asking participants to use their own experiences and understandings to identify the major barriers they saw to developing a system where preschool teacher development opportunities were coordinated. Here we were asking them to not only think back but also to project a personal view from their standpoint within the system.

Role of the facilitator. Entire books have been dedicated to the process of moderating focus groups (e.g., Krueger, 1997). This is because interviewing people in a way that allows them to provide a lot of input while also ensuring that the interview questions are answered adequately and from everyone in the group is a job requiring great skill. Aside from keeping the conversation going in the right direction, the facilitator must also pay attention to the nonverbal behavior of participants, what in the context of the group seems to spark various speakers, as well as the ideas that are put forth. Finally, the moderator also has to have a solid understanding of the topic as well as strong interpersonal skills so that s/he is able to show interest in what people are saying (even when she may disagree with the content of the conversation), and be able to prompt individuals in a respectful manner in order to follow up on a comment or topic. Without a good moderator, the quantity and quality of data gathered may be compromised.

We found that the best way to moderate the focus groups was to work as a team. One of us took the official title of facilitator at each interview, while the other took notes on the content and context of the talk. We also had a third member of the team who had the onerous task of transcribing the focus group interviews. Her task was to note who spoke when in the conversation and monitor the audio-recording devices. Having one person focused on the speakers and turn taking within the interview enabled whoever was in the note-taking role to support the facilitator if she redirected too early, overlooked a question on the protocol, or was just having a hard time rephrasing a comment. This team work was especially advantageous in the policy maker group when some participants interrupted and spoke over one another regularly, and it was difficult to keep track of who had spoken and which question they had been addressing at the time of the interruption. Working as a team also enabled us to begin engaging in a form of preliminary analysis. At the end of each focus group, we would sit down and reflect on the interview, noting particular ideas, comments, or issues that seemed to stand out to us about the conversation. When we actually sat down to conduct the formal analysis of the transcribed data, these earlier reflections often helped us to think about the context in which the data for particular stakeholder groups were generated.

Data Analysis and Writing of Report

There is no specific approach to analyzing focus group data. However, no matter how one approaches formal analysis, the work cannot begin without first organizing the data record. Aside from noting the general information regarding date, time, place, and participants for each focus group interview, it is also necessary to think about whether to use line numbering and how to differentiate between the facilitator and other members of the focus group. These decisions should be made early on so that if a transcriptionist is hired s/he is able to create the transcripts in a form that is useable to the researcher. We chose to use line numbering as well as a specific labeling scheme for each type of stakeholder group so that when we coded transcripts and grouped data according to the codes, we were able to use the line numbers and labels to go back to the original transcript and examine the data within the context of the original conversation. Similarly, for ease of reference, each stakeholder group was assigned a particular color. This color scheme enabled us to make easy visual comparisons across stakeholder groups. For example, we could see at a glance which stakeholder group spoke the most in response to particular questions and conversely where there were relative silences to some questions by a specific group.

Once organization of the data record has been accomplished, like other qualitative studies, it is then a matter of determining the best way to proceed given the purposes of the study. We decided to begin by using a typological analysis (Hatch, 2002) in that we divided the dataset into particular categories before beginning any kind of in-depth content analysis. These categories were directly derived from the research questions and comprised (a) knowledge and skills teachers need to have, (b) training experiences that contribute to the development of teacher expertise, (c) barriers and supports to effective professional development and teacher preparation, and (d) needed changes. The first sort of the data involved reading the transcripts for each stakeholder group and identifying the data according to those categories. The sorted data were then transferred into their own computer file in preparation for coding. Thus, we had data from all the stakeholders referring to a specific category and research question in one file.

All qualitative research involves inductive analysis of some kind (Hatch, 2002), and this detailed examination of the dataset is usually conducted through coding. A code is simply a tag assigned to a line, or a small piece of data, that captures the meaning of the excerpt in some way (Coffey & Atkinson, 1996). Thus, to try and make sense of the data within each of our typologies, members of the research team (three at the time) individually coded the dataset before meeting and going through the data again line by line comparing codes to ensure consistency. This process, while time-consuming, helped to ensure a kind of internal validity in the final coding scheme. If there was disagreement on a particular code, we went back and looked at the original transcripts to think again about the context of the words we were analyzing, rather than making the data fit one researcher's assumptions.

The next step involved chunking the data record within each typology to its assigned code. Using the process of categorical aggregation outlined by Stake (1995), the chunked excerpts of text related to each code within a question were then read carefully, first to generate a sense of the meanings given to the code across all participants, and second to ascertain whether there were any differences among stakeholder groups. At the end of this step, a general summary narrative of the data pertaining to each question was developed that also described points of consensus and difference within and between stakeholders. Each summary was presented as a set of one or two overarching themes with data derived from particular codes grouped under them.

Writing up the findings of a focus group study to inform policy and practice requires determining the right balance between direct quotations from the interviews and some kind of interpretive narrative. Policy makers are not really interested in stories; rather, they prefer a clear and authoritative text that shows them what is happening and provides clear recommendations about what might be done. One way we achieved this tone was to present the findings in relation to each research question in a very logical and linear format. Within each research question, however, we were able to show that most of the issues raised about the system of teacher preparation and professional development were consistent across all stakeholder groups. While the way particular issues were viewed by each stakeholder group varied to some degree, the fact that people working at various levels of a system and with differential status and authority within that system all identified similar concerns provided a convincing narrative. For example, all stakeholder groups identified three barriers impacting the system: a bureaucracy that seemed to hinder rather than support teachers upgrading their skills and credentials, a lack of early childhood expertise at all levels of the system, and a lack of coordination and partnerships between and across agencies (Lobman, Ryan, & McLaughlin, 2005b).

To further add to the credibility of the narrative, we also highlighted the distinctions between policy and state standards and what was happening in the field from the perspectives of those who had participated in our study. For example, while every stakeholder group identified traditional theoretical foundations (child development knowledge, curriculum content, etc.) as necessary knowledge to be an effective preschool teacher, very few stakeholders talked about receiving or giving training to enable teachers to respond effectively to students from diverse populations (e.g., English language learners and special needs students). Yet, knowledge of working with diverse student populations is one of the core standards for effective teacher preparation (Hyson, 2003). Similarly, despite preschool standards for math, science, and literacy, there was limited discussion of domain-specific knowledge outside of the area of literacy (Lobman & Ryan, 2006). In summary, while a focus group study with 38 participants cannot provide a comprehensive or representative assessment of what is taking place in the field of preschool teacher development in New Jersey, our study illustrated that the coming together of stakeholder groups provides valuable insights into why there may be gaps between policy and practice.

Challenges and Possibilities of Focus Groups as Qualitative Research

Focus groups are not frequently employed in early childhood qualitative studies. It would seem that their prevalent use in market research has clouded their allure for educational researchers. However, as we have tried to demonstrate in this chapter, with adequate attention given to sampling, interview design, and analysis of the data, focus groups can be an efficient and effective means of giving voice to those involved in the implementation of early childhood policies and practices. Moreover, from our experience in bringing people together, focus groups can also serve as a motivator and catalyst for change. As one policy maker put it:

> This kind of focus group is a great way to do research when your research is aimed at change. It is so much more useful to me than reading a report because it both collects data and information and makes me think. All of us are writing notes about what we need to do now as a result of this conversation.

Too often, we are so caught up in complexities of our day-to-day work that we do not get the chance to talk with one another even though we all work in the same field. As this policy maker points out, focus groups are not just a means of gathering and reporting data on a phenomenon; the opportunity to talk with others also leads professionals to think anew about their work.

Like all qualitative methodologies, the findings from focus group studies will be suspect in comparison to the supposed rigor and scientific nature of quantitative methods. One way around this ongoing challenge is to employ focus groups as part of a mixed methods design. In this way, trends within the quantitative data can be explored more deeply and used to consider pathways for action. For example, the limited attention to educating preschool teachers to respond effectively to diversity issues is also a pattern that emerged in our quantitative data. When we surveyed 689 teachers in the *Abbott* districts, 96.9% reported participating in child development classes, whereas content that dealt with teaching special needs children (78.3%) and those whose first language is not English (66.1%) had the lowest participation rates. Similarly, when we surveyed institutions of higher education, coursework in addressing the learning and development of children from diverse educational and cultural backgrounds, although available, was less likely to be offered at all institutions and often not as a separate class. The focus group data, however, showed us that different stakeholders talked about addressing diverse student populations in different ways. While 2-year college professors talked about the need to integrate diversity content into all areas of the curriculum, some teachers did not even recognize this kind of knowledge as necessary for every preschool teacher to have. Rather, they saw this kind of expertise as being context specific. As one preschool teacher responded, "No, I don't think it should be a part of teacher preparation because maybe you don't have any Spanish speaking children."

Mixed methods designs may be a compromise, but they allow the possibility of garnering funding to conduct qualitative research and ensure that qualitative perspectives are heard. In the current policy context, it is important that qualitative researchers also continue to pursue methodologies that are policy capturing. As we have argued in this chapter, focus groups are a methodology well suited to this kind of work. While there is still much to be done to ensure that policy makers understand and welcome the use of this methodology in its own right, one way we can begin to move the field is to start generating more focus group studies that can serve as a model for other researchers. At the same time, all of us who identify ourselves as qualitative researchers must remain vigilant about the quality of our work and continually be able to demonstrate the credibility of our methods and the trustworthiness of our findings. One day there may be a policy context where the qualitative is valued over the quantitative, but until that time, focus groups provide a bridge that more of us should begin to cross.

References

Abbott v. Burke, 153 N.J. 480. (1998).

Abbott v. Burke, 163 N.J. 95. (2000).

Coffey, A., & Atkinson, P. (1996). *Making sense of qualitative data: Complementary research strategies.* Thousand Oaks, CA: Sage.

Creswell, J. W. (1997). *Qualitative inquiry and research design: Choosing among five traditions.* Thousand Oaks, CA: Sage.

Division of Youth and Family Services, Department of Human Services, & State of New Jersey. (1998). *Manual of requirements for child care centers.* Trenton, NJ: Bureau of Licensing.

Hatch, J. A. (2002). *Doing qualitative research in education settings.* Albany: State University of New York Press.

Hyson, M. (2003). *Preparing early childhood professionals: NAEYC's standards for programs.* Washington, DC: National Association for the Education of Young Children.

Krueger, R. A. (1997). *Moderating focus groups.* Thousand Oaks, CA: Sage.

Krueger, R. A., & Casey, M. A. (2000). *Focus groups: A practical guide for applied research* (3rd ed.). Thousand Oaks, CA: Sage.

Lobman, C., & Ryan, S. (2006). *Differing discourses on preschool teacher development.* Manuscript under review.

Lobman, C., Ryan, S., & McLaughlin, J. (2005a). Reconstructing teacher education to prepare qualified preschool teachers: Lessons from New Jersey. *Early Childhood Research and Practice, 7*(2). Retrieved March 6, 2006, from http://ecrp.uiuc.edu/v7n2/lobman.html

Lobman, C., Ryan, S., & McLaughlin, J. (2005b). *Toward a unified system of early childhood teacher education and professional development: Conversations with stakeholders.* New York: Foundation for Child Development.

Morgan, D. (1997). *Focus groups as qualitative research* (2nd ed.). Thousand Oaks, CA: Sage.

New Jersey Department of Education. (2003). *Provisional teacher program information and application packet.* Retrieved September 12, 2003, from http://www.state.nj.us/njded/educators/license/1113.htm

Patton, M. Q. (1990). *Qualitative evaluation and research methods.* Newbury Park, CA: Sage.

Ryan, S., & Ackerman, D. J. (2005). Using pressure and support to create a qualified workforce. *Education Policy Analysis Archives, 13*(23). Retrieved March 15, 2006, from http://epaa.asu.edu/epaa/v13n23/

Stake, R. (1995). *The art of case study research.* Thousand Oaks, CA: Sage.

Strauss, A., & Corbin, J. (1998). *Basics of qualitative research: Techniques and procedures for developing grounded theory.* Thousand Oaks, CA: Sage.

5

Wanderings

Doing Historical Research on Early Childhood Education

JANICE A. JIPSON

National Louis University

In this chapter, I present three interwoven narratives of historical research in early childhood education. The first tells of my own research journey, relating chronologically my actual experiences as I conducted research on Elizabeth Peabody, founder of the American kindergarten. The second story, woven within the others but also in footnote form, is told by the data itself, as it reports Elizabeth Peabody's life in 19th-century New England. The final narrative tracks my intellectual process as I consider the methodological and ethical issues of doing historical research.

By juxtaposing the three narratives, my hope is to create a nonunitary, multiperspectival essay on the process of doing historical research in early childhood education. While the first narrative provides a somewhat linear structure for the essay, and the second narrative illustrates the research process with specific historical data, it is the final narrative that perhaps disrupts and complicates the doing of historical research. I raise issues about the practical and autobiographical concerns of framing and integrating research issues and contexts; the seductive allure of archives, eBay, Abe's Books, and living history museums; the application of analytic perspective including biographical, philosophical, and historical; and the implications for "reading the text" of any interpretive frame.

Research in the history of education is, at its core, about seeking, finding, and analyzing the past. It is also, however, framed by one's identity as a researcher, first in choosing the subject of the research, then in selecting and arranging the information, and finally in creating the narrative that illuminates one's perspective on the ideas, issues, and concerns related to the topic. Doing historical research in education can, and perhaps inevitably does, become a personal exploration of the past. The significance and meaning given to the facts of history extend from one's own conception of one's self and one's work. In essence, then, my interests, values, and motivations as a researcher influence my decisions as to what data are incorporated, what interpretations are made of those data, and how my analysis is ultimately presented.

The research that forms the core of this chapter focuses on Elizabeth Peabody and the early kindergarten. Initially it was intended to "restore" the contributions of women to the history of the kindergarten, thereby refocusing the history of early childhood education.* The details of Elizabeth Peabody's life as a 19th-century spinster, teacher, philosopher, and social reformer, along with the discourse surrounding "women's separate sphere" and "hidden maternal pedagogy," initially attracted me to this historical research project and to the construction of new understandings of the complex interrelationships between individuals and ideas. I sought to understand not only the roles of women such as Elizabeth Peabody as advocates of the thoughts and ideas of others but also their roles as central contributors to the emerging educational philosophies and practices of their time. In beginning this research project, I also wanted to explore the resistance of 19th-century kindergarten activists to traditional women's roles as well as their advocacy of progressive social and educational reform.

My interests were not new. Throughout the history of the kindergarten, educators have expressed interest in the roles of mothers and teachers. Among the earliest educators to consider the contributions of women to the education of young children were Johann Pestalozzi, author of *How Gertrude Teaches Her Children* (1801), and Friedrich Froebel, his German colleague. Froebel's *Mutter and Kose Lieder*, a collection of songs, rhymes, finger plays, and instructional commentaries, was written to direct mothers in guiding the development of their children toward a life of unity and harmony. Froebel believed that he best understood the process of educating young children and could help mothers regain what he assumed to be their lost child-rearing skills. He asserted that in a healthily constituted family it is the mother who first cares for and watches over the child. He believed that all-embracing mother love seeks to awaken and to interpret the feeling of community between the child and the father, brother, and sister. He felt that the natural mother does this instinctively, without instruction and direction. But Froebel also believed that modern industrial society had separated the roles of "mother" and "woman"

---

* Bruce Ronda (1984) has argued that while Elizabeth Peabody was a serious figure in the social and intellectual history of America, she was prevented from being recognized as such because her concerns centered on children and on women. Barbara Beatty (1995) has suggested that Elizabeth Peabody used the early 19th-century gender ideology of domesticity and "women's sphere" to promote "kindergartening" as a woman's occupation ... an ideal solution to the problem of what educated American women should do with their lives. It was Froebel's genius, Peabody believed, to have discovered a means whereby women might again assume a useful, natural role in society—"It was the noblest vocation to which a woman could aspire, the perfect development of womanliness." Beatty suggests that Elizabeth Peabody meshed Froebelianism with the philosophy of Transcendentalism and with the domestic ideology of the time. Beatty believes that "the kindergarten offered women like Peabody a respectable, meaningful cause and the possibility of self-respecting, autonomous work" (p. 58).

whom he saw as previously bonded in "primordial union." He deplored what he felt was the shameful ill-management of children, attributable to ignorance, perversity, and the absence of what he thought of as womanly, child-loving sensibility.

According to Shapiro (1983), Froebel deplored the position of women in society where woman's work was rigidly defined by man's will, even to the fettering of some of its "noblest impulses," suggesting his belief in an essentialized maternal knowledge that could be appropriated into conventional educational practice. Shapiro thought that Froebel's concern with the separation of women's roles as teachers and mothers had a direct influence on early "kindergartners" such as Elizabeth Peabody.

Elizabeth Peabody, in turn, believed that a loving mother was the first principle of Froebel's gospel of child culture. She also believed that a child should be taken care of by its mother in early infancy because only the mother could respect a child's personality sufficiently. When the age for kindergarten came, however, she felt that mothers needed to be relieved of ever-increasing responsibilities for child care and that children needed other influences than could be had in their families, particularly in families where parents worked outside of their homes. She believed the kindergarten to be a necessary adjunct to the family because a mother with more than one child would lack time and energy to properly care for them. She asserted that 4-year-olds should be handed over to "matronly kindergarteners" with a knowledge of Froebelian pedagogy and an innate feminine penchant for nurturance.

A Research Journey

My particular interest in Elizabeth Peabody was motivated by the discovery of the Louise Tharp (1950/1988) biography, *The Peabody Sisters of Salem*, in a used book store in Concord, Massachusetts. Several colleagues and I had traveled to Cambridge, Massachusetts, to attend a conference on "Development and Diversity" at Harvard University. Succumbing to food poisoning the first evening of the conference, I prevailed upon a college friend who lived in Western Massachusetts to allow me to recuperate at her home. By the time we began our drive across the state, however, I had sufficiently recovered to be interested in her suggestion of a bit of local sightseeing. Our shared passion for collecting used books took us to the village of Concord and a tiny second story bookstore. As I climbed the narrow staircase, I noticed a well-used paperback copy of *The Peabody Sisters of Salem* displayed against the back railing. Faint graduate school memories of Elizabeth Peabody's role in the history of the kindergarten must have surfaced in my mind because I immediately purchased the book and took it with me back to Oregon.

The book sat on a shelf for much of the next year until, traumatized by the turmoil of program closures at my university, I sought refuge in reading "outside my scholarly interests." The story of the Peabody sisters' lives immediately engaged my attention when I realized that Elizabeth Peabody was not only a "kindergartner" but also a New England Transcendentalist of some importance. Invoking my undergraduate school English major passion for the writings of Ralph Waldo Emerson and Henry David Thoreau, I became fascinated by the story of Elizabeth Peabody's relationships with Nathaniel Hawthorne, Horace Mann, and the Transcendentalists. I learned that, as a young woman, Elizabeth Peabody studied Greek with Ralph Waldo Emerson, transcribed sermons for William Ellery Channing, taught in Bronson Alcott's Temple School, published Thoreau's "Civil Disobedience" and the early stories of Nathaniel Hawthorne, and became an "ardent friend" of Horace Mann. I read about how Ralph Waldo Emerson, Margaret Fuller, Bronson Alcott, William Ellery Channing, and Elizabeth Peabody met frequently to discuss philosophy and the works of Rousseau and Coleridge, and how Emerson's "Nature" was a core reading selection for the Transcendentalist Club's study group, which met in Elizabeth Peabody's Boston bookstore. Elizabeth Peabody's life had become personal and I became "hooked" on doing history.

Shortly thereafter, while attending the American Educational Research Association (AERA) meetings in Boston, I noticed an advertisement for a café, which was described in the hotel brochure as "located on West Street in the former bookstore of the sister-in-law of Nathaniel Hawthorne and Horace Mann." No direct mention was made of Elizabeth Peabody or of the fact that her bookshop had also been a salon for the intellectual community of that time as well as the site where she published writings of Margaret Fuller, Nathaniel Hawthorne, and the Transcendentalist journal, *The Dial*. *How typical to ignore the contributions of women*, I thought, as I contemplated refocusing my research on the life and work of Elizabeth Peabody and other 19th-century "kindergartners," as kindergarten teachers were called at that time. Later, when I sought out the West Street location hoping to have lunch at the site of the bookshop, I discovered a lovely brick building with a brass plaque noting Peabody's residence and bookshop. Unfortunately, it was closed. I have returned to the site many times since, hoping to walk into Peabody's home, but have never found the café open.

At about the same time, one of my doctoral students, Petra Munro, was completing her research on the working lives of women teachers and I accompanied her to the archives of the National College of Education at National Louis University where we accessed the writings and materials of the college's founder, Elizabeth Harrison, who was another 19th-century promoter of kindergarten education. Petra suggested, with my complete agreement, that we join our interests in these 19th-century early childhood educators and collaborate on a project on the history of the kindergarten. We determined that a readers' theater would be an appropriate format to use for portraying both the individual and interrelated ideas of our separate subjects. Once I had gathered primary source materials on Elizabeth Peabody, mostly through interlibrary loan from Wheelock College, I enlisted several other colleagues in the project and requested that they send me copies of their primary source materials from their chosen historical figures (Sylvia Ashton Warner, Maria Montessori, Caroline Pratt, and Friedrich Froebel). After reviewing their materials and identifying themes that seemed to cut across the works of these various educators, I merged the materials into a script featuring a discussion of the nature of childhood, the role of the mother and teacher, work and play, "appropriate" curriculum for early childhood education, and so forth. I chose to contextualize the voices by placing them together for coffee at the home of Margarethe Schurz, founder of the first (German-language) kindergarten in the United States, at Watertown, Wisconsin, and invented Margarethe Schurz's "hostess" dialogue to facilitate the flow of the conversation. The resultant readers' theater (Jipson, Hauser, Lozano, Kim, & Melzoff, 1993) was then presented at the opening session of the Reconceptualizing Early Childhood Education conference in Ann Arbor, Michigan, in 1993.

Boston, 1859

Elizabeth Peabody: Margarethe, do you remember meeting me in Boston? We were houseguests at the same home in that family with four children whose father had a theory that children should only be dealt with as irresponsible beings before they were 6 years old, at which age he proposed to put on the screws of discipline. The advent of your sweet little daughter, Agatha, had the effect of a calm coming upon the storm of young life, and I said, "That child is a miracle, so childlike and unconscious, and yet so wise and able, attracting and ruling the children, who seem nothing short of enchanted."

Margarethe Schurz: And I said, "No miracle, but only brought up in a kindergarten."

Elizabeth Peabody: But I was puzzled. "A kindergarten!" I replied, "What is that?"

Margarethe Schurz: I remember telling you "A garden whose plants are human." I asked you, "Did you never hear of Froebel?"

Elizabeth Peabody: And I asked, "Who is he?"

Margarethe Schurz: And I replied, "He is a greater discoverer in education than Pestalozzi even." Herr Froebel, you came to Hamburg to lecture to mothers and instruct children's nurses and kindergartners. All the liberal people went to hear and see you. I kept a journal report of what you said to mothers and did with the children. You reasoned, "Children learn by doing things and their play can be organized to teach as well as to amuse." (Jipson et al., 1993)

The Peabody project was compelling and began to take over my research life. As I located additional letters, manuscripts, articles, and books written by Elizabeth Peabody and the others, the script was revised and re-presented in multiple venues including local and national early childhood conferences and the 1996 AERA annual meeting in New York City (with my son Erik in the added role of a young Frank Lloyd Wright, playing with Froebel blocks). We called it our off-Broadway debut!

Several years later, after joining the faculty of the National College of Education, I became increasingly interested in the life of Elizabeth Harrison, who, as a contemporary of both Jane Addams and John Dewey, worked with mothers' clubs in the settlement houses of Chicago and who sought to formalize the education of kindergarten teachers. Elizabeth Harrison's work was part of the legacy of a larger network of Chicago women activists such as Alice Putnam, Anna Bryan, Alice Temple, and Edna Dean Baker who were central in shaping educational norms before and during the Progressive era. Despite their activist, intellectual, and scholarly work, I found that these turn-of-the-century Chicago educators were seldom discussed as serious intellectual thinkers who helped shape the discourse of progressive education. When mentioned at all, these women intellectuals tend to be represented as "disciples" of male theorists such as Friedrich Froebel, John Dewey, William T. Harris, or G. Stanley Hall, or, as was the case with Elizabeth Peabody, as women who carried out the ideas of others.

I continued my research, rediscovering the rich collection of Elizabeth Harrison and Edna Dean Baker's notes, journals, and teaching materials in the archives of the National Kindergarten College (now National Louis University). Access to original sets of Froebel blocks and scrapbooks of the weavings and paper work of 19th-century kindergartners-in-training refocused my research, for a time, on the early training of kindergarten teachers. I had learned earlier that Elizabeth Peabody had visited Wisconsin on several occasions in support of the kindergarten movement[*] and that Elizabeth Harrison had taught kindergartners and mothers' club groups in Milwaukee. Paging through the large collection of turn-of-the-century issues of the *Kindergarten Magazine* and the *Kindergarten Review*, I discovered that several of the women who taught in the early kindergartens in Wisconsin or who initiated kindergarten teacher training programs in Wisconsin Normal Schools had themselves been trained at the Chicago Kindergarten College. A new direction for my research emerged and I enthusiastically contacted all of the state colleges in Wisconsin, requesting information about their early kindergarten and kindergarten teacher training programs. I was, and still am, excited by each connection I find between my Chicago-based university and the kindergartens of Wisconsin. My research had gone in a new direction.

---

[*] The Society of Superintendents and Principals invited Peabody to come to Chicago and address them on the "Genuine Kindergarten versus Ignorant Attempts At It." She repeated her lecture at the Teachers' Convention in Watertown, Wisconsin.

But then I became sidetracked, as researchers often do. I became eligible for a sabbatical and decided that I would set aside the Wisconsin kindergarten project, and use the opportunity to continue my research on Elizabeth Peabody and the history of the kindergarten. I applied for and was awarded a Research Associateship at the Five Colleges Women's Studies Research Center at Mount Holyoke College in Massachusetts and in September of 2004 took up residence in South Hadley, Massachusetts.

Paradise

The wonder of this 4-month sabbatical is difficult to describe. Imagine finding yourself in academic paradise, or at least next to Paradise Pond in the faculty dining room at Smith College. Looking back I cannot help but romanticize my experience. It is fall and the leaves are starting to change but it is not the often rainy and dreary autumn of Wisconsin or Illinois. New England is in the full glory of long sunlit days and crisp evenings as I criss-cross Massachusetts from one archive to another. Colleagues from the Women's Studies Research Center read my work, offer suggestions, extend assistance in tracking down sources. I listen to faculty from the five colleges present colloquia on their own research projects. And during one 2-week period, I hear Jim Hightower and Jonathan Kozol talk about their work and the politics of the times. I fall into a routine of productivity and respite … sleep in, read, lunch with colleagues, archival work, coffee breaks, more reading, with no regard for clocks or schedules. It is the academic life of dreams.

My office is on the second floor of a lovely old Victorian house with creaking wood floors and beautifully tiled fireplaces located on the far edge of the Mount Holyoke campus. I have what I need—an old wooden teacher desk, a big window looking toward campus, a comfortable reading chair—but I find I can't get work done here. There are colleagues with interesting research projects to talk to just across the hall; a kitchen downstairs where I can make tea and toast; my computer with its ding-ding of ever-available email coming in. I am on sabbatical, I tell myself, and I need a change from the usual workday surroundings. I develop the wonderful morning habit of wandering across campus to the college library and finding a cozy nook in the huge gothic reading room. Often the morning sun streams through the cathedral-like divided glass windows as I claim an overstuffed chair and ottoman in the corner. I pile my books and papers at my feet and start to read. With a coffee shop just down the stairs and thousands of books, it is exactly what I need, a release from the conventions of the typical academic work world. The library, after all, has always represented heaven to me.

Sabbatical evenings, at home in my not so cozy apartment, are my own. I realize that for the first time in my life I am living alone … no parents, sisters, husband, or children, so no constraints on what I do, eat, or listen to. I could watch re-runs of *Law & Order* for hours at a stretch, if I want, or listen only to

Bob Dylan and do yoga. Alternatively, I might write books and articles about my research on the little desk under the window. But instead, my evenings become Web time and I extend the pleasure of my day's work to another endless library—eBay, Abe's Books, and the online sites of the New York Public Library and the Peabody-Essex Museum. As I peruse their sites I resolve to travel to Boston, Salem, and New York City as soon as possible to see for myself the treasures they hold.

I become addicted to Web searches and crave the excitement of winning an eBay bid. I acquire Elizabeth Peabody's 1893 edition of *Lectures in the Training Schools for Kindergartners*, a book that I had previously seen only in the archives of the National Louis University library. I bid on and win an affordable copy of Henry Barnard's (1890) *Papers on Kindergarten and Child Culture*, a collection of articles from the *American Journal of Education*, which a colleague had purchased several years ago in an Evanston, Illinois, bookstore and which I had coveted ever since. I delight in finding a second edition translation of the Baroness Marenholtz-Buelow's (1889) *The Child and Child-Nature* at a reasonable price on the Abe's Books Web site. And after winning several eBay bids away from me, Scott Bultman, a Froebel scholar in Grand Rapids, Michigan, sends me a set of Froebel's First Gift, the multi-colored yarn balls, which I display in a round wooden bowl on my desk as if they were jewels or perhaps apples. Another site yields a map of Massachusetts from the mid-1900s that I place in a wood frame from the Salvation Army. I place a glass with some dried weeds next to it. My living room is gradually beginning to resemble a 19th-century study with the books and objects signaling that time.

Even my children are drawn into the search—Erik serves as my library courier, watching for the re-appearance of books I need in the Amherst College library, using his interlibrary loan privileges to access things I cannot from the Five Colleges libraries. Emily finds a rare copy of Matilda Kriege's (1872) translation of Marenholtz-Bulow's book in a shop on Boston Common and sends it to me. I open the worn green cover embossed with a gilt image of a young woman and child encircled by ivy leaves and begin reading. From the moment I note the title of the first chapter, "The New Education," and her opening lines, "The process of remodeling society, the reforms that have been going on in the last century, make a reform in education an absolute necessity" (p. 5), I am entranced.

Most Tuesdays I spend in the Sophia Smith Collection at Smith College where they have the oldest and largest collection of women's history manuscripts and archives in the United States. The winding drive along the narrow road between South Hadley and Northampton allows me time to decide what I will look for when I get there. The Alumnae Gymnasium, where the collection is housed, is an old brick building not far from Paradise Pond, offering me easy access for lunch in the faculty dining hall and study-break strolls through the Conservatory and Botanical Gardens. The collection holds documents I never expected to actually see. I find a letter written by Elizabeth Peabody to a friend and can hardly believe I have her actual handwriting in my own hands. I tell myself that this is what archival research is all about—the thrill of each discovery and the desire for more. I become obsessed with the story of Elizabeth Peabody's relationship with Nathaniel Hawthorne and nearly cry in frustration when the pamphlet I seek is missing from the artifact file. But I am comforted by the marvelous humor and helpfulness of the librarian who each week brings my research materials to my table. She worries that I may not find "enough" material in the Sophia Smith collection of letters and papers. She takes my quest on as her own, calling around the community so that I can have my own personal copy of *Hawthorne's Two Engagements*.

I learn the strengths related to my research of each of the libraries in the Five Colleges Consortium. Occasionally I go to the relatively modern Robert Frost Library at Amherst College, which, I have learned, has the largest collection of check-out-able books written by Elizabeth Peabody and her sister Mary. I often first meet my son, who is a student at the college, for breakfast at The Black Sheep, just down the street from Emily Dickinson's house and gardens. Amherst shares with Northampton the distinction of several excellent used book stores and I often find myself sidetracked all morning looking for used copies of Peabody's or Froebel's work. Eventually, however, I trudge up the hill to the library and find my books, then head back to the Women's Center for a brown bag symposium presented by one of my colleagues.

I love the libraries. There is so much to discover in each place and I keep on going back to look again and again, to make yet another marvelous discovery, to let it all seep into my being. I particularly enjoy the unexpected pleasures of the hunt—the footnote that leads you to an obscure reference in a book you would never have imagined you would be looking at, or a biographer's note that takes you to a remote small town historical society collection. Sometimes I think I am storing up all these experiences so that I can remember the time when I did research "the good way."

Road Trips

With the long autumn break weekend ahead of me, I drive to Boston. The Big Dig is in full progress and I have trouble finding my way into the city and my hotel. Luckily Boston is a walkable city, the MTA provides good connections to Cambridge, and I can park my car in the lot for the next few days. After a late dinner in my hotel room, I plot my next day's activities—visiting all the places in which Elizabeth Peabody lived and worked. I want to absorb Boston, to the extent still possible, as it was in the 19th century. Little do I know that by the end of this weekend I will be so immersed in old Boston that I will daydream of being Elizabeth Peabody, or another woman of her generation.

The next morning, I walk to the Old Corner Bookstore, located in one of the oldest buildings in Boston (built in 1712), but the bookstore is no longer there and in its space some sort of construction is taking place. According to my brochure, it was the early center of Transcendentalism in Boston and many famous books were originally published there, including *The Scarlet Letter* and *Walden*, as well as the *Atlantic Monthly* magazine. I note the loss of what is to become a long list of historic places that I can no longer visit. And next time, I remind myself, I will stay at the historic Parker House hotel while I still can, no matter how expensive.

I continue walking the Freedom Trail path past the site of the Boston Latin School on School Street that Ralph Waldo Emerson had once attended, the King's Chapel on School and Tremont Street, and the King's Chapel and Granary Burying Grounds on Tremont Street until I reach 13 West Street and the site of Elizabeth Peabody's bookshop.* The sign in the door tells me that the café is closed on Saturdays so, after peering in the windows in disappointment and trying to imagine the little shop and reading room with Peabody's father's homeopathic apothecary in the back, I appease my annoyance with a visit to the Brattle Book Shop down the street. Oddly, in this large antiquarian bookstore, I find little that I need—perhaps my Abe's Books habits have exhausted my mental bibliographic wish list, at least for the time. Or perhaps it is because I am frustrated that Boston has, of course, changed and I will never be able to actually visit the places I have re-created in my mind.

Cutting back to Boston Common, I note the site of Tremont Temple at 88 Tremont Street, where Bronson Alcott held his famed Temple School and where Elizabeth Peabody worked as his unpaid assistant in yet another of her many efforts to assist and promote the men she admired.† I make a note to further explore this inclination so common not only in Elizabeth Peabody but in many other women as well. Lost in speculation, I proceed across the Common to Beacon Hill. My goal is 15 Pinckney Street, the site of Elizabeth Peabody's early kindergarten. As I climb the hill it occurs to me that perhaps I should have done this walking tour in some more chronological order.‡ But

---

* In 1840, Elizabeth Peabody opened her bookshop on West Street and began her Wednesday afternoon "Conversations" featuring lectures by Margaret Fuller, among others. During this time, she also published Channing's pamphlet *Emancipation* and several of Nathaniel Hawthorne's works, and took over the publication of the Transcendentalist journal, *The Dial*.

† Megan Marshall (2005) suggests that Peabody, like other educated women of her time, faced questions such as should she put forward her own genius, or cultivate talents in others?

‡ In 1860, Peabody opened an English-speaking kindergarten at 15 Pinckney Street in Boston. In 1861 she relocated her school to 24 Winter Street. In 1862, she wrote "Kindergarten—What Is It?" for the *Atlantic Monthly* and in 1864, with her sister Mary, she published her *Guide to the Kindergarten and Moral Culture in Infancy*. In 1867, she traveled to Europe to find the "true kindergarten." In 1868, she returned to Boston eager to correct her mistakes in interpreting Froebel's kindergarten model. Repudiating her first *Guide to the Kindergarten*, she replaced it with a corrected edition and vowed to establish a real kindergarten based on the proper training of kindergarten teachers.

what, if any, order might I adopt? Each, whether chronological, geographic, or genealogical, might preclude some chance discovery that will change my thinking in every way. It becomes clear to me that this historical research project is turning into my own romance journey with Transcendentalism and the people of the 19th century, not unlike that of my childhood hero, Richard Halliburton, and his 1925 *Royal Road to Romance*. I now seem to be less interested in getting the facts than I am in absorbing their lives.

I walk the length of tree-lined Pinckney Street, distracted by the lovely old buildings. I imagine renting one of the houses, caring for the compact flower gardens in front. I could live here, I muse. I stop at 4 Pinckney Street, where Henry David Thoreau once lived, and walk on to 15 Pinckney Street only to discover that the house I had imagined being here was actually now a newer condominium complex. I stop at the house next door at 17 Pinckney Street, said to be a mirror image of the house in which Elizabeth Peabody had opened her second kindergarten in 1860. I imagine myself looking out of Peabody's window at the gardens below—but how am I to know if she lived on that side of the house or could see the gardens from her room. I wonder, did the children in her kindergarten classes play here, create their own child's garden? Momentarily distressed by the lost opportunity to visit her actual kindergarten rooms, I walk on. Across the street, I find 20 Pinckney Street where a plaque informs me that Louisa May Alcott's family had rented rooms, before moving to the Transcendentalist farm called Fruitlands. I made a mental note to check the period of Peabody's and Alcott's residencies across the street from each other. How could one street house so many wonderful authors? I proceed up the street to 43 and 81 Pinckney Street, where my guidebook informs me that the Alcott family had rented rooms. I wonder which house Louisa May Alcott had lived in when she worked as a kindergarten teacher.* I add that to my mental checklist. Finally, I come upon the house just around the corner at 10 Louisburg Square that Louisa May Alcott bought for her father, Bronson Alcott, and herself once her books started producing income. They lived in that house from 1885 to 1888, when they died within 2 days of each other and Elizabeth Peabody outlived them all.

The following week becomes a blur of research frenzy. Initially, the Internet directories of various library holdings structure my searches, but when I actually enter the reading rooms and archives I revert to the research strategies of my undergraduate days at Wisconsin. Look at everything. Peruse the stacks

---

* Peabody convinced Louisa May Alcott to become a kindergarten teacher, which she did, but then quit when she discovered it did not pay. Peabody indicated that such behavior characterized a poor-spirited teacher with avowedly mercenary ends and added that she did not think it was one's duty to wear oneself out and half starve, for the sake of keeping a kindergarten, but that only those who are sufficiently free from other obligations should have the privilege and luxury of "working with God, on the paradaisical ground of childhood" (Jipson et al., 1993).

and dig through the archival boxes, if allowed. Allow the librarians and archivists to be my informants because often they know where the "good stuff" is. Don't allow any technological device to determine what I find.

The Massachusetts Historical Society yields a rich harvest of materials including letters to Elizabeth Peabody as well as letters from family members and friends. The Bostonian Society's collection of photographs and other images is likewise a fertile source for my research activity and my desire to have a photo image of everything I could. The Schlesinger Library on the History of Women and the libraries at Harvard University allow me to fill in some missing spaces in my research and also to identify what I need to locate elsewhere. I could spend my life in these Boston and Cambridge libraries and never feel as though I had completed my work. Piles of photocopies accumulate in the backseat of my car. But I am becoming fussy, I suppose; microfilm copies, for instance, of the *Kindergarten Messenger* no longer suffice—I need to hold the actual journal in my hands and turn the pages one by one, finding the surprises that I did not know I was seeking.

When I finally reach Concord, a week later, I am stunned by the beauty and the history of the village. I arrange to stay at the Colonial Inn overlooking the town common, which had been, for a brief time, the home of Henry David Thoreau. According to local history, in the 1830s, Ralph Waldo Emerson, Bronson Alcott, Margaret Fuller, Henry David Thoreau, and Elizabeth Peabody spent much time in Concord, sharing their philosophical and religious interests, but also their commitments to social reforms such as education, abolition, temperance, and woman suffrage. I imagine the Colonial Inn, as it was when the Emersons, Alcotts, and Peabodys lived in Concord, not yet an inn but rather a store and then private home and boardinghouse. I smile at my growing fascination with the lives of these people and my attempts to also experience it through their eyes. The documenting of history is now rapidly fading from my priorities, replaced with the desire to actually live it, as much as I can.

The most exciting event of the day is visiting the Sleepy Hollow Cemetery, just down the road from the Colonial Inn. Despite the late afternoon rain, I find my way to Author's Ridge and climb the steep, slippery path to the top where I locate the graves of the Alcott family, and also those of the Emersons, the Hawthornes, and Thoreau, all clustered quite near each other overlooking a wooded ravine. But I cannot seem to find Elizabeth Peabody's tombstone, although I am quite sure she is also buried here. Finally, as darkness settles over the cemetery I give up and return to my hotel. Discussing my futile search with the helpful woman at the reception desk, I am offered a map of Concord that reveals the exact location of Peabody's grave as well as the location of other sites of interest in the village.

A bright, sunny morning greets me as I plan today's activities in Concord. First the cemetery where, with the help of the map, I find Elizabeth Peabody's grave marker on the flat ground below Author's Ridge … I wonder how she might have felt, outliving her friends and colleagues and being finally separated in her plot on the flats, still lovely in the autumn sun, but alone. I knew she had sometimes strolled to Sleepy Hollow with Emerson, debating the materialism of contemporary scientific thought or the relationship of spiritualism to their Transcendental ideals. As I exit the sad and peaceful cemetery, I wonder about the choices Elizabeth Peabody made in her life—did she regret her late-in-life decision to focus on the kindergarten and the more practical issues of pedagogy and teacher preparation? Did she envy her friends who were better known as philosophers, men of ideas, or the marriages of her sisters to important authors? Or did she remain proud of the work she had done and her commitment to education, emancipation, and equality? I will visit Sleepy Hollow Cemetery again, in the rain, and again, and again. It draws me against all other places.

My plan is to go calling on the homes of the Concord Transcendentalists, but first on my route is the Concord Museum where I read they have a collection of Thoreau's furnishings from his cabin at Walden Pond and also the furniture and books from Ralph Waldo Emerson's study. One of the curators at our local historical society has suggested I talk to her daughter who works there and who can help me access the materials I seek.

Inquiring, I am told that the daughter now works in Lexington, but I am offered, instead, enthusiastic assistance by the local staff—most significantly for me, they provide me with the location of Mary Peabody Mann's house which she shared with her sister Elizabeth during some of their later years. I also learn that the Concord Free Public Library is closed for repairs and that I will have to postpone until a future visit my perusal of their special collections and of the Elizabeth Peabody Foreign Library. That is actually okay. I am on sabbatical, after all, and time seemingly has no bounds. After all, it is a gloriously bright and sunny day and I know that the library will wait, so without regrets I proceed to the home of Ralph Waldo Emerson, just down the road.

I approach the Emerson house in awe of being in the place where so many of my heroes had dined and talked.[*] I peek into Emerson's study and then the parlor across the hall that had accommodated his houseguests including Thoreau, Margaret Fuller, and, on several occasions, Elizabeth Peabody. From the windows of the room I could view the endless fields and trees, much as they might have looked in Emerson's day. Seeing the rooms where so much important writing and talk took place I begin to get a sense of what it might have been like to be part of such a vibrant intellectual community. I also recognize, as Thoreau (1962) once suggested in his journal, how the quiet and

---

[*] Ralph Waldo Emerson gathered intellectuals, including Margaret Fuller, Bronson Alcott, William Ellery Channing, and Elizabeth Peabody, in his home to discuss philosophy and the German and French writings of authors such as Rousseau and Coleridge.

pastoral village life of Concord could inspire one to write a poem to the river, the woods, the ponds, the hills, the fields, the swamps and meadows, the streets and buildings, and the villagers. It is no wonder Elizabeth Peabody was able to so readily grasp Froebel's notion of the child's garden and of the unity of mankind and nature, imagining it as the proper basis for the education of young children. Being in Concord is beginning to allow me to understand, in a very intuitive way, the relationship between Transcendentalism and the kindergarten, much as Elizabeth Peabody herself perhaps understood it. Whereas before I had known of the connection between the two, I now feel the connection myself in an enlightening and satisfying way.

So much to see, so much to think about. My next visit is to Orchard House, home of the Alcott family. I had developed a method for my visits: listening to the curators describe the lives of the former occupants, all the while imagining myself visiting the house in their times, listening in on their conversations, watching, for instance, Louisa May Alcott write her stories or Emerson share his ideas about the nature of godliness. In the back yard west of the Orchard House, beyond the gardens and under the pine trees, stands the chapel-like building where Bronson Alcott conducted his Concord School of Philosophy. Elizabeth Peabody, Ralph Waldo Emerson, William Torrey Harris, and many others lectured there.* I think of Elizabeth Peabody there, with Margaret Fuller and all those other accomplished men and women, in passionate conversation about the work and ideas that had consumed their lives. And I treasure even more my print of Elizabeth Palmer Peabody and William Torrey Harris under a shade tree there at the Concord School of Philosophy.

I walk on down the road to Wayside, the former home of the Alcotts, which was later owned by Nathaniel and Sophia Peabody Hawthorne, Elizabeth Peabody's youngest sister. Elizabeth Peabody and her other sister, Mary Peabody Mann, had also lived there for a time, and I knew from reading the memoirs of Rebecca Harding Davies (1904) that Elizabeth Peabody had been a guest in this house and at times had caused quite a fuss:

> One evening I was with Mrs. Hawthorne in the little parlor when the children brought in their father. The windows were open, and we sat in the warm twilight quietly talking or silent as we chose. Suddenly Miss Peabody appeared in the doorway. She was a short, stout little woman, with her white stockinged feet thrust into slippers, her hoop skirt swaying from side to side, and her gray hair flying in the winds. She lighted the lamp, went out and brought in more lamps, and then sat down and waited with an air of stern resolution. Presently Mr. Emerson and his daughter appeared, then Louisa Alcott and her father, then two gray old

---

* Peabody lectured at the Concord School of Philosophy on "Emerson as a Preacher" and on John Milton and *Paradise Lost* in the early 1880s.

clergymen who were formally presented to Mr. Hawthorne, who now looked about him with terrified dismay. We saw other figures approaching in the road outside.

"What does this mean Elizabeth?" Mrs. Hawthorne asked her aside.

"I did it. I went around and asked a few people in to meet our friend here. I ordered some cake and lemonade, too."

Her blue eyes glittered with triumph as Mrs. Hawthorne turned away. "They've been here two years," she whispered, "and nobody has met Mr. Hawthorne. People talk. It's ridiculous! There's no reason why Sophia should not go into society. So I just made an excuse of your visit to bring them in." (p. 16)

My last stop of the day is The Old Manse where Emerson and the Hawthorne family had lived at various times and where Thoreau had visited and worked as a handyman and gardener. Elizabeth Peabody had also visited with her sister and her family at this house, shortly after their marriage. I wonder if she ever stood looking out at Thoreau's garden, regretting her own loss of Hawthorne's affections and the domestic tranquility that her sister had found with him. I climb to the room on the second floor that was used as a study by Emerson when he wrote *Nature* and later by Nathaniel Hawthorne when he began writing *Mosses from an Old Manse*. From one of the western windows, according to legend, the Rev. William Emerson's family had watched the battle between the Minutemen and the Redcoats at Old North Bridge, only a hundred yards away. I wonder if it is the same window where Sophia Peabody Hawthorne and her husband, Nathaniel, scratched messages in several of the windowpanes:

Man's accidents are God's purposes. Sophia A. Hawthorne, 1843.

Nath'l Hawthorne. This is his study. 1843

The smallest twig leans clear against the sky.

Composed by my wife, and written with her diamond.

Inscribed by my husband at sunset, April 3, 1843 On the gold light. S.A.H.

As I walk along the Concord River, I can hardly imagine all that has happened on these grounds, and yet they remain so beautiful, peaceful in the fading afternoon sunlight.

I wake early to another glorious Concord day. Today I go to Walden Pond— have I saved the best for last? But first I must walk past Mary Peabody Mann's house at 7 Sudbury Road, so kindly pointed out to me by the helpful women at the Concord Museum. The house is still privately owned so I must content myself with looking at the gardens and imagining which rooms Elizabeth

Peabody used during her residence with her sister. When Horace Mann died in 1859, his wife, Mary, had returned to Concord, purchasing a house for herself and her sister Elizabeth. It was here that Elizabeth Peabody's interest in kindergarten and the work of Friedrich Froebel was more fully developed. Perhaps it was in this house that Elizabeth Peabody and her sister Mary conceived of their *Guide to the Kindergarten and Moral Culture of Infancy* (1864) in the hopes of bringing Froebel's ideas to the attention of American educators. Influenced by Horace Mann's commitment to public education and the eradication of social injustice, Elizabeth Peabody became interested in the possibility of a free public kindergarten. Her lectures and work editing the *Kindergarten Messenger* promoted the notion of kindergarten across the East and Midwest and led to broad interest in the opening of kindergartens and the training of kindergarten teachers. I began to recognize the significance of the ideas that emanated from this home base in Concord.

Finally, I reach Walden Pond! If ever there was a place where ideas form and dreams are made, it is here at Walden Pond. It would be a stretch to say that Thoreau's Walden outpost had anything directly to do with Elizabeth Peabody and the formation of the kindergarten, although she did at least once tour Walden Pond with Emerson. It is here that I sit at the edge of the pond and finally begin to put it all together for myself. It must be the hidden necessity of historical research—time to do nothing but reflect on where I have been and what I've learned and what it all means, at least to me. I think about Elizabeth Peabody and how her life's work was really about linking history and philosophy with society, about the possibilities of the kindergarten as an initial agent of social change. I think about her efforts to link Transcendentalism with the kindergarten and how that is perhaps for me the key to the history of early childhood education, the notion of nurturing the transcendence of the child. I think about the need for interpretive creativity when dealing with what happened in the past. Can I imagine conversations and events or must I merely chronicle them as they occurred, chaining them together according to some external logic of sequence? Or dare I make it my story, my journey through the life of Elizabeth Peabody? Sitting here at Walden Pond, I determine that the part I like most in the research, in the finding of patterns and themes, is the creation of my own dream-visions of how it might have been.

On the Road Again

At first Salem seems an afterthought to the drama of Concord. The "Grimshawe House," as it was named by Nathaniel Hawthorne in one of his stories, is easy to find, located next to the old burial ground. The Peabody family moved to the house in 1835,* and it is here in 1837 that Elizabeth Peabody first got to know Nathaniel Hawthorne and later introduce him to her sister Sophia. Hawthorne (1890) used the house as the base for his story "Dr Grimshawe's Secret" and describes it in vivid detail, better than I ever could.

> It grieves me to add an additional touch or two to the reader's disagreeable impression of Doctor Grimshawe's residence, by confessing that it stood in a shabby by-street, and cornered on a grave-yard, with which the house communicated by a back door; so that with a hop, skip, and jump, from the threshold across a flat tombstone, the two children were in the daily habit of using the dismal cemetery as their play-ground. ... As I remember it it did not appear to be an ancient structure, nor one that could ever have been the abode of a very wealthy or prominent family—a three-story wooden house perhaps a century old, low studded, with a square front, standing right upon the street, and a small enclosed porch, containing the main entrance affording a glimpse up and down the street through an oval window on each side, its characteristic was a decent respectability, not sinking below the boundary of the genteel. It has often perplexed my mind to conjecture what sort of man he could have been who, having the means to build a pretty spacious and comfortable residence, should have chosen to lay its foundation on the brink of so many graves; each tenant of these narrow houses crying out, as it were, against the absurdity of bestowing much time or pains in preparing any earthly tabernacle save such as theirs. (pp. 1–3)

I can imagine Elizabeth and her sisters looking out the upper windows at the place where the witches are memorialized and at all those other revolutionary-era graves. It reminds me in a way of Sleepy Hollow Cemetery—the witches' stones placed outside the walls entombing the successful. What might it have been like for the Peabody sisters to look out over the graves of the great founding fathers and patriots but also the supposed heretics? I wonder if Elizabeth Peabody might have liked to see herself as one of those women outside the bounds of tradition.

My great finds in Salem are, however, books. The Essex-Peabody Library seems to have everything I need to supply background information to the narrative I have been constructing in my head. I find myself on a whole new path for this research, and indeed, one of the great pleasures in doing the project has been the ability to happily follow any and all sidetracks that present them-

---

* Also in 1835, Elizabeth Peabody published *Record of a School*, based on Bronson Alcott's dialogues with his students at Temple School. She stated that children possessed an intuition of God and goodness that teachers can help them recognize and cultivate. Megan Marshall (2005) notes that with the publication of this book, she was able to recognize her vocation in life to nurture and promote the men she admired, "helping them achieve a greater range of action than she could ever hope to attain as a woman" (p. 316).

selves, trusting that whatever I find will in some way enrich my understanding of my subject. But for now it is biographies of women in the mid-to late 19th century and histories of women's lives at that time. As I carry my armload of books back to my car, I wonder at the spiral of my research, moving from the text, to the place, and then the imagination before starting the cycle all over again on another plane. It seems as though, for me at least, the text must always be grounded in the specificities of location and time.

Home Again

Sabbaticals, like dreams, must end, and in December I find myself back in Wisconsin, trying to put together all that I have learned. There is the written report for the sabbatical committee due soon and the presentation I must give to my colleagues at the next autumn faculty retreat. There are the other presentations at conferences … AERA, Sarah Lawrence College, Reconceptualizing Early Childhood Education … all requiring me to create permutations of my theme.

The cold, snowy days give me the time, once again, to reflect on my experiences doing this research and to decide what form my new understanding will take. But as in any successful research project, I now have more questions than I began with: Is there ever such a thing as a completely accurate account of any period of history or any person's life? Even in doing biographical or historical research, the scholar's task is to imaginatively piece together selected details to create meaningful narratives. The one thing I know for sure is that the research is never done. So next fall I am going back to Concord, the library will be reopened by then, and to Boston to the little café on West Street, this time at noon and during the week. I will retrace my research journey, filling in the missing pieces until I once again get sidetracked in a new direction. And then I will go wherever it takes me.

An Epilogue?

In this chapter, I have attempted to re-create the meanderings that actually characterized my research process, complete with dead-ends, subjective interpretations, unintentional distortions, and suspect interpretations from sometimes-insufficient data. Perhaps like other researchers of history, I selected fragments, altered texts, created contexts, and reconstructed ideas and events to fit the narrative image in my mind rather than some unitary historic chronology. As I reflect back on this project, I am again confronted with the questions of research method that first troubled me when I began my academic career.

From my earliest days as a teacher struggling to teach John Donne to high school sophomores, I have been concerned with the questions of what counts as valid knowledge; how knowledge can be acquired, verified, and textually represented; and, given my belief that knowledge is socially constructed, how can I identify the multiple factors that inform my understandings? One major aspect of my concern has been with the nature of the relationship between the researcher and the researched.

Conventional definitions posit a finite, permissible range of relationships that clearly articulate separations between researcher and researched. These distinctions, constructed in the cause of objectivity, minimize, the researchers' cultural beliefs and practices, while directing attention to the beliefs and practices of their research subjects (Roman, 1990). Within contemporary feminist research are a variety of practices that deliberately violate the strict separation between researcher and researched, encouraging a plurality of voices and narratives and promoting reflexivity as a strategy for confronting the inevitable imposition of research interpretation. Rather than positioning myself as an objective observer and recorder, my choice to employ autobiographic as well as biographic research strategies placed me, as nearly as was possible, in the center of Elizabeth Peabody's life and provided me with a perspective from which I could revisit her life experience through my own. My very choice of Elizabeth Peabody as my subject was, in fact, autobiographically motivated by my own life history and professional interests. In retracing her life, I could almost viscerally experience the many influences that formed who she was, and, in turn, could use her life as a lens through which to understand my own.

Beginning this project, I wondered how a collaborative approach, as advocated by many feminist researchers, might be useful in a research process focused on educational history. Much of the "method" in the research project described here was informed by my desire to create a kind of an "imagined collaboration" with Elizabeth Peabody in experiencing 19th-century Boston, Salem, Concord, and the Transcendentalist community, and I was quite satisfied with my immersion into that world and with the insights it evoked. Central to this sort of research process, however, are assumptions that authentic depictions of subjective experience can only be generated through personal reflections on one's own lived experience and intuitive examination of one's own ideas and beliefs. The problem, of course, was that the opportunity to reflect on the research experience was very one-sided. I could never really know what Elizabeth Peabody actually felt and experienced as she transited the world of 19th-century male intellectuals. The events I focused upon and the meaning I gave them were rather arbitrarily defined by my own interests and motivations. Even the use of this three-part narrative to represent my work is dictated by my own interest in alternative forms of research representation and the use of juxtaposition as an analytic device rather than by the conventions of either historical research or 19th-century discourse. For all the certainty of my understandings, they are only my own.

It is clear that I must continue to vigorously interrogate the imposition of my personal meaning on the life experience of my subject and reconcile the apparent discomfort with "truth" and "value" that are inherent in my chosen methodology of autobiographic analysis. But I also am aware that restricting the construction of my own interpretations can obscure the emergent insights inherent in my lived experience with my subject and thereby limit the creation of new understandings that may be unexpected and multifocused. Attentive to these realities, I continue to explore the contradictions, struggles, and negotiations inherent in my efforts to demystify this research process through the inclusion of my own subjective, emergent experience.

References

Barnard, H. (1890). *Papers on kindergarten and child culture*. Hartford, CT: Office of the American Journal of Education.

Baylor, R. (1965). *Elizabeth Peabody, kindergarten pioneer*. Philadelphia: University of Pennsylvania Press.

Beatty, B. (1995). *Preschool education in America*. New Haven, CT: Yale University Press.

Davies, R. H. (1904). Boston in the 60's. In *Bits of gossip*. Boston: Houghton Mifflin.

Doyle, Margaret. (1899). Notes from Milwaukee. *Kindergarten Magazine*, 11, pp. 333–334.

Froebel, F. (1826/1887). *The education of man* (W. Hailmann, Trans.). New York: Appleton.

Froebel, F. (1911). *Mutter- und Kose-Lieder*. Leipzig: A. Pichler's Witwe und Sohn.

Halliburton, R. (1925). *The royal road to romance*. Garden City, NY: Star Books.

Jipson, J., Hauser, M., Lozano, T., Kim, M., & Melzoff, N. (October 1993). Gertrude's secrets: How we (historically) educate our children. Paper presented at the conference on Reconceptualizing Early Childhood Education: Theory, Research and Practice, Ann Arbor, MI.

Kriege, M. (1872). *The child, its nature and relations*. New York: E. Steiger.

Marenholtz-Buelow, B. (1889). *The child and child nature*. Syracuse, NY: Bardeen.

Marshall, M. (2005). *The Peabody sisters: Three women who ignited American romanticism*. Boston: Houghton Mifflin.

Peabody, E. P. (1862). Kindergarten—What is it? *Atlantic Monthly*.

Peabody, E. P. (1893). Lectures in the training schools for kindergartners. Boston: D.C. Heath.

Peabody, E. P., & Mann, M. (1864). *Guide to the kindergarten and moral culture in infancy*. Boston: Burnham.

Pestalozzi, J. (1801/1977). *How Gertrude teaches her children*. Washington, DC: University Publications of America.

Roman, L. (1990). Is naturalism a move away from positivism? Materialist and feminist approaches to subjectivity in ethnographic research. In E. Eisner & A. Peshkin EdSc), *Qualitative Inquiry in Education*. New York: Teachers College Press.

Ronda, B. (1984). *Letters of Elizabeth Palmer Peabody, American Renaissance Woman*. Middletown, CT: Wesleyan University Press.

Shapiro, M. (1983). *Child's garden: The kindergarten movement from Froebel to Dewey*. University Park: Pennsylvania State University Press.

Tharp, L. (1950). *The Peabody sisters of Salem*. Boston: Little, Brown.

Thoreau, H.D. (1962). *The Journal of Henry David Thoreau*. New York: Dover.

6
Action Research in Early Childhood Contexts

FRANCES O'CONNELL RUST

New York University

Every day in every classroom, teachers act in response to data that they have collected around questions of practice. They try to determine who is paying attention, who is tired, who needs help, who needs some independence, what is working, what is not working, and much, much more. Sometimes, they have learned in their teacher education programs to shape a question and follow through with a systematic study; sometimes, they just ask a question that leads them into inquiry around practice. However they get there, when teachers engage in questioning, collecting data, and following through by taking action, they are engaging in the signature activities of teacher research. When this process incorporates what Schön (1983) describes as "reflective practice"—a stepping back and weighing of possible actions, following through on those deliberations with purposeful action, and assessing the outcome of the actions taken—teacher research becomes a very powerful catalyst for the improvement of practice as well as for professional development.

In this chapter I work from action research studies that my students, early childhood teachers with whom I work as members of the Teachers Network Leadership Institute (TNLI), and I, myself, have conducted in our efforts to understand our settings, our students, and ourselves. I use these studies or parts of them to lay out what we have come to see as essential tools for inquiry and to describe how we have used them and what we have learned in the process.

Practitioner Research

Teacher research, action research, practitioner inquiry—each of these describes a special type of qualitative research that draws on techniques that are, for the most part, already part of the instructional tool kit of most practitioners. They have to be! In the midst of the complexity of the average classroom and early childhood setting, teachers have neither the time nor the luxury of doing large-scale, experimental studies.

Practitioner research fits generally within the traditions of qualitative research in education (Eisner & Peshkin, 1990; Ely, Anzul, Freidman, Garner, & Steinmetz, 1991; Erickson & Christman, 1996; Spindler, 1982). Qualitative research is, as Rist (1982) writes,

> a model of research that brings the study of human beings *as human beings* to center stage. It represents a fundamental rejection of the ultimately irrational pursuit to quantify different aspects of human belief and experience. (p. x)

The methodological precedents for data collection in this form of research emerge from anthropology and sociology—from fields that seek to describe the human condition in all of its variety. In anthropology, the effort is to understand cultures that are quite different from those of the investigator. In sociology, the effort is to make the familiar strange, to gain some distance from a phenomenon so as to really see what is happening. Thus, giants such as Boas (1928), Benedict (1934, 1946), and Mead (1928) in anthropology; and Becker (1963), Becker, Geer, Hughes, and Strauss (1961), Geertz (1973), Mills (1959), and Whyte (1955) in sociology provide models of traditional qualitative approaches.

In recent years, as Hatch and Barclay-McLaughlin (2006) note, "Qualitative research approaches have contributed substantial understanding to the field of early childhood education" (p. 497), and early childhood educators could look to the well-crafted studies that Hatch and Barclay-McLaughlin review, such as those by Graue (1993), Lubeck (1985), Quintero (1999), and Tobin, Wu, and Davidson (1989), to find models of qualitative research that are appropriate to understanding early childhood settings and interpreting practice in early childhood.

Action research is situated in the qualitative tradition. It is, as Bogdan and Biklin (1982) describe it,

> the systematic collection of information that is designed to bring about social change. ... [It is] a type of applied research in which the researcher is actively involved in the cause for which the research is conducted. (p. 215)

Hatch (2002) asserts that the focus of action research is not with generating findings that can be applied in other settings. Practitioner research may provide a basis for theory generation and knowledge production, but its "primary purpose is as a practical tool for solving problems experienced by people in their professional, community, or personal lives" (Stringer, 1999, p. 11).

Thus, teachers who seek to understand life in their classrooms and schools and to make local change based on the data of their inquiry are working within the parameters of action research. Although much of teacher action research is qualitative in design, both qualitative and quantitative methods can be used for data gathering (see Meyers & Rust, 2003). According to Ritchie (2006), practitioner research relates to more common forms of educational research in that it is contextually specific and investigates questions that are central to teaching and learning. Like qualitative research, it focuses on process. Like quantitative research, it looks for relationships among datasets. However, teacher action research is different from more traditional qualitative and quantitative research in that it is conducted by "insiders" in real classrooms and school settings; it is practical; it values individual and group reflection; and its conclusions inform practice-specific contexts.

The Process of Inquiry

Much of the action research that my students, my colleagues, and I do is done in settings where we can work with others—not necessarily to actually conduct the inquiry with them but to have the company of knowledgeable others who will listen, help us refine our thinking, and keep to our focus. Although the work that I cite here focuses entirely on early childhood settings, the methods of inquiry, the protocols that we follow, the techniques that we use, and the ways in which we report our work fit within the traditions of teacher research across the grades (see Cochran-Smith & Lytle, 1993; Hollingsworth, 1997; Hubbard & Power, 1993; Meyers & Rust, 2003; Zeichner, 1993, 1995; Zeichner & Noffke, 2001).

Developing Questions

We begin by shaping questions. Often our questions emerge from wonderings: "I wonder what would happen if …" "I wonder whether I spend more time with boys than with girls." "I wonder how the various areas of the room are used during choice times." We work with these wonderings, moving from them into researchable questions, that is, questions that require systematic inquiry if they are to be answered.

Sometimes our questions seem pretty straightforward. Take, for example, the wondering: "I wonder whether I spend more time with boys than with girls." This easily becomes a researchable question by simply asking, "Do I spend more time with boys than with girls?" But, it could be that we have a theory behind the wondering that makes its way into our questions and leads us to a new or slightly different focus. For example, a theory about the relationship between activity and teacher–child interaction might change the question of who a teacher spends time with to something slightly different, as it does here: "Does the activity I choose, for example, working with kids in the block corner, doing a read-aloud in the library corner, engaging in making play dough, determine who I spend time with?"

As we shape a question, we try to avoid asking "why" questions, questions that could easily be answered with a "yes" or a "no," and questions that do not invite any action on our part. "Why" questions require a depth of knowledge about others' thinking that we simply are not equipped to ascertain. The easily answered questions take us nowhere. Questions such as "What is the relation-ship between parental income and children's language skills?" is interesting for a large-scale research study but not for action research, which is intimate in that it relates to our practice and our interactions with our students.

As we zero in on a question that we will pursue, we are mindful that it seems as if in doing this we're ignoring the many questions that we, as teach-ers, are asking all the time. Experience has taught us, however, that by focus-ing on one aspect of our practice, we inevitably touch on the broader context of the classroom and that in the end, we will have begun to think in new ways about those unanswered questions. Focusing on one question also allows us to develop our plans for intervention—our action, what we will do to ameliorate the problem or to change the situation.

Describing the Context

Inevitably, one's question emerges in a context. It is vital to think about why the question is important, the circumstances in which it has emerged, and what we hope to accomplish by looking more deeply than we already have into the issue of concern. A nice example of this description of context comes from one of my students, Paola Higuera (2000), who was student teaching in a first grade classroom where several of her students were simultaneously learning English as a second language and learning how to read and write in English. She wondered if, given a degree of latitude in how the teachers could approach reading, the kids might have ways of combining the two tasks—learning the language and learning to read and write in it. She chose to follow one child, but she situated her study in the complex context of emergent literacy in a first grade classroom.

Another example comes from a study by MetLife Fellow Rachel Zindler (2003) who focused on the 7 of 24 children who were classified as special education students in her second grade inclusion classroom. These 7 chil-dren struggled with a variety of developmental delays, such as expressive and receptive language processing disorders, physical disabilities, and social and emotional issues. All but one was a child of color who lived outside of the local community. Given this context, Zindler questioned how truly "inclusive" her classroom was.

In my own multi-age preschool and kindergarten classroom, where 28 children ranging in age from 3 to 6 years had 2 hours of choice time every morning, I wanted to know what areas of the room were favored by the chil-dren, when these areas were used most heavily, and whether their preferences changed during the choice time.

The point here is that one needs to think about what makes the particular question or focus of inquiry important. Paola, like many teachers in urban environments, wanted to understand the complex phenomenon of second language learning. Her concern emerged in a context in which children's learning to read and write in English is critical to their success in school. She needed to be able to try to gain an understanding of how this works. Rachel and her teaching partner had an obligation to the special education children in their inclusion classroom, but they also had an obligation to the entire class. They needed to see whether and how the supposed benefits of inclusion actually played out. For my co-teachers and me, knowing how the room was working for our kids was important in helping us to know whether our arrangement of the room and our decisions about the materials and activities that we made available to them enabled our students to develop the understandings and ways of knowing that were critical to the school that we had set up.

Situating a Study

If we were in settings where we and our colleagues shared the inquiry, then we would be talking with one another and sharing information about the topic, but such learning communities are rare. Instead, most teacher-researchers need to seek colleagueship and information about a topic by reading about the topic. I suggest doing an ERIC (Educational Research Index Clearinghouse) search through your local library or university. Teachers Network maintains a huge digital library of teacher research and other relevant literature (see http://www.teachersnetwork.org). Google searches can also be helpful in identifying articles and books that can be useful.

Paola read about second language learning and about emergent literacy behaviors. Rachel read up on inclusion as well as on the relationship between children's social interactions and learning. I read about open classrooms, and I read into Montessori's work looking particularly for what she had to say about the prepared environment and children's decision making.

These forays into others' research help to situate an inquiry in what is an increasingly robust literature of practice. They show what others have done about similar issues. They can help teacher-researchers to plan their studies, determine appropriate research strategies, and gauge the success of their interventions.

Permission

If you are doing your study for a class as Paola did or anticipate publication as Rachel did, then you should get permission from your school's director or principal as well as from parents. Teachers Network has model forms available for download from the Internet (see the website above). If you are like my co-teachers and me and are simply trying to figure out what is working in your classroom, letting your principal or director know is useful (because of the long-term possibility for changing the discourse within the setting) but not essential. Such inquiry is, as I said at the beginning, the normal activity of a thoughtful teacher.

The Tools of Inquiry in Classrooms

Embedded in most questions are the tools that one will use to answer that question. In teaching, most of the tools that we use are, in one way or another, the tools of classroom observation: classroom maps, anecdotal records, time-sampled observations, samples of student work, drawings and photographs, audio and video recordings, interviews, conversations, surveys, and teachers' journals.

Paola used conversations with her student, samples of his work, observations of him alone and interacting with other children, and her journal entries to help her figure out how her student was progressing. Rachel used observations of the children in and out of the classroom, interviews with students concerning social choices and with parents regarding children's after-school activities and their attitudes toward school, recorded comments of students made during class discussions, samples of student work, her own journal, and notes from her planning meetings with her co-teacher. I used classroom maps, time samples taken daily at two distinct moments during the free choice time, notes that my colleagues and I made daily about each child in the class, and my own journal.

Paola did her data collection over a semester of student teaching. Rachel did hers over an entire academic year. I did mine over a 2-week period in my classroom in the fall and then repeated it over another 2-week period in the spring.

Classroom Maps

Classroom maps are one of the easiest and the most informative observation tools to use. They are a staple of classroom research, a way of situating and referencing action. Using a classroom map, one can begin to look critically at the setup and decoration of the classroom—whose work is up on the walls? How is the seating arranged? How does the way in which the classroom is set up shape behavior of both teachers and children? (Montessori, 1965a). For example, using multiple copies of a map or transparency sheets laid over the map, teachers can plot their own, a child's, or several children's movements around the classroom. This is called *tracking movement flow* (see Acheson & Gall, 1990; Adams & Biddle, 1970) and it is particularly helpful (as it was to me) in figuring out what parts of the room are working, where children like to congregate, even how a child or group of children is making use of the room and interacting with other children in the room.

Classroom maps are useful, too, for charting verbal flow—conversation between teachers and students and conversation among students (see Acheson & Gall, 1990). Instead of movement, one plots verbal exchanges. This is useful for looking at question and response patterns as well as other patterns of conversation. It is hard to measure verbal flow without either videotaping or having an observer record the data, but learning to do this can help teachers figure out who they are calling on, who gets their attention, what parts of the classroom figure in children's talk, and what parts are ignored.

Anecdotal Records

Anecdotal records are another observation tool. These are essentially notes that teachers keep on particular children or on particular activities. They are a time-honored technique for child study. The date and time of an anecdotal record should be recorded. I generally encourage preservice students and my TNLI colleagues to develop anecdotal records using a *time sampling* technique of making notes at specific intervals—every 5, 10, or 15 minutes. In that way, one not only records misbehavior, one actually catches children being good! And it is the good behavior that we can build on. I also encourage a format in which students draw a line down the center of a page and record their observations on one side of the line and their theories about what they see and hear on the other. This enables them to separate observation from interpretation—an important discipline in any inquiry.

In my first year of teaching, I was trying to figure out why I was having so much difficulty with certain children. To answer my question, I kept notes on myself. Every 10 minutes I simply stopped what I was doing and wrote down where I was, who I was with, and what I was doing. Within 2 or 3 days, I discovered that in my multi-age, Montessori-oriented, preschool classroom, I was rewarding misbehavior. If a child wanted my attention, all she had to do was to knock over someone's block building, hit someone, yell, or otherwise misbehave. I would be there. Knowing what I was doing enabled me to change my own behavior to catch children being good! Acting on the data of my observations, I was able to turn that classroom around in a matter of a week.

Photographs

Photographs can be enormously useful for documenting the life of the classroom. If one looks at materials out of Reggio Emilia (see Edwards, Ghandini, & Forman, 1993), one sees excellent examples of documentation using photographs. For children, photographs hold tangible memories of activities in which they have been engaged. For teachers, photographs have the power to capture progress—in the block area, with art materials, writing, math—any area where children's work is both progressive and cumulative and where the teacher is interested in determining whether and how children's skills have developed.

Samples of Children's Work

Collecting samples of children's work over time is an important way of documenting students' progress. There is a rich literature around using children's work as a means of determining curriculum and gaining insight about children's strengths. See, for example, the documentation materials from Reggio Emilia (Edwards, Ghandini, & Forman, 1993), or those from the Prospect

School (Carini, 1975), or classics in the field of early childhood such as the work of Dorothy Cohen and her colleagues (Cohen, Stern, & Balaban, 1997) or that of Almy and Genishi (1979) or of Genishi (1992).

In my own classroom of children ranging in age from 3 to 6, I kept portfolios of children's artwork, drawings, and efforts to write letters and numbers. Over time, these provided strong evidence of their skill development and, often, of their conceptual development. Paola Higuera, who was trying to figure out whether and how her students were learning English, collected samples of a child's writing over a period of 3 months. What she saw was a remarkable shift from using mostly Spanish to a blending of Spanish and English in which English structures and idioms began to predominate.

Video and Audio Recordings

Video and audio recordings are among the most powerful research tools available to teachers. Video offers what Acheson and Gall (1990) describe as "a wide lens" on classroom activity because there are so many ways to study a video. One can look at verbal flow, at children and teacher interactions, at nonverbal behavior, and at management patterns (Kounin, 1970), and one can look at a video over and over again exploring new questions. Audio offers a narrower but nevertheless powerful lens that, as the teachers of Reggio Emilia (Edwards, Ghandini, & Forman, 1993) and Vivan Gussin Paley (1997, 1998, 2004) have shown, has the potential to help teachers understand how their students are making sense of the classroom, the world, and their own lives. One can also use audiotapes in very focused ways: to study teacher talk, to study the progress of a child's speech, or to study classroom conversation.

In the hands of skilled teachers who share these tools with their students, quite interesting things can emerge. See, for example, Matt Wayne's video "Fishbowl" on the Teachers Network Web site (http://teachersnetwork.org) where Matt's students decide to monitor their efforts to develop accountable talk. One of my colleagues audiotaped each child in her preschool class three times a year. Each time, the children told the story of the Gingerbread Man. They loved to hear how their language had changed over time, and she learned how to focus her interactions with individual children to maximize their strengths.

Teachers' Journals

Teachers' journals can be rich with data as well as theory making. In my classes and in my work with the TNLI teachers, I encourage them to write for 10 minutes—no more, no less—each day, every day. Ten minutes is possible, and doing it daily strengthens the habits of writing and reflecting. If using a notebook, I suggest opening the notebook wide and using the right-hand page for journal writing and the left-hand page for comments one might make after going back and re-reading what one has written. It is here, on the left-hand side, that one might jot down notes about patterns that are beginning to emerge in one's data collection or about the similarities between one's notes and something one has been reading.

Journals can work like logs where one tries to remember and record what happened vis-à-vis the focus of one's study. They can also function as diaries where one tries to remember and record what one was thinking, feeling, and experiencing. They can provide insight on ourselves as well as about a problem or concern. Best of all, the habit of writing and reflecting and focusing on a particular issue daily makes us better writers and thinkers and, when used to support teacher inquiry, better researchers! (see Fulwiler, 1987). In the end, journals are what Clandinin and Connelly (1995) describe as "narratives of knowing."

Data Collection and Analysis

Each time my students or the TNLI teachers try a new tool, I ask them to bring in the data that they gathered with it. What they discover is that the various tools they have used—whether tried specifically for their studies or because they were interested in what the tool offered—provide lenses on the classroom that enable them to see beneath the surface. Generally, this is the time we begin to look for patterns in data and for ways to represent those patterns that are consistent with the research literature we have read. For example, using samples of her student's work and carefully calling attention to the changes over time, Paola Higuera (1993) developed her own theory of the way in which children learn to speak, read, and write in a second language.

Zindler's Study of Inclusion

From her interviews with students, Rachel (Zindler, 2003) and her colleague created sociograms (see Hubbard & Power, 1993) to depict their observation data and looked to these sociograms to provide a barometer of social grouping and alienation with the class. Inclusion of the seven special education students would signal to these teachers that their interventions were having an impact on the general education students' acceptance of the special needs students.

They tried several interventions designed to facilitate friendships among students and across social boundaries. They held community meetings, set up structures in their classroom to support new friendships, paired "isolates" with popular students for fun and for academic activities, and tried to capitalize on the strengths of the children with special needs.

Although the sociogram data, which Rachel depicts in the form of five graphs developed over the year, showed that "overall, the class population became more inclusive" and the "children with learning disabilities became increasingly popular" (Zindler, 2003, p. 15), the status of the seven special needs students remained "lower than that of all the other children." It appeared as if "they had formed a social network on the margins of the class" (p. 16).

Buttressed by the data she collected from interactions with service providers in the school, notes about in-class and after-school activities, and notes from planning sessions with her colleague, Rachel's analysis connects in a variety of ways to research on learning disabilities, inclusion, and education policy and pushes the reader toward consideration of the ways in which schools could better organize to support inclusion.

Rust's Study of Children's Activity Choices

In my study of my students' choices over the 2-hour choice period, I discovered that there was a remarkable shift in children's activity choices after what Montessori (1965b) calls "false fatigue"—a time when the noise level goes up and children seem to be ready to stop what they are doing but are really just taking a breath and getting ready to settle into what Montessori calls their "real work of the day."

I collected data in my first study by using a classroom map and noting where children were at two times during the morning: 9:30 and 10:15. In later studies, I used a list of the room areas and wrote children's names beside the area that they were in at one of the two times I checked. I did this because I wanted to know if the room worked differently for boys and girls. I simply counted at the end of each day and recorded my findings on a chart that I created. Over a period of 2 weeks, I was able to document a fascinating portrait of my children's activity.

In my classroom, the children arrived at 9:15 and immediately went to work at what I discovered to be activities that were familiar and comfortable. Between 9:15 and 9:45 a.m., the fives (6 children) went to the blocks, art table, jigsaw puzzles, and manipulatives such as pattern blocks and tangrams. The fours (15 children) went to the workbench, sand table, art table, blocks, puzzles in frames, looking at books, food preparation, writing and drawing with magic markers, and dress-up. The threes (7 children) went to the sand table, book corner, easel, Montessori manipulatives such as cylinder blocks and knobless cylinders, and the art area.

Between 9:45 and 10:00, a gradual shift took place. Buttressed by Montessori's notion of "false fatigue," observations of children's choice patterns (Rust, 1971), and my own experience of seeing children seeming to shift gears, I let this rise in noise level and activity go on. By 10:00 a.m., most of the children were into new and quite different activities. These were activities that seemed to require a different level of concentration. The fives would go to reading and writing activities, checkers, math games such as chip trading, working with Lego diagrams, and board games. The fours would move into writing and drawing, math games with fives, jigsaw puzzles, pegboard and pattern block work, Lotto games, blocks, sand table, workbench, and dress-up. The threes moved into the block area, puzzles, dress-up, manipulatives, food preparation, and listening to stories.

Not only did collecting these data twice a year help me to see the pattern of work that Montessori had so accurately described, it also helped me to see which areas of the room were working and which were not. The first time I did it, for example, I discovered that the math area was hardly being used. My colleagues and I moved the math area opposite the entry to the room and decided that there would always be one of us there to work with kids. Within 10 days of having made these changes, the math area had become a beehive of activity. We applied the lessons of this research—the data regarding children's preferences, our understanding that the kids valued our presence and our interest—to our shaping of other areas of the room over the years so that the classroom became what Rambusch (1962) described as a "responsive environment," a place that suited the children who used it and enabled them to take responsibility for their learning.

What We Can Learn From Teacher Action Research

My work with preservice students over many years has told me that in a semester, they will have learned to use from four to six research tools, read broadly around two or three topics, and begun to develop lenses for studying their own practice. They will also have begun to examine and describe teaching and learning in their student teaching classrooms, to question their own and others' assumptions about teaching and learning, and to shape their work as teachers and researchers of teaching. They seem to come away from their first study of teaching with a heightened sense of awareness of the complexity of teaching and a more nuanced understanding of the ways in which teachers' actions as planners, decision makers, and doers affect the life of classrooms. They begin to think like teachers.

But one course is not enough. It is a time to begin—a place where the bigger picture of reflective practice and practitioner inquiry is framed and becomes a model for future professional interaction. I recognize that there must be a coherence of support both during and after preservice preparation so that the ways of knowing and being that teacher educators begin in courses such as mine are nurtured and encouraged to grow. Being reflective and inquiring is a fragile stance, especially for a new teacher. This is where the need for a professional group such as the Teachers Network Leadership Institute (TNLI) comes to the fore. Such networks offer support for what Clark (1995) describes as "thoughtful teaching" and for what Florio-Ruane and Clark (1993) describe as "authentic conversation," that is, thoughtful, face-to-face interchanges in which participants sincerely try to get to know one another and judgment does not enter in.

TNLI teachers claim that their engagement in action research positively affects their teaching. They describe themselves as "becoming more reflective, more critical and more aware, regardless of how many years they had been teaching" (Rust & Meyers, 2006, p. 81). They claim that the research helped them to become "stronger teachers" (p. 81) and enabled them to assume a voice in policy making in their schools, communities, and beyond.

Rust and Meyers (2006) write that "action research in the classroom is incredibly hard work" (p. 80). It takes time to learn to do it and it takes practice. The first study is always the most difficult, but as the habit of inquiry takes hold, each subsequent study becomes easier and the relationship between practice and student achievement becomes clearer. Good teaching, thoughtful teaching, my students, colleagues, and I have come to understand, is by its very nature research. It is "asking questions, … paying systematic attention to the outcomes of our instruction; determining what has been learned; figuring out what might work better; and refining, reshaping, and assessing our own work" (Meyers & Rust, 2003, p. xvii).

In early childhood settings where so many of our children are just developing their verbal skills and often do not have the words to tell us when and why things are not going well for them, it is essential that we find ways to figure out what we can do to make each day and each moment with them the best it can be. Action research provides rich opportunities and a wealth of tools for doing this and for looking deeply at ourselves, our settings, and our practices—the heart of good teaching and place where we can make a difference for the children in our care.

References

Acheson, K. A., & Gall, M. D. (1990). *Techniques in the clinical supervision of teachers*. White Plains, NY: Longmans.

Adams, R. S., & Biddle, B. J. (1970). *Realities of teaching: Explorations with videotape*. New York: Holt, Rinehart, & Winston.

Almy, M., & Genishi, C. (1979). *Ways of studying children* (Rev. ed.). New York: Teachers College Press.

Becker, H. S. (1963). *Outsiders: Studies in the sociology of deviance*. New York: The Free Press.

Becker, H. S., Geer, B., Hughes, E. C., & Strauss, A. (1961). *Boys in white: Student culture in medical school*. Chicago: University of Chicago Press.

Benedict, R. (1934). *Patterns of culture*. Boston: Houghton Mifflin.

Benedict, R. (1946). *The chrysanthemum and the sword*. Boston: Houghton Mifflin.

Boas, F. (1962). *Anthropology and modern life*. New York : Norton. (Original work published 1928.)

Bogdan, R. C., & Biklen, S. K. (1982). *Qualitative research for education*. Boston: Allyn & Bacon.

Carini, P. (1975). *Observation and description: An alternative method for the investigation of human phenomena* (Monograph series). Grand Forks: North Dakota Study Group on Evaluation.

Clandinin, D. J., & Connelly, M. (1995). *Teachers' professional knowledge landscapes*. New York: Teachers College Press.

Clark, C. M. (1995). *Thoughtful teaching*. New York: Teachers College Press.

Cochran-Smith, M., & Lytle, S. (1993). *Inside/outside: Teacher research and knowledge*. New York: Teachers College Press.

Cohen, D., Stern, V., & Balaban, N. (1997). *Observing and recording the behavior of young children* (4th ed.). New York: Teachers College Press.

Edwards, C., Ghandini, L., and Forman, G. (Eds.). (1993). *The hundred languages of children: The Reggio Emilia approach to early childhood education*. Norwood, NJ: Ablex.

Eisner, E. W., & Peshkin, A. (Eds.). (1990). *Qualitative inquiry in education: The continuing debate*. New York: Teachers College Press.

Ely, M., Anzul, M., Freidman, T., Garner, D., & Steinmetz, A. M. (1991). *Doing qualitative research: Circles within circles*. New York: Falmer Press.

Erickson, F., & Christman, J. B. (1996). Taking stock/making change: Stories of collaboration in local school reform. *Theory into Practice, 35*(3), 149–157.

Florio-Ruane, S., & Clark, C. M. (1993, August). *Authentic conversation: A medium for research on teachers' knowledge and a context for professional development.* Paper presented at the meeting of the International Study Association on Teacher Thinking, Goteborg, Sweden.

Fulwiler, T.(Ed.). (1987). *The journal book.* Portsmouth, NH: Heinemann.

Geertz, C. (1973). Thick description: Toward an interpretive theory of culture. In *The interpretation of cultures.* New York: Basic Books.

Genishi, C. (Ed.). (1992). *Ways of assessing children and curriculum.* New York: Teachers College Press.

Graue, M. E. (1993). *Ready for what? Constructing meanings of readiness for kindergarten.* Albany: State University of New York Press.

Hatch, J. A. (2002). *Doing qualitative research in education settings.* Albany: State University of New York Press.

Hatch, J. A., & Barclay-McLaughlin, G. (2006). Qualitative research: Paradigms and possibilities. In B. Spodek & O. N. Saracho (Eds.), *Handbook of research on the education of young children* (pp. 497–514). Mahwah, NJ: Erlbaum.

Higuera, P. (2000). The little computadore: A study of emergent literacy. Unpublished paper for Study of Teaching, New York University.

Hollingsworth, S. (1997). *International action research: A casebook for educational reform.* London: Falmer Press.

Hubbard, R. S., & Power, B. M. (1993). *The art of classroom inquiry.* Portsmouth, NH: Heinemann.

Kounin, J. S. (1970). *Discipline and group management in classrooms.* New York: Holt, Rinehart, & Winston.

Lubeck, S. (1985). *Sandbox society: Early education in black and white America.* London: Falmer Press.

Mead, M. (1928). *Coming of age in Samoa.* New York: William Morrow.

Meyers, E., & Rust, F. (Eds.). (2003). *Taking action with teacher research.* Portsmouth, NH: Heinemann.

Mills, C. W. (1959). *The sociological imagination.* London: Oxford University Press.

Montessori, M. (1965a). *The Montessori method.* New York: Shocken Books.

Montessori, M. (1965b). *Spontaneous activity in education.* New York: Shocken Books.

Paley, V. G. (1992). *You can't say, "You can't play."* Cambridge, MA: Harvard University Press.

Paley, V. G. (1998). *The girl with the brown crayon* (Reprint ed.). Cambridge, MA: Harvard University Press.

Paley, V. G. (2004). *Wally's stories* (Reprint ed.). Cambridge, MA: Harvard University Press.

Quintero, E. (1999). The new faces of Head Start: Learning from culturally diverse families. *Early Education & Development, 10,* 475–497.

Rambusch, N. M. (1962). *Learning how to learn: An American approach to Montessori.* Baltimore: Helicon Press.

Rist, R. (1982). Foreword. In R. C. Bogden & S. K. Biklen, *Qualitative research for education* (pp. ix–xi). Boston: Allyn & Bacon.

Ritchie, G. V. (2006). *Teacher research as a habit of mind.* Unpublished doctoral dissertation, George Mason University.

Rust, F. O'C., & Meyers, E. (2006). The bright side: Teacher research in the context of educational reform and policy-making. *Teachers and Teaching: Theory and Practice, 12*(1), 69–86.

Rust, L. W. (1971). *Attributes that differentiate boys' and girls' preferences for materials in the preschool classroom: A systems design approach.* Ann Arbor, MI: University Microfilms.

Schön, D. (1983). *The reflective practitioner.* New York: Basic Books.

Spindler, G. (Ed.). (1982). *Doing the ethnography of schooling: Educational anthropology in action.* New York: Holt, Rinehart, & Winston.

Stringer, E. T. (1999). *Action research* (2nd ed.). Thousand Oaks, CA: Sage.

Tobin, J. J., Wu, D. Y., & Davidson, D. H. (1989). *Preschool in three cultures: Japan, China, and the United States.* New Haven, CT: Yale University Press.

Whyte, W. H. (1955). *Street corner society.* Chicago: University of Chicago Press.

Zeichner, K. (1993). Action research: Personal renewal and social reconstruction. *Educational Action Research, 1*(2), 199–220.

Zeichner, K. (1995). Beyond the divide of teacher research and academic research. *Teachers and Teaching: Theory and Practice, 1*(2), 153–172.

Zeichner, K., & Noffke, S. (2001). Practitioner research. In V. Richardson (Ed.), *Handbook of research on teaching* (4th ed., pp. 298–330). Washington, DC: American Educational Research Association.

Zindler, R. (2003). *Trouble in paradise: A study of who is included in an inclusion classroom*. New York: Teachers Network. Available online at http://www.teachersnetwork.org/tnli/research/achieve/zindler.htm

7

Critical Pedagogy and Qualitative Inquiry
Lessons From Working With Refugee Families

ELIZABETH P. QUINTERO

New York University

> To survive the Borderlands
> you must live sin fronteras
> be a crossroads.
>
> **—Anzaldúa, 1987, p. 195**

The poet Anzaldúa (1987) speaks of surviving in borderlands ... of being a crossroad. I believe that in the current world, in which borders are in a state of flux, peace is tenuous, and governments come and go, families and schools become the crossroads. The voices of teachers, of students, of families and friends in our communities around the world can be voices of possibility if only we can listen and learn from each other.

In the social and political contexts of communities and schools serving refugee, immigrant, and asylum-seeking families, regressive "scientifically-based" research methods are not only ineffective, but often misleading. Professionals involved in early childhood qualitative research have shown that it is through rigorous qualitative methods that we see more aspects of what is really going on in various contexts (Bateson, 2004; Brooker, 2002; Hatch, 1995).

No one develops or learns outside of the contexts of family, community, country, and world or without a connection to the past—the stories of those who have gone before. Learning happens among particularities, among persons and objects in families and communities. I believe that by using critical theory and critical literacy as a perspective in our interactions with immigrant and refugee families, the stories of people who are not currently "heard" will open up an environment of possibility for students and society. The way to study, document, and analyze the participatory activities in these endeavors is by using qualitative research methods.

My research and teaching are based on a deep commitment to critical theory, critical pedagogy, and critical literacy. The underlying elements of participation by all, respect for multiple points of view and ways of knowing, and responsibility for transformative action lead me to carry out my teaching and research within a critical qualitative methodological framework. I have found over years of working with teacher education students and community participants (adults and children) that qualitative approaches provide a framework for addressing complex, critical issues, among multiple participants, in an honest and collaborative way. While no research and teaching methodology can be a panacea and should never be a recipe, the combination of qualitative methods and critical theory give my students, our community participants, and me ways to collaborate and learn from each other. This chapter describes how my commitment to critical qualitative inquiry takes shape in an annual study abroad program through which graduate students work with refugee children and families in the United Kingdom.

A Graduate Education Class: Critical Theory and Qualitative Research

In a graduate class built around an intensive 2-week study abroad program, most participants were master's-level students majoring in early childhood education, international education, or bilingual education. Two participants were doctoral students. All were enrolled in the course *Working With Parents: Cross Cultural Collaborations* because they wanted information, experience, and transformational perspectives regarding issues of refugee and immigrant families and their young children.

As the professor, from the outset I elucidated my personal theoretical and philosophical perspective, which is strongly influenced by the work of Paulo Freire (1973, 1984, 1997, 1998). My teaching and research are based upon critical theory and critical literacy, and I am passionate about qualitative methods as the most effective way to probe and analyze issues of participants' agendas and transformation. The combination of a critical theoretical framework and qualitative methods promotes educational researchers' connecting their own lives and experiences with the study and brings to the fore the potential for transformative action.

Some scholars label critical theory "critical social theory" (Leonardo, 2004). Whatever the label, most scholars believe that, through critical social theory, discourses will be broadened in terms of the horizon of possibility (Leonardo, 2003). The multidisciplinary knowledge base of critical social theory affirms the role of criticism and rejects the radical differentiation between theory and practice as two separate poles of a dualism. Critical social theory encourages the production and application of theory as a part of the overall search for transformative knowledge.

According to Freire (1997), freedom can only occur when the oppressed reject the image of oppression "and replace it with autonomy and responsibility" (p. 29). Those who adopt Freire's pedagogy must be aware that it is not made up of techniques to save the world. Instead, he felt that "the progressive educator must always be moving out on his or her own, continually reinventing me and reinventing what it means to be democratic in his or her own specific cultural and historical context" (p. 308). Freire's work has given education a language with which we can discuss the effect of oppression on people and their ability to intervene on their own behalf.

As a teacher-researcher, I believe that all of us must consistently reflect on our work and our convictions. This constant clarification of our own values and actions in all areas of pluralistic work with students ought to be the ongoing aim of education. I see this clarification as Freire (1984) does when he defines "conscientization" (based on the Brazilian *conscientizaçao*) as "the process by which human beings participate critically in a transforming act" (p. 106). I see our world as a community of learners that reflects characteristics of the many contexts from which students come and the global community where we all struggle to live together peacefully. I make the case throughout this chapter that critical theory as a framework for study and analysis combined with qualitative research methodology is potentially an effective way to address the complexities of our changing world.

The power of critical theory relates to Said's (2000) call for intellectuals to speak truth to power and to provide a dissenting voice in conflicts with authority. A young child labeling a drawing of himself and a friend in his home language as well as in English, a refugee parent demanding that information from her child's school be written in her home language, and a musician using his song writing and performing to address issues of once being a child soldier in Africa are all forms of critical theory that speak truth to power.

This particular course involved the study of relationships among families, communities, and educational programs. As a class, we addressed the challenges and the nature of collaboration among families, schools, and communities for the purpose of supporting all children's success in educational settings. Emphasis was placed on culture, models and levels of parent involvement, forms of communicating with parents, parent education, working with families in crisis, and identifying resources for families. I used qualitative research approaches to structure our learning activities in ways that enabled critical theory to help us to foreground the underlying question, "What is really going on here?" for the community participants (children and their families) and for us as qualitative researchers.

The course is offered in an intensive format (2 weeks) each January in London, England. The course is conducted once a year in London because, in spite of ongoing in-country and international contention, London is an active center of collaboration among advocacy groups supporting refugee parents, educational programs, and community agencies. The contexts are often complex combinations of many cultures, languages, styles of child rearing, and daily living. Professionals in many agencies (both government sponsored and private) strive to meet daily challenges of supporting families in their desire and need to maintain their cultural roots while learning the skills and ways of life for successful living in a modern, democratic, technological society. We visited schools, early childhood programs, community centers, and government programs of the Refugee Council UK in various neighborhoods in London as part of the course activities. We had opportunities to interview family members and children from a variety of situations to inform our work.

Students are assigned to read several texts. One, *Becoming a Teacher in the New Society: Bringing Communities and Classrooms Together* (Quintero & Rummel, 2003), gives the students a review of critical theory, critical pedagogy, critical literacy, and examples of ways that this theoretical perspective is used to address learning in multicultural contexts. Another text, *Funds of Knowledge: Theorizing Practice in Households, Communities and Classrooms* (Moll, Gonzalez, & Amanti, 2005), is used to point out the impact of research that focuses on participants' strengths. In addition, two novels, *Brick Lane* (Ali, 2003) and *White Teeth* (Smith, 2001), are assigned reading because of the complexity and depth in addressing issues of family, culture, and contexts of change and migration through literature.

Students participated in three aspects of a problem-posing format (Listening, Dialogue, Action) as one of the requirements for course completion. This format facilitated our processing of complex course content in a way that values students' prior knowledge and current professional responsibilities. The theoretical framework underlying the pedagogy also demands a critical treatment of new information and a responsibility for using this information in an action format. Furthermore, the framework is a structured way to expose beginning researchers to some basic forms of qualitative methods for approaching fieldwork. The format also allowed students choice in pursuing specific aspects of their areas of scholarly interests. Final project guidelines are based on a model of qualitative research that is straightforward enough for beginning researchers to grasp, while addressing deeply complex issues.

For the purpose of this chapter, I follow a chronological path through the 2 weeks as the clearest way to show the progression of the activities and the developing insights of the student participants. The students have chosen to remain anonymous and therefore will be referred to as "student" throughout the chapter. The composite experience is a mosaic comprising the thinking of the participating students; the complex intertwining of qualitative inquiry, critical theory, and other theoretical and experiential backgrounds brought by the students and the profoundly sensitive issues involved when working with refugee families who bring their knowledge, experiences, cultures, and histories to the activities.

The First Day

I had assigned readings in Moll, Gonzalez, and Amanti's (2005) *Funds of Knowledge* and Monica Ali's (2003) novel *Brick Lane* before we arrived in London. Then, on the first day we had arranged to meet Harry Jackson from "London Walks Tours" for a walking historical tour of "The Old Jewish

Quarter." The historical tour begins near Tower Hill in London by a section of the excavated Old Roman Wall as a point of departure for talking about immigrants and refugees coming from other lands to London. The walk ends on Brick Lane, described at length in Ali's novel, in a neighborhood of East London that has been settled by many different immigrant groups over the past 4 centuries.

As we traveled to the meeting place, I told the students a story about a recent immigration conference when I participated on a panel and spoke about a family of refugees I had met doing a qualitative study in Turkey. Following the panel was a keynote address by Mary Robinson, former president of Ireland and former director of the United Nations Commission on Human Rights. She implored us to "put a human face on migration" (Robinson, 2005). Later, she approached me at the conference to talk more about my participants' stories. She believes, she said, that talking about the people involved in global migration and their experiences is important; it gives a human context to the statistics. I explained to the students that this "putting human faces" to our research is a characteristic of qualitative research. I also told them that our tour guide, Mr. Jackson, is a longtime London resident whose parents and grandparents were refugees from Poland and had settled in the neighborhood where he was taking us. He is adept at mixing historical facts and stories of his family. I encouraged the students to make connections between the factual information and the human stories. I told them that this was a point of departure for our study.

This walk traced the history of London's Jewish community in the East End. The story embraces the poverty of the pogrom refugees and the glittering success of the Rothschilds; the eloquence of the 19th-century prime minister Disraeli, and the spiel of the Petticoat Lane stallholder. Set amid the alleys and back streets of Spitalfields and Whitechapel, this is a story of synagogues and sweatshops, Sephardim and soup kitchens. We visited the historic Bevis Marks synagogue, the oldest Jewish house of worship in London, established by the Sephardic Jews in 1698.

During the tour we worked to connect the history of the neighborhood to the political and cultural contexts of the present. As we discussed the migration of different groups of people to this city, we asked about the neighborhood during and after the bombings in July of 2005. One site of the bombings was an underground station a few blocks from where we were walking. Mr. Jackson said that he had been watching and asking Muslim friends in East London if there had been any sort of a backlash against them after the bombings in July 2005. He said that everyone he asked told him that there had not been any retaliatory incidents. Likewise, university volunteers working with asylum seekers and refugee groups in London whom we later interviewed also reported that there had been no retaliations.

The Second Day

The class meeting on the second day began with the following quote from Mary Catherine Bateson (1994):

> ... there is a powerful link between presence and care. ... I believe that if we can learn a deeper noticing of the world around us this will be the basis of effective concern. (p. 109)

I used the quote as a way to introduce the variety of experience we had planned in various refugee communities, the rigor of my expectations for the students' reading, dialogue, and collaborative and individual actions. I pointed out that the act of "noticing" is a big part of qualitative methods.

Right away, I used the problem-posing format for class activities to show students the importance of connecting personal experience; new information through reading, interviews, and lectures (often on-site at schools, parent programs, and the refugee council); and action outside their classroom. I explained that the problem-posing activities of our methodology provide a nonlinear framework in which complex information can be connected with our lives.

We began an activity designed to connect student participants' personal lives to our study and activities. I asked students to write a short journal entry about either the history of a tradition or a celebration in their family or a story that had been retold in their family or in a group of friends.

Then the class members were asked to discuss the family stories in small groups and analyze how the stories were similar and how they were different. They were also asked to consider whether or not the stories give glimpses of the students' educational experiences. I asked the groups to continue the discussions and relate their personal stories to the Moll readings, the *Brick Lane* novel, and Mr. Jackson's stories from the previous day.

One student reported later in a journal reflection, his response to the initial problem-posing activities.

> The openness in our dialogue enabled such a deep level of communication—on a level that goes beyond "sharing" of facts and into our understanding others' lives and cultures. As we move into the interviews of the action plans we will be striving to achieve this confidence in the possible absence of the university context and the benefit of two days of getting acquainted. We will be trying to develop relations for our productive and enjoyable conversations.

After a lunch break we began the problem-posing again and I gave information about the definitions of immigrants, refugees, and asylum seekers. Immigrants are people who move from one country to another for the purpose of permanent residence. It has become accepted knowledge that a refugee is a person seeking asylum in a foreign country in order to escape persecution. Those who seek refugee status are sometimes known as asylum seekers and the practice of accepting such refugees is that of offering political asylum. The most common asylum claims to industrialized countries are based upon political and religious grounds. Refugee status may be granted on the basis of the 1951 Convention relating to the Status of Refugees (http://www.unhchr.ch/html/menu3/b/o_c_ref.htm).

I then introduced examples of qualitative research that describe the efforts of educators (parents, community elders, and teachers using critical literacy) in several countries and document the ways the families and educators use various funds of knowledge (Moll, 1990, Moll et. al., 2005; Quintero, 2004) for advocacy. I then explained that with my early childhood teacher education students, I have been addressing what such understandings might mean for creating environments for learning and for developing classroom practice. Through a series of journal reflections, video- and audiotaped observations, and feedback discussion, we all document our journeys as we experience this combination of critical theory and critical literacy and qualitative fieldwork in teacher education classes and in work with young children. We also focus on creating literacy opportunities that extend beyond the classroom to use the words of their families and communities for education.

We then discussed the general instructions for the final individual project assignment. Each student was asked to focus on an area of special interest relating to education and the opportunities that our particular studies in the refugee communities in London provide for a short qualitative study that leads to designing an "action plan." Students were given a basic framework for qualitative study, including theoretical stance, research questions, review of literature, methods of observation, interviews, forms of representation, data collection, and analysis. They were also given a general set of guidelines for conducting their action plan. They are asked to include information that answers the following questions:

- What are the main goals or purposes of your plan?
- What priorities have been identified by the group of participants?
- What are the strengths of the group(s) you will be working with?
- What needs of the group are unmet?
- How does the educational and academic literature inform you about these issues? (minimum of 15 sources, synthesized in a very brief Review of Literature format)
- Who are your collaborators for this plan? What resources do they bring, and what limits do they set? How will you gain their support?
- What resources will you need?
- What will be your obstacles? How will you overcome the obstacles?
- How will you evaluate (or measure) your action as it progresses?

The discussion of the expectations, challenges, and possibilities of students' individual work related to these guidelines for the action plan opened up more opportunities for the complex exploration of critical theory, the students' specific interests, and the qualitative methods for conducting the complicated orchestration of the activities. For example, when discussing the goals of action plans, some students were already focused on what they planned to do; others were very general in their thinking at that point. One student knew she wanted to investigate how to collaborate with Ecuadorian women in order to design and implement a project that would provide information and support for women regarding issues about the schooling of their young children. Another student knew she wanted to "support young teenagers with babies in Mississippi" but she was unclear about what she would eventually do. Both students could benefit from a session about forming research questions to inform goals. Likewise, regardless of the topic or exact context in which a student wanted to work, in order to answer the questions about obstacles and allies, methods for observation, interviews, and documentation were important.

For the action homework on this evening, I wanted to focus on the critical theory premise that participants' histories are integral in any educational endeavor. I asked the students to reflect and write about how they describe or define their racial or ethnic identity. I asked them to think about what is important and not important to them about this aspect of their identity. I asked them whether their ethnic identity is tied to a particular place and what are some of the details of that place that are a part of life now or of a memory that is important to them.

The Third Day

At the beginning of this seminar session, I asked, and tried to listen critically to, how the students felt about the previous day's work and the homework reflective writing assignment. Many students were excited about the activities as they provided ways to connect personal experiences to issues we were studying. Yet, one student said, "I don't like it!" I asked if she would clarify which parts of previous activities she didn't like. She said that she liked the readings, the history tour, and our previous class discussions. She didn't like the homework reflective writing activity about her family history.

She explained,

> My mother tends to live in the present and you have to get her in a really good state of mind to even hear about things that went on in her past. Most of it is negative stuff anyway that was used to point out how she had suffered or how "if she had been taught better she would have gone further in life." Such short snippets, only served to place upon me a burden which I should, but do not want to bear.

After we listened to this student and critically analyzed her stance, we listened to each other give glimpses into the connection between her comments and some issues of life for refugee and immigrant families. We reviewed the important aspect of critical theory that demands that participants' knowledge and opinions be respected and a part of every dialogue and activity. We discussed the complex task of remaining sensitive and creative in our work because every activity in our work will not be embraced by everyone and for very good reasons.

The students *who chose to share* reflections then discussed their personal stories, including the following:

Racial identity has been a running theme in my life. For the first decade of my life I didn't think about being Hispanic. I just was me. When I moved from a large urban city to a suburban community, all that changed. Being the only Hispanic in an entire primary school was devastating to me. All of a sudden I was "different." I quickly learned how cruelly "different" can be treated. My goal for that whole year was to do everything I could to blend in. Before I knew it I had begun the process of hiding who I was. I changed my dinner on my nutrition logs. I stopped talking Spanish and wouldn't listen or dance to the music. I pretended that race was only the color of my skin. This process involved different levels of intensity at different periods of time. I remember that towards the end of high school there were several Hispanic girls in my class. They all hung out together, but I didn't. By this time my race and my cultural ties were so suppressed that I didn't fit in socially with them. Yet, I didn't completely fit in with my "white" friends either.

As I started to travel more and more I began to value other cultures. Through that I began to look for the value in my own. I realized that I have many more questions than answers. Am I Latina or Hispanic? Am I Ecuadorian or Ecuadorian-American? What does it mean to be who I am? How much of who I am is connected to my racial identity? I am not sure of the answers but I feel that "race" is only the tip of the iceberg to culture. When we explore our culture or try to articulate our racial identity what we really try to do is see how each small piece of language, food, music, customs, shape who we were yesterday, today, and tomorrow.

Another student who grew up in the Deep South wrote,

My racial identity has always been the word black. However, what that means is hard to say. My family is more religious than cultural, so no one ever really talked about our ethnic history. To be honest, most people my age where I come from don't even know about Zora Neale Hurston and Billie Holiday. They only have heard mention of those more noted leaders of our culture, like Rosa Parks and Martin Luther King, but still couldn't share much knowledge about their beliefs and struggles. It became more important for me to learn more about my culture once I came to New York, a place of cultural diversity. Being from a place where there is only white and black leaves little need for explorations of any culture.

Finally, a student from the same group who comes from different life circumstances perhaps asks the most provocative questions at the end of her reflection.

I do not recall having any particular conceptions of it (racial identity) and the reason why I say this is because I did not feel disappointment like some immigrants who come to the U.S. and feel as if it was not living up to their preconceived expectations. I did have a picture in mind, but it is hard to put into words. I think that it does not solidify itself until after real life experience. ... I am still trying to reconcile what the difference is between personal philosophy, personality, and culture. I find myself making statements about all, after seeing the actions of a few ... unable to see, think or believe what is outside of the racial check boxes. Why do we have to check the box? Why are the boxes there in the first place? Who does it benefit? ... I feel that the process of migrating, in itself, changes the migrant ... The Jamaican culture is neither racial nor ethnic, but it is what I identify with most strongly. Yes, most of the population is Black and so I guess many of us do not use the Blackness as a unifying factor in the way we view potential friends. It is hard to understand the concept that those identifiers are now used to judge us when we do not necessarily do the same to ourselves.

As a critical theorist, teaching introductory qualitative methods, I asked whether the class participants saw any connections between this student's story and the stories we might hear from refugees and asylum seekers. A complicated discussion ensued. Two students commented on the discussions that day. One said,

Today our group discussion was so informative. It put so much into perspective for me. One connection that jumps out for me is the concept of culture within education. Gonzalez, Moll, & Amanti refer to social theory that legitimized marginalization of minority students by perpetuating an idea of "a culture of poverty," the idea that the culture of the poor (or minorities) was the cause of educational failure. They warn that this theory is flawed because it lacks a holistic approach. This spoke to our discussion of how, as minorities, our family history shaped our college selection process.

And the other said,

As Funds of Knowledge addresses the culture of students as important to classrooms when addressing multicultural perspectives, when speaking in our group we found that we learned a significant amount of cultural knowledge by interaction with peers from other cultural backgrounds than our own. The "funds of knowledge" that the students possess can be important too for teachers to build and develop a multicultural community.

Fourth Day

On this day, we visited one office of the Refugee Council. In the United Kingdom, the Refugee Council operates a number of programs for the vast needs of migrating families. This is the largest organization in the United Kingdom working with asylum seekers and refugees. Just to name a few of the many services provided for asylum seekers and refugees in the London area, there is a One Stop Service in which assistance is given, with the assistance of a staff of interpreters of a wide array of world languages, in the tasks of registration for needed services, application issues, and multiple family supports. There is a large Children's Sector that provides general services for families with young children and, through their work with the Medical Foundation for Victims of Torture, very specific services for children and unaccompanied minors. The office in Brixton supports a large Day Center where a staff cook and a few volunteers provide hot meals for 250 people a day. The Day Center has hot showers available, toys for children, and space and volunteers for various classes such as English as a Foreign Language.

Although the work of the Refugee Council is by and large very effective, a critical perspective requires a closer look at difficult issues affecting the work of the organization. The Refugee Council has the complex job of being a strong advocate for asylum seekers and criticizing the Home Office for not enough support and lack of strong enough-action, while at the same time being required to work with this political government bureaucracy.

In the afternoon of this day, we met with a leader and a university student volunteer from an organization giving university students and young people the opportunity to learn from and be advocates for migrating families. This group, Student Action for Refugees, or STAR, has a threefold mission to (1) learn about and raise awareness of refugee issues in innovative ways, (2) support refugees in a practical way in their local communities through volunteering, and (3) campaign with and for the rights of refugees everywhere.

The STAR network is made up of university-based student groups, other young people involved in the STAR Youth Network, and Friends of STAR (individuals and organizations who support the work of STAR). The group believes that refugees and asylum seekers are a vulnerable group of people who often have a long and difficult struggle to secure their safety in another country. As people fleeing persecution, torture, and prejudice, they need and deserve support. Furthermore, as a new generation it is vital that students and young people have a positive attitude toward refugees, asylum seekers, and displaced people.

Natasha King, the Student Outreach Officer for STAR, said, in response to a question about maintaining and sustaining work in contexts where the needs are so great and the issues so complicated, that

> At the national level of issues, racism, lack of information, fear on the part of native Britons about their jobs being "taken" by asylum seekers is really depressing, but that at the local university-by-university level the small projects can be so effective that it is really encouraging.

Fifth Day

On this day, our school visit to Star Primary School was an opportunity to address questions that exemplify critical theory and that are served by using qualitative methods to explore them:

> What are the aspects involved in educating children of refugee and immigrant families?
>
> In communities with a high population of refugee families, students who speak the language of the school as a second, third, or fourth language, and a high rate of poverty, what can schools do?
>
> How can a curriculum be designed and delivered that supports and respects the history, language, and culture of newcomers while at the same time providing students with knowledge and skills to give them an equal chance for success in their new homes?
>
> How can schools provide support for the entire family of its students?

These are questions that exemplify critical theory and questions that are served by using qualitative methods to explore them.

Star Primary School is a community school for pupils aged 3–11 years. It is located in Canning Town in the East End of London, an area of economic deprivation. It is surrounded by prewar properties used mainly for temporary accommodation. The school provides education to pupils from a wide range of cultures, faiths, and languages. There are 750 students in the primary school, and 75 in the nursery. Half of the pupils are speakers of languages other than English and for those who are children in asylum-seeking families, their potential for resettlement causes additional complications and stress. Teachers have to become legal advisors, helping families negotiate the minefields of immigration, housing law, and social security benefits.

Marion Rosen, principal, explains that her intentions for teachers at Star School have to do with moral purpose and social justice: "Teachers have to be the best they can be ... It's about building for the future ... You don't write anybody off." "I'm really interested in change," she says. Ms. Rosen urges the public to not judge our kids in our communities. She says that "our kids are not intellectually less able than kids anywhere else in the country; it's just their circumstances. They're already disadvantaged when they come in." She believes strongly that the kids and the parents have an entitlement for change.

Sixth Day

This day began with problem-posing activities to help process all the information gleaned during the previous few days. Then, information was shared that had been summarized from "Ethical Conflicts in Classroom Research" (Hatch, 1995). Our discussion related issues of conflicts in doing classroom qualitative research with young children to the conflicts we were seeing arise in our own qualitative research in refugee communities. I then gave students an overview of qualitative research characteristics, such as participant perspectives, emergent design, inductive analyses, and research paradigms; and I described types of qualitative studies. We touched on post-positivist and critical/feminist paradigms and summaries of major philosophical and theoretical considerations. I reminded students that my theoretical perspective is critical theory, that there are many other perspectives that are compatible with studying migrating families and their children, and that these perspectives can also be supported by using qualitative methods.

Then, I asked students to identify the theoretical and philosophical assumptions that currently guide their professional and academic study. I explained that we would later connect these assumptions to their research interests and the qualitative methods to explore these interests. Some students were able to identify philosophers upon whose work they based their own work. Others were more general in terms of identifying what their intentions were. A few of the Identified Assumptions were as follows:

> An assumption from my field that heavily guides my work is that human motivations and behaviors are largely determined by their cognition. Something Ms. Rosen said about the impact of "talking up" the community that she works in really rattles me and hit close to home. Most of the time, we Mississippians spend so much of our time sharing all the negative aspects of our community in an effort to find help for it and to possibly change things. I think if we spend more time "talking up" the more positive aspects and possibilities, it will encourage those within that community to help themselves rather than sitting around waiting on someone else to rescue them. This doesn't indicate that I feel their struggles should be forgotten, but rather use them to support their efforts and accent where they are now versus where they came from.

Another:

> Children have a compassion and empathy for the "other," and there is a danger of base propaganda and uninformed citizens. We need to expand foreign understanding of the human side of Americans, but moreover we need to bring understanding of other cultures here to the U.S. ... As global citizens we carry social responsibility.

And:

> Learning the language and history is not all you need to know to understand a culture. You need interaction, conversation, a true understanding of the individuals themselves in order to really learn. How does this individual use the language? How the history of that area or group applies to that person's individual life and personal choices ... reading in texts cannot teach you about the individuals you have to try to integrate into a new culture. Only through sincere and empathetic cross-cultural conversations, can these adjustments take place.
>
> Customs are stronger than love.

And:

> I am influenced by Seyla Benhabib: Cultures are fluid and porous and thus there is definitely a way that we can understand one another ... if only we try ... societies need to be able to access the layers of our shared and unique histories with the ability to question the ideas and philosophies behind the creation, transmission, and perpetuation of thought.

Another student wrote:

> Children are seen as individuals with personality, temperament, family culture, experience, and historical contexts, driving desire for young children and families to develop deep relationships over time with those who provide their care and education.

And:

> Geertz believed that learning about a community's local culture was the only way to truly understand. I take Geertz's idea of local culture as a guiding principle to understanding the many people throughout the world.

I encouraged and led discussions about the importance of theoretical and philosophical assumptions in our qualitative research, which relies on primary data from our participants, not just datasets of secondary quantitative data.

Seventh Day

This day was devoted to community visits in small groups for observation and interview contributions. Time was scheduled throughout the day for individual tutorials.

Eighth Day

Again, using a problem-posing methodology for our class activities, we spent the day working on analysis of information gained so far in our journeys, according to our theoretical perspectives. I gave examples of how what I had planned for the class activities provided information to be used with a critical theory lens. I asked students to give examples of experiences they have had over the 2 weeks that they see as examples of their using critical theory as a framework for rethinking some information about children and families. The critical reflections using personal history combined with qualitative methods of interviewing and observation and ongoing analysis (in various forms) led to a daily increasing capacity for depth in thought. One student wrote about personal history reflections related to critical theory:

> Why have I, as a Jewish woman with a strong connection to my Jewish cultural traditions, not had the desire to go to Israel? Why don't I feel the sense of attachment and would I feel otherwise if I were to actually go? Other questions I would have would most definitely relate to the history of the Jews in the region and how the different factions in Israel can account for their feelings toward a multi-state solution and justification for the ancestral claims to the land. How can the Jewish people in Israel justify the treatment of Palestinians as second-class citizens after they have suffered such a long history of persecutions? Some general questions I have relate to how the history of the Middle Eastern region is taught around the world and how that shapes views of both Israelis and Palestinians (and Arabs in general) in the United States and in other countries. What are some of the political reasons for supporting one side over the other and how does that shape perceptions both in and out of the country?

Another student wrote about a challenge to his thinking about parents:

> Funds of Knowledge claims parent involvement creates a domino effect, and that we need to rethink the levels of parent involvement. This challenges my thinking. Perhaps in immigrant contexts, is involvement essential for success while parents may know very little about education, be poorly educated themselves, or not consider education a value? Yet, the families know their own culture and are the mediators between structured western educational stands and foreign culture.

Another student struggled with her belief that the well-being of children is intimately tied to the well-being of their communities, and she was as impressed as we all were with the Star School, but she was surprised by the use of "time outs" as a behavior management technique at the school. The interviews and observations led her to identify a dissonance that is important for her to grapple with in her research and practice.

Finally, a student struggled with some facts we learned through the Refugee Council:

> We learned that many refugees possess degrees above the university level— so that begs the question of, what, in the eyes of the Home Office, constitutes a human being? Clearly, not education. Also by denying refugees the right to work and then hoping they will disappear (subjecting them to a very rough life) … the Home Office commits an inhuman act …

The students' analyses of interview data, observations logs, and underlying philosophical assumptions pointed out discontinuities in their ideas about aspects of teaching and learning.

Ninth Day

On this day we had a visiting lecturer, Liz Brooker, from the Institute of Education, University of London. She (Brooker, 2002) had studied the pedagogical patterns of Bangladeshi families and compared those to the pedagogical patterns in native British families and analyzed both in relation to the early years program in a quality school. She looked at how home language, home culture and school language, and school culture influence children's school success and later position in society. She studied (1) culture in home … how is it transmitted and what is it? (2) how pedagogy is done in home, and (3) how might policy be influenced (Brooker, 2006).

Brooker (2002) also found, through her research involving preschool children and their families in a community in England, that none of the Bangladeshi children had had experience with the materials of preschool. When the children from the Bangladeshi community came into the classroom they did not know how to interact with the materials. Furthermore, the Early Childhood Development model encourages children to be active, self-initiators, and communicators. However, the Bangladeshi children did not approach teachers. Curious about this, Brooker (2002) asked mothers what they had told their children about school. All mothers said, "I told him to sit quietly, don't speak, listen to the teacher, and study hard." This directly conflicts with one of the most consistent expectations placed on primary children in Western cultures, which is to be actively engaged (verbally and kinesthetically) in their learning.

Brooker (2006) also explained that the early childhood program in her study claimed to have proactive pluralistic policies such as an open door policy for parents. However, there was no open door policy because there were no practices structured into the school such as having an interpreter available consistently. These observations pointed to our recurring critical theory question, "What is really going on here?" She did find a few glimpses of simple steps initiated by the program that provided real interaction with all the families and that were examples of transformative action. These activities involved (1) bilingual staff to engage parents in what they need in order to communicate, (2) a parent coordinator from their culture who could be direct with parents when a member of another cultural group cannot, (3) a sewing class and various small literacy projects, small parent-led arts and crafts projects for the school. She explained that, as simple as these steps sound, parents were good at making things and interested in contributing to the school.

Tenth Day: Glimpses of Preliminary Findings, Overlapping Critical Themes

On the final day of class meetings, each student participant gave a brief presentation that was an update on his or her qualitative study and action plan direction to date. There were a variety of plans and studies discussed. Some were family-based, some community-based, and some were classroom- and school-based. The qualitative methods led to the students' pursuing interests of their own and to the creation of action plans for transformative, participatory projects that exemplify critical theory in action. Some examples follow.

One project flips the discussion of "participating in a culture other than one's own" so that the educators hold the responsibility for participating in their newly composed classroom and school culture, which now involves immigrants and refugees from many cultures. The National Literacy Trust of England asserts that "teachers need to know about immigrant children's previous education if they are to help them progress" (www.literacytrust.org .uk/Database/refugees.html). It has been the practice in the past to produce a document that details backgrounds on the pupils' countries of origin and that shows ways to adapt the curriculum. This information is vital but not put to adequate use. A document that sits stagnantly in a staff room is insufficient. The information must be shared and discussed. Who better to share the information than the students and families themselves? Immigration Consultant Educators will support teachers using their immigrant populations as knowledge brokers and will demonstrate universal methods for improving immigrant accessibility to learning in the classroom; however, culture-focused methods must also be taken into account.

Another student embarked upon a study that addresses a multicultural curriculum for refugee children. She said that refugee children struggle with the balance of adopting a new culture while maintaining their own culture. She agrees with Pinar (2004) that curriculum must be an example of the Latin *Currere* (p. 14). "Curriculum" is a verb and it cannot be developed for others. It must be a self-driven, self-study activity. Qualitative interviews and observations at Star School were the basis of her multicultural curriculum planning.

One student, who is the director of an Early Childhood Program at a YMCA in a large city in the United States, planned research and action to create more culturally inclusive staffing and programming for infants and toddlers. Another student is taking her study and action to her home community in Mississippi in a youth development, school, and family connection project. Another student took his investigation back to his Korean community in the United States to study the dynamics of first-generation Korean immigrants to the U.S., one and a half-generation immigrants, and second-generation immigrants. Two students are involved in an international qualitative study investigating support and advocacy for Ecuadorian immigrants around the world.

One student, who plans to move to Madrid after graduation, became very interested in issues involving African refugees and their migration to Spain. She wrote:

> Xenophobia and anti-immigrant politics have entered the Iberian Peninsula and the feelings are increasing despite the fact that their history reminds them of their strong connection to North Africa. Over the past 2 decades, there has been a flood of North African immigrants making a new life for themselves throughout Spain.

Another student chose to comment upon her interviews with Unaccompanied Minors through the Refugee Council:

> So far, this endeavor has been very enlightening. Before traveling to London, I was under the impression that the biggest problem faced by refugees was political. The only time we hear about refugees is typically when a law is being changed or contested. Sometimes we may hear about how refugees are draining away tax dollars. We never hear about the hidden psychological trauma experienced by refugees living in our own communities. We never hear about the problems that are not solved by counselors. We never hear the personal stories. When we do, however, we might be open to change. After meeting Pierre, I felt shock, disbelief, anger, and sorrow. The way that refugees are treated needs to be changed. They should no longer be thought of as people who cause problems; in reality, they are the effect of problems.

Conclusion

While the information gleaned from these experiences has different tones and tenors, there are overlapping themes. Insights from the diversity of students and their investigations illustrate a mosaic of possibility for early childhood educators and qualitative researchers. Experiences such as these, with a critical theoretical frame that lends itself well to the application of qualitative research approaches, may be the nexus of hope for crucial understandings in an ever-more-complex world. If we will only listen to the stories, we can organize for change and learn to support the efforts of others. This is especially true within the social and political contexts of communities and schools serving refugee, immigrant, and asylum-seeking families.

References

Ali, M. (2003). *Brick lane*. London: Doubleday.

Anzaldúa, G. (1987). *Borderlands: The new mestiza = La frontera*. San Francisco: Spinsters/Aunt Lute Press.

Bateson, Mary C. (1994). *Peripheral visions: Learning along the way*. New York: HarperCollins.

Bateson, Mary C. (2004). *Willing to learn: Passages of personal discovery*. New York: Steerforth Press.

Brooker, L. (2002). *Starting school: Young children learning cultures*. London: Open University Press.

Brooker, L. (2006, January). Lecture presented to the New York University Intensive Graduate Study Program, London.

Freire, P. (1973). *Education for critical consciousness*. New York: Seabury Press.

Freire, P. (1984). *The politics of education: Culture, power, and liberation*. Granby, MA: Bergin & Garvey.

Freire, P. (1997). *Pedagogy of hope*. Granby, MA: Bergin & Garvey.

Freire, P. (1998). *Pedagogy of freedom: Ethics, democracy, and civic courage*. New York: Rowman and Littlefield.

Hatch, J. A. (1995). Ethical conflicts in classroom research: Examples from a study of peer stigmatization in kindergarten. In J. A. Hatch (Ed.), *Qualitative research in early childhood settings* (pp. 213–222). Westport, CT: Praeger.

Jewish Encyclopedia. Retrieved January 28, 2006, from http://www.jewishencyclopedia.com/view.jsp?artid=1002&letter=B

Leonardo, Z. (2003). *Idealogy, discourse, and school reform*. Westport, CT: Praeger.

Leonardo, Z. (2004). Critical social theory and transformative knowledge: The functions of criticism in quality education. *Educational Researcher 33*(6), 11–18.

Moll, L. C. (1990). *Vygotsky and education*. Cambridge, England: Cambridge University Press.

Moll, L. C., Gonzalez, N., & Amanti, C. (2005). *Funds of knowledge: Theorizing practices in households, communities, and classrooms*. New York: Erlbaum.

Pinar, W. F. (2004). *What is curriculum theory?* Mahwah, NJ: Erlbaum.

Quintero, E. P. (2004). *Problem-posing with multicultural children's literature: Developing critical early childhood curricula*. New York: Peter Lang.

Quintero, E. P., & Rummel, M. K. (2003). *Becoming a teacher in the new society: Bringing communities and classrooms together*. New York: Peter Lang.

Refugee Council. Retrieved January 21, 2006 from http://www.refugeecouncil.org.uk/refugeecouncil/therefugeecouncil.htm

Robinson, M. (2005, October). Lecture, IGEMS Conference, New York University, New York, NY.

Said, E. (2000, October 30). The end of Oslo. *The Nation*, p. 12.

Smith, Z. (2001). *White teeth*. New York: Vintage.

STAR. (2005). Who stays? Who goes? Who decides? *The National Newsletter of STAR* (pp. 1–2).

II
Issues in Early Childhood
Qualitative Research

8

Surviving a Methodological Crisis
Strategies for Salvaging Your Classroom-Based Research When Things Go Wrong in the Field

LISA S. GOLDSTEIN

University of Texas at Austin

My 15 years as a qualitative researcher studying early childhood teachers' practices have given me clarity, certainty, and confidence about one thing: if I plan a research study designed to investigate any aspect of a teacher's classroom life, I am guaranteed to experience some sort of problematic, brain-rattling, nerve-shredding crisis that convinces me that my project is doomed to fail, that I have wasted my participant's time, and that I made the wrong career choice when I left kindergarten teaching to go to graduate school.

I have experienced at least one epic disaster in every classroom-based research project. Because difficulties inevitably arise when I am in the field, I have had the opportunity to develop a range of effective strategies for managing most types of methodological crises. In this chapter I describe two moments of crisis that occurred during the fieldwork portion of my recent study of kindergarten teachers' instructional decision making, discuss my experience managing and resolving each crisis, and share some of my tried-and-true, field-tested strategies for salvaging classroom-based research studies when it seems that things have suddenly gone terribly wrong in the field.

Framing the Study

U.S. kindergarten teachers are presently facing changing expectations, confronting conflicting demands, and managing multiple sources of pressure (Graue, 2001; Hatch, 2002). The commitment to learning environments supporting young children's development in the cognitive, social, physical, and emotional domains that has shaped kindergarten for many years is under siege as public schools continue to push their emphasis on student mastery of academic skills and achievement of predetermined learning outcomes down through the primary grades and into kindergarten (McDaniel, Isaac, Brooks, & Hatch, 2005). Now, in addition to providing educational experiences that support the development of the whole child, kindergarten teachers must also work to ensure that their students have had suitable exposure to all of the knowledge and skills mandated by their state and school district.

I knew that kindergarten teachers in the school districts surrounding my university were dealing with difficult challenges caused by these changing expectations. The undergraduates in my early childhood teacher education practicum course came to class each week brimming with stories from their field placement classrooms that revealed the levels of frustration, desperation, and despair their cooperating teachers were experiencing as they struggled to find ways to meet their multiple and complicated obligations.

A number of kindergarten teachers quoted in the recent empirical litera-ture describe difficulties similar to those reported by my students' cooper-ating teachers. One teacher expressed frustration about the new academic demands placed on her students, pointing out that "kindergartners are now expected to learn what had once been in the domain of a first grade curric-ulum" (DeVault, 2003, p. 91). Another stated, "as a kindergarten teacher in today's public education system, I think it is impossible not to feel the pres-sure for academic achievement" (McDaniel et al., 2005, p. 22). A third admit-ted that the clash between her commitment to developmentally appropriate practices (DAP; Bredekamp & Copple, 1997) and her obligation to meet new expectations for academic outcomes left her feeling "torn between what she knew children needed and the principal's mandates" (Da Ros-Voseles, Danyi, & Aurillo, 2003, p. 36).

As can be seen in this final quotation, the research literature examining the challenges currently facing kindergarten teachers generally depicts two con-flicting and irreconcilable goals: using developmentally appropriate practices on one hand and teaching a standardized curriculum comprising predeter-mined academic skills and mandated curriculum content on the other (Wien, 2004). Journal articles bearing titles such as "Achieving High Standards and Implementing Developmentally Appropriate Practices—Both ARE Possible" (Egertson, 2004) and "Implementing Developmentally Appropriate Practices in a Developmentally Inappropriate Climate" (Dever, Falconer, & Kessenich, 2003) are further evidence of this trend.

Similarly, in her foreword to Wien's (2004) book, *Negotiating Standards in the Primary Classroom: The Teacher's Dilemma*, Lillian Katz positions devel-opmentally appropriate practices and standardized, academically oriented curriculum in opposition to each other and presents the tension between them as a significant problem that shapes the lives of early childhood teachers. She writes:

> Every day these teachers' lives present them with a major dilemma: should they focus on satisfying the detailed requirements of the standardized curriculum and risk forfeiting many important aspects of the children's developmental needs? Or should they focus primarily on

the children's needs and risk failing to satisfy the regulations that govern their employment? Such is the nature of a dilemma: addressing one of its two horns means neglecting the potential benefits of addressing the other. (Katz, quoted in Wien, 2004, p. x)

Fascinated and troubled by these complex circumstances, I designed a qualitative study that would allow me to gain insight into kindergarten teachers' experiences managing these seemingly contradictory obligations and responsibilities. I drew on my knowledge of the literature and of the circumstances my students were witnessing in the field to frame the following research question: How do kindergarten teachers satisfy both their commitment to developmentally appropriate teaching practices and their responsibility to teach the predetermined knowledge and skills mandated by their state?

Designing the Study

To answer this question, I intended to spend time observing full-day kindergarten teachers with at least 3 years' experience who had self-identified as strongly committed to teaching the mandated curriculum in developmentally appropriate ways. I planned to document their teaching practices, and then interview them to gain insight into their instructional decision making.

The initial aspects of the research process unfolded smoothly. I had no trouble identifying potential participants through my established relationships with local elementary school principals and easily found four teachers who I believed would have a great deal to offer and who would enjoy participating in the study. The bulk of my observations took place over a period of 10 weeks in October 2003–January 2004; I spent close to 25 hours in each participant's classroom. I was also presented with the unexpected opportunity to work with a kindergarten teacher in Hawai'i whose work with indigenous children came highly recommended by a Native Hawaiian teacher educator. I relished the opportunity to see how these dilemmas and challenges played out in a different sociocultural context in a different state. I spent 2 full weeks in May 2003 observing this participant at work (a total of approximately 70 hours of participant observation).

All five participants were observed during the course of their typical working day engaging in their usual teaching practices with the kindergarten students in their classrooms. During my observations, I documented aspects of the participants' practice including the skills and knowledge selected for each lesson and the ways in which the participant organized the classroom and educational materials, created conditions for learning, and structured instructional activities. I took notes on a laptop computer or in a notebook during these observations, describing in detail what was occurring in the classroom.

I engaged in ongoing data analysis and interpretation throughout my fieldwork. My observations in the classrooms raised questions that I would ask my participants in informal conversations held during recess, on yard duty, while walking the children through the halls, or immediately after school. Their responses to those questions focused my future observations, which in turn led to more questions and further informal conversation. Slowly, I began to shape tentative interpretations and build my understanding of each participant's teaching practices based both on my own observations and on the insights he or she offered.

I used my tentative interpretations to develop specific interview questions for each participant. Interviews lasted 45 to 60 minutes and were audiotaped and transcribed. The goals of these one-on-one interviews were

1. To allow the participants to discuss their teaching practices, offering more detailed information about their planning, decision making, and problem solving
2. To allow the participants to offer explanations or clarifications regarding instructional experiences I observed in their classrooms
3. To explore in detail the pedagogical and curricular challenges facing the participants as kindergarten teachers
4. To provide the participants with opportunities to raise issues, ask questions, or direct my attention to significant aspects of their professional lives that I had not mentioned

After leaving the field, I began a three-level process of formal data analysis, using the constant comparative method (Strauss & Corbin, 1990) to develop categories and identify themes in the data. The three-level data analysis process allowed me to develop a clear, nuanced, and thoughtful understanding of each participant's teaching practices. I analyzed the data for each participant separately using the same three-level procedure.

First, I reviewed my field notes and interview transcripts repeatedly to identify the characteristic practices of the teacher. I looked for multiple examples of a particular practice or behavior and also gave close consideration to strongly unique "signature" aspects of the teacher's work. Second, I attended to individual elements of the teacher's classroom practices. I examined both the regular features of the daily schedule, such as opening activities, instruction in language arts and math, and transitions and routines, and also the ordinary but unpredictable features of classroom life, such as the presence of parent volunteers or special education aides, holiday or birthday celebrations, episodes of unusually inappropriate student behavior, school assemblies, and so on. I looked across all of my documented examples of each element (approximately 5–10 examples of opening activities, language arts lessons, and math lessons in each classroom, plus many transitions and routines) seeking recurring instructional practices or pedagogical decisions. My intent here was to establish a sense of the practices that could be considered typical and representative of the participant's work. Finally, I went back to the field notes and interview transcripts to look for disconfirming evidence in an effort to uncover relevant information I had overlooked in earlier readings.

The three levels of analyzed data were brought together to create narrative portrayals of each participant's work. I used these narratives to craft vignettes depicting a variety of effective strategies for integrating DAP and academic standards. I believed that these vignettes would be a useful and welcome addition to preservice early childhood teacher education courses, a valuable discussion tool for administrators and mentor teachers to use with teachers on their faculty, and an opportunity for my participants' excellent practices to be recognized and celebrated. Three of these vignettes are featured in this chapter.

Problems in the Field

I grounded my research question in the literature and designed my study with deliberate care and consideration to ensure that I would be gathering the precise data needed to answer my research question. But my careful planning did nothing to prevent a methodological crisis in my Hawaiian site and a second crisis in one of my local sites.

The Hawaiian Crisis: Mrs. Neill's Practices

The purpose of my study was to learn how experienced kindergarten teachers satisfy both their commitment to developmentally appropriate teaching practices and their responsibility to teach the predetermined knowledge and skills mandated by their state, and I believed I had done a thorough job of selecting participants who would be able to offer meaningful insight into the instructional decision making that allowed them to integrate DAP and standards. When I arrived in Mrs. Neill's classroom, however, I was distressed to find that her practices were not well aligned with my understandings of developmentally appropriate practices. This brief vignette illustrates a typical lesson I observed during my fieldwork.

The kindergartners sit at their tables, heads bent over worksheets and fingers clutching brightly colored crayons. They chat quietly to each other as they work on the task at hand, coloring in the outline of a carp on a page that will later be cut and glued to form a Boys' Day kite. Mrs. Neill, wearing a flowered dress and a pointy origami hat, walks over to the CD player at the side of the room. "Let's listen to some music while we work," she suggests.

The music fills the sunny classroom and the children begin to sing along. Absorbed in their work and their song, the children barely notice the older woman in the corner of the classroom who has just begun to prepare their lunches. Grandma Mary, a beloved classroom volunteer, has set out 19 partitioned styrofoam trays on the table before her and is carefully doling out chicken, rice, macaroni salad, and apple slices, placing a small amount of each item on every tray. As Grandma Mary leaves the room to fetch the tray of milk cartons from the fridge, Mrs. Neill circulates around the room checking on the children's progress, hoping that most of the group will be done before it is time to sit down to lunch.

She stops beside one of the boys at Table 1 and bends down to look at his carp. Speaking in a nice, loud, teacher voice, Mrs. Neill proclaims, "Look at how well Martin cut out all those little edges. … Martin, you are doing a really great job!" She checks in with the children at Tables 2, 3, 4, and 5, and then looks up at the clock. It is 11:15. She exchanges a silent glance with Grandma Mary, who appears ready to serve the children their meal.

"It is time to stop your work and get ready for lunch," Mrs. Neill tells the class. "Please put away your materials and go wash your hands."

From the perspective of the NAEYC guidelines for developmentally appropriate practices, this peaceful and harmonious classroom scene is a train wreck of inappropriate practices and problematic instructional decisions. Rather than offering a range of experiences presenting different degrees and types of challenge, providing interesting materials to use in creative ways, and allowing the children to make choices about how they wanted to spend their time (as the DAP guidelines recommend), Mrs. Neill selected a simple, closed-ended coloring worksheet that "provide[d] no real challenge for the children" (Bredekamp & Copple, 1997, p. 124) and then expected all the children "to do and presumably learn the same things at the same time without attention to their individual needs or differences" (p. 125). And rather than allowing the children to prepare their own lunch trays, thereby turning the meal into an opportunity for maximizing children's independent accomplishment and "encouraging children to do what they are capable of doing for themselves" (p. 126), Mrs. Neill had Grandma Mary prepare and serve the children's lunches.

Methodological crisis! How would I be able to answer my research question with data gathered in this classroom if Mrs. Neill wasn't using any practices that I could identify as developmentally appropriate?

The Local Crisis: Jenny Aster's Practices

My first fieldwork experience in a local kindergarten classroom was also marked by a disjuncture between my understanding of developmentally appropriate practices and the teacher's instructional strategies. The following vignette is representative of the opening activities I witnessed each morning in Jenny Aster's classroom.

Once all of the children have arrived and unpacked their belongings, Jenny begins the daily opening activities. She engages the children's attention with a question. "Kevin is our calendar helper, right? Come on up and grab a pointer, Kevin."

Kevin, a coltish boy whose skinny ankles protrude from khaki pant legs that were the right length just a few weeks ago, tentatively leads the class in singing their customary song about the months of the year, using his pointer to identify the names of each month on the brightly colored bulletin board that faces the open carpet area.

Like an enthusiastic game show host, Jenny directs the students' focus with her voice and her body. Swinging her arm toward the large tag board calendar page hanging on the bulletin board, Jenny says, "Over to the calendar! Yesterday was January 20th so today is … " Jenny pauses to allow the class the opportunity to respond. And respond they do, loudly chiming, "January 21st!"

Tightly clutching a felt-tipped pen, Kevin writes the date on the calendar. Suddenly, a low rumble of muttered comments begins to spread across the carpet like spilled apple juice as the children see what Kevin has written: "it's backwards … backwards … backwards," they inform each other, heads whipping to the right and the left as they share and confirm the news. Kevin has written the number 2 backwards. As the rumble grows louder, Jenny defuses the situation easily. "Kevin, take a look at what you have written. Is there something you would like to change?"

Jenny picks up a roll of white correction tape that sits in a basket of supplies beside her chair—apparently Kevin is not the first student to make an error on the calendar—as Kevin puts his finger on the backwards 2. "Good job, Kevin! It's really hard to write up on the board with everyone watching, and it's easy to get confused. And good eyes, everyone on the carpet! You know the number 2 well enough to be able to tell when it's backwards."

The opening activities continue, unfolding just as everyone expects. The children count the number of days they've been in school—by ones, by fives, by threes, using a large 100 chart for guidance—and figure out how many days are left till they reach the one-hundredth day of school. As they count, Jenny redirects children who aren't paying attention—with a glance, with a hard look, with their whispered name, with a sharp snap of her fingers. The class recaps yesterday's activities and decide together that the highlight was a math lesson using T. Rex teeth as a unit of measure: Kevin's next job is to write a sentence about that lesson in yesterday's calendar square.

All eyes are on Kevin as he writes the word "We" independently and correctly. Jenny takes the pen from Kevin, writes the words "measured with" on the calendar, and returns the pen to Kevin, who writes "T. Rex" with ease. Jenny helps the class sound their way through the word "teeth": "Tttttt, T, right! Now eeeeeeeeee … E, good. There are two of them. And then th-th-th ... what makes that? TH, TH makes that sound. And the sentence needs an ending mark—what kind? Right, a period." Kevin, listening closely to the class and to Jenny's carefully articulated letter sounds, finishes the sentence.

As the children begin to talk (and sing) about the days of the week, Kevin goes to the window to check the weather. When he returns, he adds a small colored marker to the "cold" column on the weather chart. Jenny asks if any of the children would like to make an observation about the information on the weather chart, and many hands shoot up. Children point out that "cold" has four more markers than "rainy" and that "foggy" and "windy" have the same number of markers.

After a detailed review of the lunch menu, the class moves on to the Morning Message. Jenny has written a brief letter to the children on a chart tablet. The sentences are written incorrectly; a quick look at the chart suggests that the class has been learning about the rules for capitalization and the proper punctuation for the end of a sentence.

Volunteers are called up to the chart tablet. Some are asked to correct Jenny's errors, adding punctuation or capital letters. Others are given the opportunity to circle the letter of the week or to underline a sentence. Jenny encourages the children to help each other: as one boy slowly underlined a sentence, for example, his classmates said "go-go-go-go-go-go-go-go-go-STOP!"

Jenny reported that she has opened each day of school in this manner since she began teaching 4 years earlier and sees no reason to change this practice: the skills and knowledge that form the core of her opening activities are skills and knowledge included in the state-mandated kindergarten curricula for language arts, mathematics, and science. For example, Jenny pointed out that the Texas learning standards require kindergartners "to do this special unit on weather. Well, we talk about the weather every day. So I don't worry about [doing a special unit]."

Jenny's opening activities are certainly familiar kindergarten fare, and she did an admirable job of integrating the standards into her practices. However, her expectation that the children would remain seated quietly for upwards of 45 minutes while they watch one classmate engaging in the very same tasks that are completed every morning is not evidence of a commitment to developmentally appropriate practices.

Methodological crisis! How would I be able to answer my research question if Jenny's practices emphasized the standards but did so in developmentally inappropriate ways?

Seeking Understanding and Finding Solutions

When I entered Mrs. Neill's classroom, I found her using teaching strategies and making instructional decisions that did not match my expectations. This was a jarring surprise that caused a great deal of intellectual turmoil and hours of frantic scribbling in my reflective journal. Mrs. Neill's recommendation as a study participant came from an experienced teacher educator whose knowledge of early childhood practices and whose understanding of my research agenda I trusted completely. Further, Mrs. Neill self-identified as a teacher who taught academic content to kindergartners in developmentally appropriate ways—that was a criterion for participation in my study. My challenge, then, was to make sense of the gap between my understanding of developmental appropriateness and Mrs. Neill's understanding of that concept.

The answer came in the form of a document entitled *Na Honua Mauli Ola: Hawai'i Guidelines for Culturally Healthy and Responsive Learning Environments* (NHMO; Native Hawaiian Education Council, 2002) that describes the key features of educational contexts that are culturally appropriate for Native Hawaiians. From the perspective of the NHMO guidelines, educational activities, experiences, and materials are appropriate if they lead to the perpetuation of Hawaiian heritage, traditions, language, and cultural knowledge and practices; forge bonds between past, present, and future; and sustain the family and the community as a whole. The NHMO guidelines provided me with valuable insight into the context in which Mrs. Neill's practices were embedded and allowed me to understand her instructional decisions on a deeper level.

When the NHMO guidelines' definition of appropriate practice is used to interpret the vignette of Mrs. Neill's teaching presented earlier, her work is seen as an exemplar of appropriate, culturally healthy, and responsive teaching.

To pull out a single practice to serve as an example, Mrs. Neill's decision to use whole group instruction reflects the NHMO guidelines' emphasis on the profound importance of connection with others in the creation of effective learning environments for Hawaiian children. As her class happily colored their carp worksheets, Mrs. Neill was satisfying NHMO's recommendations to "create and maintain a safe haven for learning in which all students are actively engaged and contributing members" (Native Hawaiian Education Council, 2002, p. 36) and to "reinforce students' sense of cultural identity and place in the community" (p. 39). Further, by providing her students with the opportunity to work alongside classmates on a common task, Mrs. Neill was helping to prepare the children to "assume responsibility for their role in relation to the well-being of the cultural community" (p. 26).

The NAEYC guidelines for developmentally appropriate practices emphasize the importance of providing learners with educational experiences that are culturally appropriate, and I had expected to see Mrs. Neill using culturally responsive pedagogies with her students. However, because I am an outsider with only the most superficial knowledge of Hawaiian culture, I was unable to recognize Mrs. Neill's practices as being culturally appropriate. Like a tourist, I needed a guidebook to help me appreciate Mrs. Neill's decisions and understand how her work resonated deeply with fundamental Hawaiian beliefs and practices as well as with the intent of the NAEYC DAP guidelines.

Although I felt like neither an outsider nor a tourist in Jenny's classroom, I still struggled to make sense of her instructional decisions. Jenny described herself as a committed practitioner of developmentally appropriate kindergarten teaching with greater dedication and gusto than any of my other research participants; this added to my puzzlement about her frequent use of developmentally inappropriate practices. Realizing that Jenny deliberately drew clear boundaries around activities designed to teach knowledge and skills linked to the state's academic standards and around activities designed to offer children developmentally appropriate learning experiences was my aha moment. Unlike teachers who strive to integrate DAP and standards, Jenny satisfies the district's expectations for content coverage and her own professional commitments to developmentally appropriate practices at separate times each day. This approach, used daily in her morning instructional block, is depicted in the vignette below.

"Jackson! Do you know what you are supposed to be doing right now? I need to see you on task. I know that you don't want to finish up during free centers." Jenny is on her hands and knees next to a round table, picking up the small snips and scraps of paper that fell to the floor as the children working at that literacy station colored, cut, sequenced, and glued a series of pictures representing the life cycle of the pumpkin. Jackson is seated alone at a nearby table; he gazes off into space, thoroughly unconcerned about the blank handwriting worksheet in front of him.

There are four different literacy stations set up in Jenny's classroom each morning, and the children are divided into four groups based on Jenny's assessment of their literacy skills. Each group moves through the four stations in turn, spending approximately 15 minutes at each station. In my field journal, I noted:

The literacy tasks that are assigned during stations generally include handwriting and letter-sound matching worksheets that are linked to the basal reading series, free journal-writing, and something related to the science or social studies curriculum that involves writing a word such as "seed" or "pumpkin" in the appropriate spot, or sequencing pictures. The kids are practicing basic skills, doing typical kindergarten seatwork.

Jackson and a few other stragglers are the only children still seated at their stations. The other children in Jackson's literacy group left the station one by one as they completed their worksheets—one girl was done in the blink of an eye, the other two children took a bit longer but approached the task with forbearance and were soon wandering around the room, chatting with their classmates and looking for something to occupy their time until the groups are allowed to move on to their next assigned station.

Jenny crawls out from under the table and looks at her watch as she walks toward Jackson. She stops, then claps her hands in a rhythmic pattern to get the class's attention: "It is time to clean up the room so we can have free centers. The quicker we clean up, the sooner we can start." The children quickly scurry around the room picking up scraps of paper, returning scissors, glue, and other supplies to their proper locations, and collecting completed work. Energized by the promise of free centers, Jackson finishes his handwriting worksheet in a flash and begins pushing in chairs with gusto.

When free centers begin, it is easy to see why the children are so motivated to straighten the room and get started. Free centers transform the space from a teacher-directed classroom to a buffet of child-directed learning opportunities. A pair of bland, unmarked cupboard doors swings open to reveal a large assortment of unit blocks, all of which are eagerly—and noisily—pulled onto the speckled linoleum floor and immediately put to use in the construction of a "racing tower." Several robber-pirates dart out of the housekeeping area, scarves tied around their heads and sacks filled with treasure clutched in their fists. Puzzles and games are pulled onto the carpet as mixed-sex clusters of children reconfirm rules and clarify procedures.

A small, businesslike group of girls hold's clipboards and stride's purposefully from center to center. They chat with their classmates, make notes on their clipboards, and move on. The group comes over to me. The first girl announces, "We are taking orders for the pumpkin patch. Do you want a pumpkin?" "Or two!" adds the second girl. "Or … uh … three-four-five?" suggests the third girl.

Unable to resist such persuasive marketing, I agree to place an order and ask the girls' advice on how many pumpkins to get. As they confer about my pumpkin needs, I take a quick peek at their clipboards. Each girl has used invented spelling or cues from the environmental print in the classroom to write classmates' names, color preferences, and numbers on the page on her clipboard; one girl even has a table with column headings and tally marks drawn in thick purple marker on a piece of red construction paper clipped to her board.

The girls recommend one pumpkin per person in my house, and dutifully mark down my order for three pumpkins. As they set off to corral the robber-pirates, one girl turns back and calls out to me: "We'll be back soon to take your order for your Christmas trees."

Jenny's approach is a unique and ingenious solution to the challenge of meeting the demands of the district and the ideals of NAEYC. Jenny uses the district-mandated Language Arts materials during literacy stations, supplementing those materials with activities linked to the state learning standards for kindergarten science and social studies. The children produce work that documents their exposure to the required skills and that can be used to demonstrate their growth over time and their progress toward the state's goals for kindergartners. Even parents, administrators, or district personnel with minimal knowledge of kindergarten are able to understand and to see clearly that Jenny is meeting those expectations. Because she can point easily to visible evidence of student learning and to compliance with district and state policy, Jenny feels justified in allowing her students a solid, uninterrupted, and protected block of free play in their curriculum each day. Her unique approach enables Jenny to spend close to 45 minutes each day teaching kindergarten exactly as she believes it should be taught, with no need to compromise, negotiate, or apologize.

Jenny's instructional decision making highlighted a serious flaw in my research design. My research question was, "How do kindergarten teachers satisfy both their commitment to developmentally appropriate teaching practices and their responsibility to teach the predetermined knowledge and skills mandated by their state?" But one of my selection criteria specified teachers who "self-identified as strongly committed to teaching the mandated curriculum in developmentally appropriate ways." This criterion is much narrower than my research question because teaching the mandated curriculum using developmentally appropriate practices is only one of many possible ways that teachers satisfy both their commitment to developmentally appropriate teaching practices and their responsibility to teach the predetermined knowledge and skills mandated by their state. For example, rather than using developmentally appropriate practices to teach the mandated curriculum, Jenny teaches the state standards and uses developmentally appropriate practices at different times, in different ways, and for different purposes. Jenny's approach added new dimensions to my thinking about the challenges currently facing kindergarten teachers and about the instructional strategies teachers might use to respond to those challenges.

Surviving a Methodological Crisis

The two methodological crises that occurred during my study of kindergarten teachers' instructional decision making, like all the methodological crises in my previous studies, were resolved using the following five strategies.

1. Remain calm.

When you first realize you have made some sort of methodological misstep, you may feel strongly tempted to charge in and straighten things out as quickly as possible. Do not give in to this urge. Most methodological emergencies are not life threatening and do not require immediate attention. Often the passage of time reveals that the emergency was a false alarm, or that the aspect of the research design that initially appeared to be causing the trouble was actually not the real problem after all. Give yourself the opportunity to think, to talk the situation over with a colleague, to gather more information from your participants. There is really no need to rush—if you truly have made a mistake, it is not going to go away on its own. Let it wait until you are prepared to address it thoughtfully.

2. Attribute positive intent to your participants.

When your participants do things or say things that don't make sense, or that you find offensive or distasteful, or that contradict other things they said or did, always give them the benefit of the doubt. If you attribute positive intent to all their actions and statements, you will be able to remain open to possibilities and alternatives. After 70 hours of observation, it would have been easy for me to conclude that Mrs. Neill simply didn't understand what the phrase "developmentally appropriate practices" meant; attributing positive intent and resisting that conclusion gave me the opportunity to learn that I was the one who had a limited, partial understanding of the complexity swirling within that phrase. Your participants have entrusted you with their thoughts and their practices. This is an act of incredible generosity and should be received with humility and gratitude.

3. Remember that unexpected findings are still valuable data.

Qualitative researchers design studies to answer questions that have emotional significance for us as well as professional implications for the field. We may enter our research site with a marked preference for certain kinds of findings, and when different findings surface, they are often unwelcome. For example, I had a strong preference for observing child-centered, play-based kindergarten teaching, and I was irritated by Jenny's regular, ongoing use of developmentally inappropriate practices, particularly in light of her frequent comments about her commitment to DAP. I had not expected to be gathering data documenting developmentally inappropriate practices, and it was difficult for me to imagine how I would include vignettes depicting long and repetitive opening activities. However, my efforts to embrace those unexpected findings helped me understand more fully the range of approaches to balancing DAP and standards, and also allowed me to catch a serious problem in my research design.

4. Continue to take detailed field notes even if you think your study is ruined.

Teachers' practices can be very difficult to understand, and researchers' minds are often a lot slower than we think they are. All the meanings embedded within the data you're gathering may not be immediately obvious to you. It is very possible that field notes taken in a classroom that feels like a fruitless research site, like Mrs. Neill's classroom felt to me, may turn out to make the greatest contribution to understanding your research topic and the impact of your study on the field.

5.

My last strategy was going to be "Learn to anticipate unexpected turns of events as a natural and unavoidable part of the research process." It sounds like good advice. But, really, it is a meaningless statement. Even if you are expecting it to happen, a methodological crisis still feels horrible. I felt shocked, ashamed, disappointed in myself, terrified, worried, and angry when I experienced my first methodological crisis during my dissertation research (you can read all about this in Goldstein, 2000, and Goldstein, 2002). Still, despite the added years of research experience and the growing tally of methodological crises successfully managed, I felt all of those same feelings (topped with a dollop of disgust that I still haven't gotten my act together after all these years) when I sat in Mrs. Neill's classroom and realized that I had probably made a terrible mistake and chosen a participant whose practices would shed no light on my research question.

What has changed, though, is my perspective on methodological crises. I have learned that if I handle these inevitable problems carefully, I can expect to come away with an understanding of my research topic much richer and deeper than I could have attained if my research had gone strictly according to plan. Methodological crises force you to think in new ways, to approach your research topic from untried angles, to experiment with alternatives you could never have imagined, and to embrace explanations you never would have been willing to consider under more typical research conditions. Learning from every crisis helps you develop your abilities to recover quickly from these setbacks, to make necessary adjustments, to complete your research project successfully, and to cope with future crises effectively and efficiently. Unfortunately, allowing yourself to learn from every methodological crisis certainly won't enable you to avoid future research problems; like death and taxes, methodological crises are an unavoidable fact of scholarly life.

References

Bredekamp, S., & Copple, C. (Eds.). (1997). *Developmentally appropriate practices in early childhood programs* (Rev. ed.). Washington, DC: National Association for the Education of Young Children.

Da Ros-Voseles, D. A., Danyi, D., & Aurillo, J. (2003). Aligning professional preparation and practice: Bringing constructivist learning to kindergarten. *Dimensions of Early Childhood, 31*(2), 33–38.

DeVault, L. (2003). The tide is high but we can hold on: One kindergarten teacher's thoughts on the rising tide of academic expectations. *Young Children, 58*(6), 90–93.

Dever, M. T., Falconer, R. C., & Kessenich, C. (2003). Implementing developmentally appropriate practices in a developmentally inappropriate climate: Assessment in kindergarten. *Dimensions of Early Childhood, 31*(3), 27–33.

Egertson, H. A. (2004). Achieving high standards and implementing developmentally appropriate practices—Both ARE possible. *Dimensions of Early Childhood, 32*(1), 3–9.

Goldstein, L. S. (2000). Ethical dilemmas in designing collaborative research: Lessons learned the hard way. *International Journal of Qualitative Studies in Education, 13*(5), 517–530.

Goldstein, L. S. (2002). Moving beyond collaboration: Reconceptualizing research relationships with classroom teachers. *Teachers and Teaching, 8*(22), 155–170.

Graue, E. (2001). What's going on in the children's garden? Kindergarten today. *Young Children, 56*(3), 67–73.

Hatch, J. A. (2002). Accountability shovedown: Resisting the standards movement in early childhood education. *Phi Delta Kappan, 83*(6), 457–463.

McDaniel, G. L., Isaac, M. Y., Brooks, H. M., & Hatch, A. (2005). Confronting K–3 teaching challenges in an era of accountability. *Young Children, 60*(2), 20–26.

Native Hawaiian Education Council. (2002). *Na honua mauli ola: Hawai'i guidelines for culturally healthy and responsive learning environments.* Hilo, HI: Native Hawaiian Education Council.

Strauss, A., & Corbin, J. (1990). *Basics of qualitative research: Grounded theory procedures and techniques.* Newbury Park, CA: Sage.

Wien, C. A. (2004). *Negotiating standards in the primary classroom: The teacher's dilemma.* New York: Teachers College Press.

9

Never Certain
Research Predicaments in the Everyday World of Schools*

SUSAN GRIESHABER

Queensland University of Technology

Introduction

Doing qualitative research is often just like the textbooks say, but it is also much more. No matter how well prepared you are, how much you have read, or how experienced you are, there is always at least one thing involved in any research project that works itself out in ways contrary to experience or what the textbooks say. In this chapter I discuss some of the predicaments I have experienced when undertaking research in the everyday social world of schools. By predicaments I mean the integral and often small parts of research design that are described generally in research textbooks but in the lived world of the research site assume a heightened significance. To this end, I consider explicit experiences of gatekeepers and gatekeeping, the effect of researcher presence in the classroom, and researcher–participant relationships that surpass the conventional. In sharing these experiences, I provide some intimate details of these situations with the aim of assisting others facing similar quandaries. Having said that, quandaries tend to be characterized by raising more questions about complex situations than they can expect to answer. The point then is to begin a conversation in the hope that others will join and the dialogue will grow.

The experiences I draw on here are from two research projects. One involved two public schools (Yucca and Layt), where data were gathered from mid 2002 until mid 2004. Participants included a range of teachers and members of the school administration. Yucca is a P–7 multi-age school of approximately 400 students located in a low socioeconomic area with a transient population. Layt is also a P–7 multi-age school of about 700 and many of the parents are young professionals. The project in which these two schools were involved was a

* The research discussed in this chapter was funded by an Australian Research Council Linkage Grant (Industry Partner Education Queensland Assessment and New Basics Branch) and a Queensland University of Technology Research Encouragement Award.

case study documenting ways in which a whole school renewal process called New Basics (Department of Education and the Arts [DEA], 2004) enhanced numeracy learning and teaching with children in the first 3 years of school.

The other research on which this chapter draws involved four classroom teachers in a P–12 public school, Teviot College, which is in a rapidly developing residential area. The school opened in 1998 with support from the state Department of Education and the real estate company that designed and developed the suburb. All house and land packages included the option of an Apple computer connected to a networked server that was maintained by the developer. The school Web site indicates that it is the first computerized community of its type in the world. Teviot was also an Apple Classrooms of Tomorrow (ACOT) school and the eighth of its kind in the world. Initially, each classroom was provided with six Apple computers, a printer, and a large monitor that could display a computer screen. The research investigated how literacy and numeracy learning was enhanced using information technologies (IT) and information and communication technologies (ICT) with children in the first 3 years of school.

Paradigms and the Like

Most of the classroom-based early childhood research in which I have been involved can be located in a constructivist paradigm (Denzin & Lincoln, 2005), has used naturalistic methods, and produced case studies, narratives, and interpretations as a result of researchers and participants co-constructing understandings (Hatch, 2002). I have also been involved in research teams using mixed method approaches in school settings that combine positivist and constructivist paradigms. In these cases, I have been responsible for qualitative aspects such as nested case studies but have had a small amount of experience piloting child measures, constructing questionnaires, and coding child measures. I have also undertaken studies that draw on feminist, feminist poststructuralist, and Marxist perspectives, as well as combinations of these that incorporate emancipatory theory, race, class, and gender (Denzin & Lincoln, 2005). This chapter provides the opportunity to move from the constructivist paradigm adopted for research in the three schools and, drawing on critical and poststructural perspectives (Hatch, 2002), reflect critically on a number of tight spots that were encountered in the course of these research projects.

Moving from constructivism to critical and poststructural theories means a change in ontological understandings. The relativist ontology of multiple realities associated with constructivism gives way to feminist and Marxist conceptions of materialist-realist ontology where "the real world makes a material difference in terms of race, class, and gender" (Denzin & Lincoln, 2005, p. 24). Epistemologically, I am moving from the constructivist assumption that knowledge is a human construction and that researchers and participants co-construct understandings, to seeing knowledge through critical and feminist lenses as subjective and political. Thus I am framing these selected quandaries in particular ways to orient the conversation toward the power relationships that were lived out while data gathering was taking place in the schools. Methodologically, the data were gathered using naturalistic, qualitative approaches. Here I turn some of it on its head and, using aspects of critical theories and deconstruction, explore the power relations that were operating.

These musings hopefully enable a re-orientation epistemologically, that is, an investigation into what can be known when the researcher's values re-frame the data and inquiry, and engage reflexively and reflectively with power relations in school sites. Of course, these attempts to re-present the world of lived experience are always partial and never complete (Hatch, 2002). They also signify an effort to allow a space for data that are typically ignored, silenced, or not treated as data. In the research and publication world, there is often little time to devote to the nuances of research relationships, particularly if they do not fit neatly into "the steps in the research process" outlined in introductory textbooks (e.g., Burns, 2000; Creswell, 2005).

Those who undertake educational research are often familiar with educational settings as they are members or former members of school communities. They bring to educational research a plethora of experience, beliefs, values, and opinions or what Gee (1999) calls "cultural models" of participation in school contexts. More than that, because of this background, the "classic tension between distance and closeness in the research setting is often blurred in educational research" (Rogers, Malancharuvil-Berkes, Mosley, Hui, & Joseph, 2005, p. 382). Thus, I attempt to position myself with others in the research team as part of the research stories that are told here. What I try to do falls outside the gamut of "the prescribed research process." To some extent, textbooks are put aside, some traditional procedures are questioned, and a space is made for writing about aspects of research processes that receive very little attention.

Part of what I try to do is tied to what Van Mannen (1988) has called "confessional tales," where researchers engage in reflection about themselves as researchers, or what Richardson (2000) talks about as researchers writing themselves into their texts as examples of how social science and the self are intertwined. Yet hopefully it is more than this. As Linden (1993) notes, there are many research "confessions" but what is less common are "reflexive accounts of how other cultures and cultural 'others' act on fieldworkers" (p. 9). Achieving some degree of reflexivity, reciprocity, and "turn[ing] the analytical frame back on the researcher" (Rogers et al., 2005, p. 381) are the aims of this chapter. To assist in this task, I bring in critical and postmodern dimensions and seek readings of how power relations position those involved in research in school sites and how cultural "others" act on fieldworkers. I begin with gatekeepers and gatekeeping.

Gatekeepers and Gatekeeping

Most introductory research books offer sound advice about what gatekeepers are, offer effective strategies for negotiating access and working with gatekeepers, and in some cases discuss maintaining access (Denscombe, 2003; Feldman, Bell, & Berger, 2003; Glesne, 2006; Graue & Walsh, 1998). What is detailed to a lesser extent are matters that arise during the course of a project that require sensitive and ongoing management or renegotiation of access as the research progresses. This may be due to changes at the research site or in the expectations and needs of researchers and participants (Feldman et al., 2003; Glesne, 2006).

One of the researchers had been involved in research at Teviot the year before this project began, and there were good working relationships between the school administration, the researchers, and the teacher (Ann) who had been involved in the earlier project. In fact, the relationship with Ann was so positive and productive that as researchers, we wished to work with her again and expressed this desire to the deputy principal, with whom we liaised. We had spoken informally with Ann about the new project, and she was keen to be involved, which we mentioned to the deputy. However, due to staff changes and the impending arrival of a new staff member who was a beginning teacher, the deputy advised that we would not be able to work with Ann in Term 3, as it was preferable to let the beginning teacher become established in the classroom and develop a relationship with Ann first. During the conversation with the deputy principal to negotiate access to Ann and her classroom for the second time, it became clear that as more research was being undertaken, the policy had altered. Research projects would now be shared as the administration team believed that all teachers were able to make valuable contributions. On this basis, the deputy had selected two teachers and we would gather data in their classrooms. It was our understanding that we would be able to collect data in Ann's classroom (as originally requested) in Term 4, after her new teaching partner had settled.

At the start of Term 4, we were ready to begin the next stage of data collection and had spoken informally with Ann and her teaching partner Jane at the end of Term 3 and both were enthusiastic. Having negotiated a visit with the teachers, we made our way to the classroom. Shortly after exchanging greetings, the teachers advised us to speak to the deputy as they were unsure that data collection could go ahead in their classroom. We were a little surprised and made a hasty retreat to "the office" to seek the deputy, where we eventually found that we had been "allocated" another classroom and that we would be collecting data there. This was disappointing as recent conversations with Ann revealed that there were exciting things happening in her classroom, and we wanted the research to be undertaken there for this reason. Having been disappointed that we were unable to collect data in Ann's classroom in

Term 3, we reconciled ourselves to returning in Term 4. However, this was not to be. Although we had gathered what we thought could be called "good" data in Term 3, what had happened in this classroom was not as innovative as what was experienced in the previous year with Ann's class. As our quest was to document highly creative and novel approaches to using IT and ICT with young children, we would have preferred the classroom of our choice, which was Ann's.

We were in the habit of chatting informally with the deputy but somehow we had missed the fact that we would not be collecting data in Ann's classroom. Schools are very busy places and gaps in communication do occur. In retrospect, we probably made an assumption that we could gather data in Ann's class but did not clarify it with the deputy, which led to our misunderstanding. But conversely, we cannot recall the deputy saying to us that we could not work in Ann's classroom, and we suspect that the statement was never made. Perhaps our motivation to work again with Ann and the anticipation of capturing what was happening in her classroom meant that we "missed" this vital piece of information. However, while having the conversation with the deputy, we tried not to lose face and to regain composure as quickly as possible. We then proceeded to make our way to the classroom to which we had been allocated, trying to be as positive as we could.

It was difficult to begin the research in this classroom immediately as we did not really know either teacher, although we had met briefly in the past. It is always a challenge to begin gathering data in a classroom when there is no time to develop rapport and build some trust with the teacher. Having a researcher in the room along with a computer, monitor, digital mixer, video camera, and so on is an imposition in any classroom; but we wondered if these teachers knew or would find out that we thought we were going to collect data in Ann's classroom and not theirs (and if they did, what would they make of it?). So, it was with some trepidation that we embarked on the data collection in this, the classroom to which we had been allocated. As it turned out, it was not one of the more successful data collection stories that I can recount. By the time we had negotiated data collection visits and begun to gather data, it was the third week of term. This was the last term of the school year, and the teachers did not want data being gathered in their classroom during the last 2 weeks of school, which left us with about 5 weeks' data collection time and two teachers who "had a lot of work to cover" and who said "please don't interrupt us" before the end of the year.

There are two things about this experience that I discuss: the power relations and, relatedly, what was said and what was not said. By power relations, I mean the layers of relationships of power that are both explicit and implicit in schools and not just those that exist between researchers and participants—that is, the material conditions of life ("race," class, gender, age, culture, hierarchy, societal structures, experience, etc.) that affect who can say what to whom, when, where, why, and how. Relations of power need to be negotiated continually as they are always challenged, contested, and resisted. In addition, the balance of power can change frequently during exchanges (Foucault, 1980).

At Teviot, we experienced several layers of power relationships: the school as an institutional structure of society; the administration team; the two teachers who shared the double teaching spaces; and the teachers individually. But these layers intersected with other everyday realities such as gender, teaching experience, the culture of the school, age, and so on. Relations of power are part of gaining access, which Graue and Walsh (1998) say can be difficult. After getting over the hurdle of being able to do further research at Teviot, we found that this was just one layer of negotiations and that what followed was not as easy as it was one year before, or indeed as easy as gaining initial access had been. In the circumstances, the power relationships that existed at the classroom level with the four teachers required some skillful negotiation that left us unsure about whether the teachers to whom we had been allocated actually wanted research to occur in their classrooms. On an individual level with each teacher, it was difficult to find times to collect data that suited the teachers. We indicated from the start that we would fit in with the class schedule but this did not seem to make the task of finding suitable times any easier as there was always a reason that a time was unsuitable.

The protracted negotiation needed to arrange actual data gathering sessions in the classrooms in Term 4 was one reason we wondered if the teachers had any choice in their involvement. Graue and Walsh (1998) acknowledge that gaining entry must be renegotiated on a daily basis with those who actually work with children (as opposed to who might grant access initially) and that daily renegotiation "never stops" (p. 99). It was also a case of how the balance of power seemed to be tipped against us. We were positioned less powerfully because we wanted access. The teachers had been asked (told?) by the administration to grant us access, yet they were able to determine exactly when we could be there to collect data and for how long. And important for us, there was no time for things such as building rapport and developing a trusting relationship with the teachers. Had there been time for this, the teachers may have been more responsive and negotiations may have been a little easier. Gaining and maintaining access is therefore a process of building, preserving, and sustaining relationships: "There is no point at which access is stable ... the access process continues throughout and sometimes beyond one's exit from the field" (Feldman et al., 2003, p. x).

The days of seeing researchers as all-powerful are long gone, and there are those who, although they acknowledge that the traditional power of researchers can be shared in several ways, conclude that the balance of power remains with the researcher (Atweh & Burton, 1995; Mayall, Hood, & Oliver, 1999). Hatch (2002), too, has commented that teachers "often perceive themselves to be in a subordinate position in relation to educational researchers" (p. 67). In this experience at Teviot, it felt like we were in a subordinate position and dependent entirely on the teachers' decisions about when we could gather data. And yet if we had asked the teachers, they may well have agreed with Hatch's (2002) position, saying that they felt that the balance of power was with the researchers or perhaps the administration, given that it was the administration team who granted initial access.

For the administration team, the important thing seemed to be equality and that more teachers had an opportunity to be involved in research. To us, this signaled not only that the administration valued all teachers and what was occurring in their classrooms, but also that what was happening was worthy of research. As the deputy knew, we were interested in novel and innovative classroom practice with IT and ICT. However, there was a definite mismatch between what the deputy knew we were interested in researching and what occurred in the classrooms to which we were allocated. Like Wright and Reid (2003), we were left wondering just how much input these teachers had in the decision about data gathering in their classrooms, and further, the "reliability of data collected under these circumstances" (p. 8).

In retrospect, what was not said was perhaps more powerful to us than what was. We cannot recall the deputy saying that we could *not* research in the preferred classroom, but we were aware of the change in policy. We knew that there was a lot of research interest in the school and that some teachers had created reputations for themselves because they had presented aspects of their classroom work at conferences and professional development sessions for teachers. It was these teachers (like Ann) and their classrooms that were in demand by researchers (like us). We suspected that the reason for the policy change was that the administration team was aware of the demands on these teachers and consequently they decided to spread the load. This fits well with literature that discusses the gatekeeping role as including protecting potential participants from harm (Minichiello, Aroni, Timewell, & Alexander, 1995).

Another explanation is that the administrative team could have drawn on their more powerful positions and decided to limit who was involved, thus inadvertently altering the nature of data gathered. We had no information about whether there had been a discussion with staff about research or whether concerns had been expressed privately to administration team members about the fairness of research occurring in the same teachers' classrooms. And we had no knowledge of whether any of the teachers were consulted, as Ann, whom we thought we were working with in Term 4, did not seem to know about the new arrangement when we spoke with her at the end of Term 3. Ultimately, even after negotiations with gatekeepers, gaining access to classrooms involves give-and-take, and in this instance we were unable to access the classroom of our choice, which has to be seen in hindsight as a trade-off for the privilege of access, albeit one littered with layers of power relations. However, what can be accessed and when also determines to a large degree the data that are gathered and the research questions that can be investigated (Feldman et al., 2003).

In this experience, we did not go down the tricky road of trying to find out how the administrative decisions had been made about our access to classrooms. Taking such action would have been an attempt to understand how the power relations were working to position those involved, which may have led to more transparency (for us and maybe the teachers) about the process. That is, it may have made the processes of the administrative team and the data collection more visible by involving participants in research conversations that are aimed at more equitable relationships. Theoretically, this should be possible within a constructivist paradigm where researchers and participants co-construct understandings. Nonetheless, our frameworks of thinking are currently shaped to see such actions within a critical paradigm, prefaced by a transformative inquiry aimed at challenging existing power structures and relations. Ideally, these frameworks of thinking should not limit our understandings of what is possible, but in the everyday world of schools and research, they are the frames in which the multiple realities of constructivism operate. If inspired by social justice, they are also the very places where our work as researchers is located.

Researcher Effect in Classrooms

As both research projects gathered data about how children used IT and ICTs in daily classroom activity and the pedagogies that teachers use, we were interested in how teachers interacted with children while they were using computers and other technologies available in the classrooms. By interaction, I mean what teachers said to children and what they did with them. For instance, how did they scaffold children's numeracy learning in individual, small group, and whole class interactions? If children needed individual assistance, did teachers provide verbal instructions or did they take the mouse from the child and "fix" the problem themselves before handing the mouse back to the child? The original intention was to observe and video-record with minimal participation in the hope that teacher–child interaction would predominate.

Because researchers are both "shaped by" and "shapers of our world" (Lather, 1991, p. 269), the intrusion of a researcher complete with computer and video-recording equipment into a classroom alters that site in ways that can be known partially and ways that are impossible to know. Suffice it to say that the degree to which the research site altered in this research project was difficult to ascertain. Although teachers may feel uncomfortable with the research imposition and alter their behavior, teachers, like the family members that Henry (1971) discussed, "cannot remain on guard constantly and everywhere as the strain is too great" (p. 192). Researchers too are subject to change in accordance with various sites and different respondents as it is difficult to adopt and maintain one style throughout a project (Burgess, 1991). Rather, several dispositions are taken up and developed throughout an investigation, depending on the nature of the exchange taking place between researcher and participants. This means that dispositions are continually "negotiated and renegotiated with different informants throughout a research project" (Burgess, 1984, p. 85). Glesne (2006) notes the importance of researchers clearly defining their research roles from the beginning of the project but acknowledges that researchers alter their behavior to maximize data collection opportunities. In what follows, I explain what we did in an attempt to maximize our data collection opportunities as we realized that fulfilling one of our research aims was quickly disappearing.

In the ten or so classrooms at Layt and Yucca in which a research assistant took up a position with computer and video-recording equipment, it soon became obvious that on the whole, the teachers avoided contact with children who were working at the computers. At first, we thought that this could have been due to the fact that in most of these classrooms, a bank of six or eight computers was located together in a cluster. In others, computers were positioned in individual spots or in pairs. When we became aware of the issue, it was recorded in field notes (Emerson, Fretz, & Shaw, 1995) and discussed among the research teams. As an initial research strategy, incidental observations continued and field notes documented in a general way the actions and interactions of the teachers. As well as this, there was audio and video evidence that the teachers interacted very little with those children who were using the computers and hardly at all with the children using the dedicated "research" computer.

After our initial strategy produced no change in the behavior of the teachers, we decided to make them aware of the situation. Before we discussed it with the teachers, we raised it at a meeting with representatives from the state Department of Education, who were partners in the research project. Considerable thought was given to how we might discuss it with the teachers. We wanted to handle it sensitively and avoid making it an issue, or worry the teachers. A decision was made to mention it subtly in the course of daily classroom activity, to attempt to fit it into a conversation that was progressing comfortably and that was related to an aspect of the data gathering process. This was achieved over a period of 2 or 3 weeks and teachers responded well to what was said, but none indicated awareness of avoiding the computers.

In general, all teachers seemed to be conscious of their actions when they were mentioned, but we had a hunch that they were not aware before we brought it to their attention. Thus, the ten teachers, who all worked in pairs in double classrooms, had not discussed it with their teaching partners (or other teachers such as their mentors). There had been no individual, pair, or small group critical reflection on this part of their classroom work and no subsequent discussion with the research assistant or the researchers. That this did not eventuate could have indicated the lack of significance the teachers attached to the research, that they had not noticed that they avoided the computers, or the extremely busy classroom life of teachers. Teachers may have avoided the area because the presence of the research assistant may have signaled that assistance was available if necessary. This was despite the fact that teachers at both schools were made aware that we were interested in the pedagogies they used to help children become numerate. It is also plausible that teachers associated pedagogies with more traditional approaches to instruction, such as "teaching" the whole group, rather than interactions with individual children, pairs, or small groups of children working at one or two computers. Whatever the reason, these ten teachers exhibited acute computer avoidance, which was of no assistance to our research whatsoever.

We were hoping that once we had made the teachers aware that they were avoiding the computers they might interact a little more with the children who were using them. This worked with one teacher for a couple of days, but after that things were just the same. For a while, we did issue gentle reminders to teachers, but as there was little or no response, we gave up. So here we were with over 2 years of data collection still to be undertaken and a group of teachers who would not go near or interact with children when they were using the computers. Thus, it turned out that what we expected would be a major source of data was just not going to materialize. This called for a revision of our data collection strategies (which was possible), but not our research questions or the research aims, as the funding for the research had been made on the basis of the aims and the questions that we were investigating. We broadened our agenda and instead of focusing specifically on numeracy, IT, ICT, and children working on the dedicated research computer, we began to consider the classroom as a whole. We used more observation techniques, took more detailed notes of classroom routines, classroom organization, and management strategies, and began to video-record whole class lessons that involved numeracy, IT, and ICT. This action increased the amount of data gathered but still fell far short of capturing the expected number of teacher–child interactions. It did mean that we had great difficulty achieving one of our research aims, which was to identify teacher talk and specific strategies teachers used to assist, enhance, and scaffold children's numeracy learning when using IT and ICT.

Our concern about not being able to meet one of our research aims was tempered somewhat (we thought) by the development of a computer lab at Yucca. For the first 2 years of the project classes at Yucca visited the computer lab once per week for a 30-minute lesson that was taught by the computer teacher. Class teachers were to be present in the lab and to assist children to complete the tasks set by the computer teacher. The idea was that the computer teacher taught a skills-based lesson and teachers were to reinforce the skills in the classroom during the week that followed. Teachers were required to attend lab classes but not all teachers did, much to the chagrin of the computer teacher (Grieshaber, 2005). For one term, we video-recorded the lab lessons for one class, which captured the computer teacher teaching a skills-based lesson using a transmission approach.

We also attempted to video-record the class teacher interacting individually and with small groups of children while assisting them to complete the tasks set by the computer teacher. However, we found that the teachers themselves were generally unfamiliar with the program being used and even though much of what the computer teacher taught was basic, the class teacher had trouble keeping up with the instructions from the computer teacher and thus found assisting children and "troubleshooting" quite a challenge. So even though we thought that we might still be able to meet our research aim by moving data collection to the computer lab, we were thwarted because teachers lacked confidence and did not know the programs being used, and because of this were able to provide little scaffolding. Most of the class teacher's interaction with children was reiterating the instructions from the computer teacher, often verbatim. This, coupled with teachers' avoidance of computers in their own classrooms, presents a case for more focused attention to how teachers "teach" and interact with young children when completing set tasks on computers in the course of daily classroom activity, especially when these two schools have as part of their mandate a commitment to multiliteracies and communications media. This raises the question of what and how long it is going to take for teachers to come to the point where they have the content knowledge of IT and ICT programs that is required to teach competently and confidently.

In some cases, then, despite the best-laid plans, researchers have little influence over the type of data that can be gathered and are so positioned that they are unable to alter in any significant way the nature of those data. In one way, this renders them powerless to access the data they thought they were going to gather, but in another, it opens other possibilities as it signals that the state of affairs may be different from what was expected and hence worthy of research in other dimensions. This situation can be problematic if there is a chance that answers to the research questions will not eventuate and the research is funded by an agency that expects particular results.

As the research at Yucca and Layt was funded by the Australian Research Council and the state Department of Education, there were specific relations of power that were operating at various levels that ranged from subliminal to overtly conscious awareness. Funded research works to motivate or even compel researchers to ensure the research finds what it seeks. In this sense, researchers working within positivist, postpositivist, and constructivist paradigms are likely to contribute to the perpetuation and reproduction of the power relations in which they are enmeshed, whereas those working within critical frames have more opportunities to engage in the transformation of social relations. As researchers we were concerned for some time that we might not produce all of what we had undertaken to produce as part of the funded research contract. We were bound by the agreement to provide evidence for what we had set out in the grant application. What would happen if we did not produce what was expected? Would that jeopardize further funding from this powerful Australian organization by which one's reputation as a researcher in this country is known and evaluated? And do these concerns mean that we were complicit in our own oppression and succumbed to, rather than resisted, the power relations that operate around and about funded research? The tensions inherent in this position are obvious but nonetheless daunting, and we hoped that this concern, which we did not mention to the teachers, would not translate itself imperceptibly into the research process. We finally resolved the uncertainty by convincing ourselves that we had done as much as we possibly could to gather data related to the phenomena under investigation and that there was nothing more that we could do.

Researcher–Participant Relationships That Surpass the Conventional

During research projects and especially longitudinal studies, there are opportunities for the development of relationships between researchers and participants that go beyond the classroom. Having a researcher in a classroom on a regular and long-term basis can result in a high degree of rapport between teacher and researcher and often a reciprocal relationship that has mutual benefits. In such situations, researchers can become involved with teachers, administration staff, or class members, which is something that within the confines of traditional sociological interview technique has been regarded as a form of "personal degeneracy" (Oakley, 1981, p. 41). More recently, however, research designed from a critical or postmodern perspective has relegated this position to the methodological backwater (e.g., Lather, 1991).

The data collection at Layt and Yucca was spread over approximately 2.5 years and resulted in the development of a close relationship between the research assistant and one teacher in each school, where the research assistant could be described as a "critical friend." Over a short period of time, a critical friend relationship developed between Eva (the research assistant) and one teacher at Layt (Nerida); and Eva and one teacher at Yucca (Ali). For Nerida and Ali, this consisted of many in-depth conversations both inside and outside the classroom, email and phone contact outside the classroom; and for Nerida, on some occasions informal meetings outside the school environment. Critical friends have been used as a way of enhancing school effectiveness (Swaffield, 2005; Swaffield & MacBeath, 2005) and were part of the New Basics school renewal program in which both Layt and Yucca were involved: both schools had employed critical friends who assisted teachers and administration staff. Costa and Kallick (1993) described a critical friend as:

a trusted person who asks provocative questions, provides data to be examined through another lens, and offers critiques of a person's work as a friend. A critical friend takes the time to fully understand the context of the work presented and the outcomes that the person or group is working toward. The friend is an advocate for the success of the work. (p. 50)

The employment of critical friends by schools is therefore consistent with research that has shown that schools are more likely to improve if they have external support (Barker, Curtis, & Beneson, 1991; Fullan, 2001).

Despite the development of a body of literature about critical friends, this project did not include a critical friend as part of data gathering. These two critical friend relationships developed spontaneously as data collection occurred in the two classrooms.

Swaffield (2005) sees the primary aim of a critical friendship as "support-ing improvement through empowerment, demonstrating a positive regard for people and providing an informed critique of processes and practices" (p. 45). It is fair to say that as part of this unplanned development, Eva acted as a critical friend in the ways described by Costa and Kallick (1993) and Swaffield (2005). As time progressed, she acquired an intimate knowledge of the two classrooms, teachers, and children and was sought frequently by the teachers as a source for discussing anything and everything that was connected to the life of the two classrooms.

The critical friend relationship that developed imposed extra responsibili-ties on Eva. Mindful of the fact that "participants are the ultimate gatekeep-ers" (Hatch, 2002, p. 51) and that it is participants who in the end decide the information that researchers can access, we set out to establish good working relationships with all staff at both schools. We were attentive to reciprocity, or the give-and-take (Lather, 1986) between researchers and participants, knowing that while we wanted to investigate classroom processes as "cul-tural insider[s]" (Hatch, 2002, p. 64), this involved the "mutual negotiation of meaning and power" (Lather, 1986, p. 263). The bottom line with these issues of negotiation, give-and-take, and power is the benefits researchers and par-ticipants get from the research. Benefits for researchers are often obvious, but the payback for participants is not always so evident.

In Eva's case, the payback for the two teachers was that they wanted what Eva could provide as their critical friend, and they couldn't get enough of it. Eva was available, responsive, reflective, challenging (but not too challeng-ing), stimulating, accepting, respectful, and empowering. She was in every sense a highly skilled and receptive critical friend, and she was in their class-rooms "on tap." As Feldman et al. (2003) noted, "Establishing a good rela-tionship in the field … can lead researchers to gain more access than they expected" (p. 28), which was certainly the case with Eva. She was in demand

and, in a kind of role reversal, at times had to limit the access that teachers had to her. Thus, the ability to relate to others becomes part of the research process (Spradley, 1979) and being involved in classroom activity can place those who are collecting data in compromising positions. Finch (1984), Oakley (1981), and Spradley (1979) have also suggested that researchers may have little influence over the relationships that eventuate between researchers and participants, citing reasons of personality matches, cultural norms, interpersonal skills of the researcher, and the development of trust and confidence. This was certainly the case with Eva, as in both instances, the critical friend relationship developed quite quickly and meant that Eva was positioned as a source of personal and professional support for curriculum, pedagogical, and assessment decisions that occurred in these classrooms.

However, all this fell apart quite suddenly when Eva was diagnosed with an aggressive form of cancer in September 2003 and withdrew permanently from the project shortly after the diagnosis. Apart from being paralyzed for a time as a result of this news, the rest of the research team was unable to support the teachers in ways that might have been helpful. There is little written about how to make a gracious departure from the research site and in this situation, we found no literature to assist with explaining Eva's unexpected and sudden departure. As team members, we were struggling with the situation ourselves but were conscious that we needed to make contact with the schools and keep them informed, particularly because of the close relationships that had developed between Eva and Nerida, and Eva and Ali.

It was Eva's choice to provide only basic information to the schools, as she was not sure of the medical implications immediately. Thus, it was not until some time later that participants found out the seriousness of the situation. Fortunately, it was close to the September school holidays when Eva withdrew, and she was able to do this without too much difficulty. Her continued absence did raise some concerns, and we provided teachers with as much information as we could at the time. We were able to call on research assistants from other projects to undertake interviews with teachers and administration staff that were scheduled for Term 4, and were able to gather a small amount of data.

Staff changes are to be expected in a longitudinal project, but the pivotal role Eva played became increasingly apparent as we attempted to replace her. We were finally able to do this after the beginning of the school year in February 2004, and we began to collect data again shortly after school resumed, but not before the team leader had been diagnosed with a different form of cancer early in 2004 and was subsequently absent for several months. To continue with the project following this news was somewhat of a challenge, but we did manage to keep up with most of the data collection that had been scheduled. The new part-time research assistant was in classrooms collecting data and the other part-time research assistants who had been called on toward the end of 2003 were still working on transcripts and collating data.

The research assistant who took Eva's place was a very different person from Eva, and none of the teachers developed a rapport with her in the same way they did with Eva.

Eva's departure marked a significant disjuncture in the data gathering process, and things were never the same. There were noticeable differences in the relationships with the schools generally and the teachers specifically, which included the necessity of regaining access to classrooms following Eva's departure and the resumption of data collection at the beginning of 2004. Returning to the schools for the first time was hard and involved challenges in providing information about Eva's health. There was also the complication of the team leader whose absence of several months was not mentioned to the schools and so made continuity of data collection and liaising with the schools demanding and almost impossible.

The extreme circumstances of parts of this project meant that the research lost impetus and momentum, which we were never able to regain or re-create. The seriousness of the interruptions impacted both researchers and participants and, although unforeseen as they were, had implications for what occurred later in terms of further data collection, relationships with participants, presence at the schools, and leaving the field. Planning an exit is an integral part of any research process (Feldman et al., 2003), but this project did not reach closure in a number of ways and possibly never will because of decisions taken by the researchers. There is no comfortable way of revealing bad news, and it was not possible to resume the same momentum following Eva's departure as everything had changed. The eventual departure from the field was low key and to some extent remains unfinished business. For instance, a decision was made by the researchers not to report verbally to participants about the outcomes of the research, although a report was prepared and made available.

The way in which Eva worked with the teachers was well received by everyone in the project. When Eva allowed herself to enter into a critical friend relationship with two teachers, both the teachers and Eva gained significantly from this relationship, although it is not certain that Eva was aware at the beginning of how the relationship might evolve. Despite evidence that external support is required for schools to improve (Barker et al., 1991; Fullan, 2001), we need to question the ways in which the critical friend relationship could have continued to produce Eva as "external expert" and the teachers as needy, inexperienced, and unknowing. Of course, this is not what they said, but because of how these teachers positioned Eva and how she positioned herself, the idea was reinforced that experts (who are inevitably positioned more powerfully than teachers) come from outside the school and they provide resources and information that is not available within the school.

While it was an extremely productive relationship for Eva and the two teachers, it is instructive to look beyond the immediate and consider the macro perspective of the frames of knowledge that shape our thinking and the relations of power that permeate them. It is more than likely that such support, advice, and expertise were available within the schools but on the whole, schools are not structures that are set up to take advantage of resources in this way. Special arrangements would have to be made and they take time and energy. At Yucca, teachers were paired with others in a mentoring relationship, but they did not have access to these teachers for lengths of time while the children were in attendance. Yet, despite it being a potentially valuable exercise, we did not talk to the teachers about the impact of Eva's presence simply because of the circumstances of her departure. While we suspect her contribution did not reinforce the idea of outsider as expert and insiders as uninformed, there are no data to support our suspicion. But we hope that the positive nature of the relationships is an indication that these existing ways of thinking were questioned and possibly re-shaped by the teachers and their experiences.

A Certain Conclusion?

With the ever-changing relationships that occur in daily classroom life, any research (particularly longitudinal research) undertaken is subject to daily renegotiation. For the teachers involved, ongoing classroom research can often be the least significant thing that occurs for them in their classrooms; while for the researchers, it is often one of the most significant parts of what they do. At the basis of all research undertaken in classrooms, but not always acknowledged as such, are power relationships. The examples provided here give some insights into the ways in which teachers, administrative staff, and researchers are enmeshed in power relations both inside and outside the classroom and how teachers and researchers can be positioned more and less powerfully depending on what is happening at the time. That is, they offer instances of how power relationships play out and how cultural "others" can act on fieldworkers: teachers and administration staff can make demands that are unanticipated; gatekeepers can require daily access rituals; teachers can inadvertently avoid the very thing one wants to research; and research workers can be lulled into deep relationships they did not begin to contemplate. And how researchers see and understand what happens depends on the research paradigm they have adopted from the start.

Although the research design was constructivist, there was a mismatch between the design and the New Basics school renewal project that was being undertaken at Yucca and Layt. New Basics is about reconceptualizing and building curriculum by "envisioning the kinds of life worlds and human subjects that the education system wants to contribute to and build" (Department of Education and the Arts, 2004, p. 3). Because it aims to develop critical and analytical thinking skills, problem solving, and lifelong learning skills, as well as deal with new student identities, new technologies, economies, and workplaces, and diverse communities and complex cultures, New Basics is placed firmly in a critical paradigm. To be consistent with the New Basics approach, a critical research design should have been adopted. Given that the New Basics set out to transform education, a research design that incorporated transformation of social relations as an integral part of its methodology was fitting. Yet as researchers, we decided to hedge our bets and write the grant application based on previous experience with case study and on our estimation of the likelihood of funding. This meant steering away from a design informed by critical theory, which as a consequence also meant strengthening existing ways of thinking as opposed to challenging or chipping away at the status quo.

The implications of this decision are still with us and are part of the reason for writing this chapter. But one cannot dwell on past mistakes for too long, and the depth of what has been learned has been an asset already and also stands as experience for future reference. Whether having a design informed by critical theory would have made a significant difference to what happened in these schools and with data collection cannot be known. But I like to think that it might have made a difference, especially in the daily life of classrooms where the micro and the macro are so inexorably interwoven and opportunities arise for research conversations that not only are more equitable but also have the capacity to reveal much more about what is being investigated.

I offer the following suggestions for early childhood classroom researchers based on the experiences related above:

- Be aware of the research paradigm in which you are operating and understand the ontological, epistemological, and methodological implications as well as the kinds of outcomes that are produced from the paradigm.
- Remember that almost everything is negotiable and therefore re-negotiable.
- Be prepared to negotiate some things on a daily basis.
- Consider power relations from all perspectives, that is, how each person is positioned and the effect that positioning has on him or her, others, and the research project.
- Keep track of relationships and how they develop.
- Clarify and confirm research expectations with gatekeepers and participants if you are unsure.
- Think about the effects that researchers may have on the research site and the implications of those effects.
- Be prepared for the unexpected.

References

Atweh, B., & Burton, L. (1995). Students as researchers: Rationale and critique. *British Educational Research Journal, 21*(5), 561–575.

Barker, P., Curtis, D., & Beneson, W. (1991). *Collaborative opportunities to build better schools.* Bloomington, IL: Association for Supervision and Curriculum Development.

Burgess, R. G. (1984). *In the field: An introduction to field research*. London: Allen and Unwin.

Burgess, R. G. (1991). *In the field: An introduction to field research*. London: Routledge.

Burns, R. B. (2000). *Introduction to research methods* (4th ed.). Frenchs Forest, New South Wales, Australia: Pearson.

Costa, A., & Kallick, B. (1993). Through the lens of a critical friend. *Educational Leadership, 51*(2), 49–51.

Creswell, J. W. (2005). *Educational research: Planning, conducting, and evaluating quantitative and qualitative research* (2nd ed.). Upper Saddle River, NJ: Pearson.

Denscombe, M. (2003). *The good research guide for small scale social research projects* (2nd ed.). Maidenhead, England: Open University Press.

Denzin, N. K., & Lincoln, Y. S. (2005). Introduction: The discipline and practice of qualitative research. In N. K. Denzin & Y S. Lincoln (Eds.), *The Sage handbook of qualitative research* (3rd ed., pp. 1–32). Thousand Oaks, CA: Sage.

Department of Education and the Arts. (2004). *The New Basics research report*. Brisbane, Queensland, Australia: The State of Queensland.

Emerson, R. M., Fretz, I., & Shaw, L. L. (1995). *Writing ethnographic fieldnotes*. Chicago: University of Chicago Press.

Feldman, M. S., Bell, J., & Berger, M. T. (2003). *Gaining access: A practical and theoretical guide for qualitative researchers*. Walnut Creek, CA: Altamira Press.

Finch, J. (1984). It's great to have someone to talk to: The ethics and politics of interviewing women. In C. Bell & H. Roberts (Eds.), *Social researching: Policies, problems and practices* (pp. 70–87). London: Routledge.

Foucault, M. (1980). *Power/knowledge: Selected interviews and other writings 1972–1977* (C. Gordon, Ed.; C. Gordon, L. Marshall, J. Mepham, & K. Soper, Trans.). Brighton, England: Harvester Press.

Fullan, M. (2001). *The new meaning of educational change* (3rd ed.). London: Routledge.

Gee, J. P. (1999). *An introduction to discourse analysis*. New York: Routledge.

Glesne, C. (2006). *Becoming qualitative researchers: An introduction*. Boston: Pearson.

Graue, M. E., & Walsh, D. (1998). *Studying children in context: Theories, methods and ethics*. Thousand Oaks, CA: Sage.

Grieshaber, S. (2005, May 30–June 1). *Young children and a computer lab: A case study*. Paper presented at the meeting of Redesigning Pedagogy: Research, Policy, Practice (Innovations in Curriculum Development and Classroom Practice), Singapore.

Hatch, J. A. (2002). *Doing qualitative research in education settings*. Albany: State University of New York Press.

Henry, J. (1971). *Pathways to madness*. New York: Random House.

Lather, P. (1986). Research as praxis. *Harvard Educational Review, 56*(3), 257–277.

Lather, P. (1991). *Getting smart: Feminist research and pedagogy with/in the postmodern*. New York: Routledge.

Linden, R. (1993). *Making stories, making selves: Feminist reflections on the Holocaust*. Columbus: Ohio State University Press.

Mayall, B., Hood, S., & Oliver, S. (1999). Introduction. In S. Hood, B. Mayall, & S. Oliver (Eds.), *Critical issues in social research: Power and prejudice* (pp. 1–9). Buckingham, England: Open University Press.

Minichiello, V., Aroni, R., Timewell, E., & Alexander, L. (1995). *In-depth interviewing: Principles, techniques, analysis* (2nd ed.). Melbourne: Longman.

Oakley, A. (1981). Interviewing women: A contradiction in terms. In H. Roberts (Ed.), *Doing feminist research* (pp. 30–61). London: Routledge.

Richardson, L. (2000). Writing: A method of inquiry. In N. Denzin & Y. Lincoln (Eds.), *Handbook of qualitative research* (2nd ed., pp. 923–946). Thousand Oaks, CA: Sage.

Rogers, R., Malancharuvil-Berkes, E., Mosley, M., Hui, D., & Joseph, G. O. (2005). Critical discourse analysis in education: A review of the literature. *Review of Educational Research, 75*(3), 365–416.

Spradley, J. P. (1979). *The ethnographic interview*. New York: Holt, Rinehart, & Winston.

Swaffield, S. (2005). No sleeping partners: Relationships between head teachers and critical friends. *School Leadership and Management, 25*(1), 43–57.

Swaffield, S., & MacBeath, J. (2005). School self-evaluation and the role of a critical friend. *Cambridge Journal of Education, 35*(2), 239–252.

Van Mannen, J. (1988). *Tales of the field: On writing ethnography.* Chicago: University of Chicago Press.

Wright, N., & Reid, J. (2003, December). *Keeping ourselves honest? The research relations in data collection.* Paper presented at the Australian Association for Research in Education Annual Conference, Auckland.

10
Researching With Children
The Challenges and Possibilities for Building "Child Friendly" Research

GLENDA MACNAUGHTON, KYLIE SMITH, AND KARINA DAVIS

*The University of Melbourne, Centre for Equity
and Innovation in Early Childhood*

Introduction

Understandings about what constitutes valid and reliable research data and the necessary protocols for developing relationships with participants are typically based on standards set within positivist science (Denzin & Lincoln, 2005a). "Real" and valid research is generally seen as objective, untainted by the researcher's experiences or understandings, and it adheres to "the stringent, technical and impersonal rules of scientific investigation" (Hughes, 2001, p. 33). These standards require that researchers conduct research in particular ways that limit the role and autonomy of research participants and deny them ownership of the research process, results, and outcomes (Denzin & Lincoln, 2005b). Hence, traditional positivist research has historically hierarchically positioned the participant as the less powerful "other" to the researcher.

This form of traditional scientific research remains the dominant form of educational research in many "Western" countries, especially the United States. For example, the *No Child Left Behind* policy, enacted in the United States in 2001, gives billions of dollars of federal funds exclusively to educational programs and strategies that are based on traditional positivist scientific research evidence (Fueur, Towne, & Shavelson, 2002).

Challenges to positivist research and its positioning of the researched have circulated for over 30 years. For instance, feminist researchers (e.g., Maynard & Purvis, 1995; Roberts, 1981; Stanley & Wise, 1983) have argued for more equitable relationships between researchers and researched that recognize the validity of the voice of the researched and their rights to shape the research process. Several strands of feminist research have also argued for research that is transformative and produces social change through participant empowerment (see Maynard & Purvis, 1996). More recent challenges to the positivist view of what constitutes valid and reliable research and ethical research relationships have arisen from within black and ethnic minority communities that have been its targets (Bishop, 2005; Kaomea, 2003; Ladson-Billings & Donnor, 2005; Moreton-Robinson, 2004; Tuhiwai Smith, 2005). These scholars argue for greater control by the researched in all aspects of the research process.

Whilst these challenges have been important in shaping the nature of transformative qualitative research for the researched adult, they are yet to significantly reshape qualitative research with young children. As young children have long been subjects of research, we believe that attention to their rights as participants to direct the research process is long overdue. To date, children as the researched have been mainly the concern of ethicists who have worked to ensure that research protocols offer particular protection to children as research subjects. For instance, they have required children's caretakers/guardians to consent to research being conducted on children. Whilst this is an essential aspect of protecting children's rights, this focus tends to ignore children's views about research and being researched. As Cannella (1998) argued:

> The most critical voices that are silent in our constructions of early childhood education are the children with whom we work. Our constructions of research have not fostered methods that facilitate hearing their voices. (p. 10)

Cannella, along with others, has sparked debate about young children's voices in research. When this debate began in the 1990s, we witnessed a move to listen to young children's voices and perspectives in early childhood research. For example, Australian researchers sought young children's perspectives on issues as diverse as migration (Candy & Butterworth, 1998), literacy (Martello, 1999), social networks (Corrie & Leito, 1999), "race" and gender equity (MacNaughton, 2001a, 2001b, 2001c, 2003), and peace (Campbell et al., 2001). This shift within the early childhood research field now intersects with an increased concern over how a civil society can recognize and enact the rights of the child.

In this chapter, we explore how framing research in and through a children's rights perspective might produce more "child-friendly" research in which children's research voices are recognized alongside their right to participate in the design and production of research. We are interested in producing research that disrupts those knowledge-power dynamics that mute children's rights as people who are the "researched." We borrow the term "child-friendly" from the UNICEF Child Friendly Cities Initiative (CFCI), which links building cities to the idea that "the well-being of children is the ultimate indicator of a healthy habitat, a democratic society and good governance" (UNICEF, 2004, p. 5). We do this to explore what it takes to build research in which the well-being of children drives democratic research governance in which children are active participants in shaping research for and about them.

Framing Young Children as Researched People With Human Rights: The UN Convention on the Rights of the Child

The 1989 United Nations Convention on the Rights of the Child made children's rights legally binding in the same way as other (adult) human rights. This includes the right of children to have a voice in decisions about them. The United Nations General Assembly endorsed the Convention unanimously on November 20, 1989, and on January 26, 1990; 61 countries signed it. The 1989 United Nations Convention on the Rights of the Child proclaimed that children have, among other rights:

> The right to express their views on all matters affecting them and for their views to be taken seriously (Article 12)
>
> The right to freedom of expression, including freedom to seek, receive, and impart information and ideas of all kinds through any media they choose (Article 13) (See also Ackroyd & Pilkingham, 1999; Reimer, 2003.)

The recent United Nations General Comment (No. 7) on *Implementing child rights in early childhood* makes clear that young children's right to express their views and feelings should be taken into account in "the development of policies and services, including through research and consultations" (Office of the High Commissioner of Human Rights, 2005, p. 7) and it stresses that these are the rights of all children, irrespective of their age.

The Convention's principles and the recent United Nations General Comment (No. 7) have intersected with new images of the child to produce a heightened concern that includes children's perspectives and voices in early childhood research (e.g., Farrell, 2005; Lewis & Lindsay, 2000; MacNaughton & Smith, 2005). As Christensen and James, working from within a new sociology of the child (2000), explained:

> [We need to treat children] as social actors in their own right in contexts where, traditionally, they have been denied those rights of participation and their voices have remained unheard. (p. 2)

Similarly, Dahlberg, Moss, and Pence (1999) caution adults against imposing their knowledge on children, as such imposition can diminish children. Their concern echoes Article 12 of the United Nations Convention on the Rights of the Child, which guarantees the child's right to be heard and to express opinions. Dahlberg et al. express their concern thus:

> This is part of a wider ethical project of establishing a culture where the children are seen as human beings in their own right, as worth listening

to, where we do not impose our own knowledge and categorizations before children have posed their questions and made their own hypotheses. (1999, p. 137)

Early childhood research that seeks children's perspectives on their world (e.g., MacNaughton, 2003; MacNaughton & Smith, 2005; O'Kane, 2000) is part of bringing children's right to participate to life. However, in our efforts as researchers to honor children's right to participate in a research project we are currently conducting, we have confronted several challenges about how best to conceptualize and enact children's participation in research. We draw on those challenges in this chapter to engender further discussion about what a rights-based approach to children and child-friendly research could look like in the early childhood field.

Conceptualizing Child Participation in Research: A Question of Knowledge–Power Relations

The increased interest in children's rights has generated debate about how best to conceptualize and enact child participation in several spheres of public life, including local government (see, for instance, CREATE Foundation, 2000b). Several models of children's participation in policy making and governance have emerged in recent years (e.g., Arnstein, 1969; Fajerman, 2001; Hart, 1992; Holdsworth, 2000; Mason & Urquhart, 2001; Reimer, 2003; Shephard & Treseder, 2002). However, the CREATE Foundation cautions:

> There is no simple prescription for enhancing participation. To impose uniformity or to simply rely on one model is counter-productive because children and young people are not all the same. The participatory process is one that continually evolves and changes to meet the needs of individual children and young people as they receive a service ... children and young people may move between the different ways of participating, even within the same process, dependent on circumstances. (2000a, p. 7)

We have reviewed these different models of child participation elsewhere (Hughes & Smith, 2005) and here we draw on aspects of that review to identify issues for (re-)considering children's participation in research from a rights-based perspective.

Arnstein's (1969) "ladder of citizen participation," a common yet contentious model of children's participation, has spawned many derivatives. For example, Hart's (1992) adaptation of Arnstein (1969) identified eight different forms of children's participation in projects. Each form of participation is represented by a "rung" on a ladder that identifies the degree of power and control that children and adults assume in a project. Hart uses the ladder metaphor to argue that the bottom rung of the ladder ("manipulation") is the least desirable form of children's participation in a project. Manipulation is present when adults influence children to participate in an adult initiated and run project. The top rung of Hart's (1992) ladder ("control") represents the most desirable form of participation. Children are in control of a project if they initiate it and direct it. Whilst Hart's (1992) model has been criticized for placing "more value for one type of participation over another" (Burfoot, 2003, p. 44), it points to the different knowledge-power dynamics that can be produced in seeking to honor children's right to participation in decisions and processes that affect them.

Applied to the research context, research projects initiated and run by adults could manipulate children to achieve adult needs and goals, such as writing a chapter like this. Cannella (1998) and Hart (1992) challenge us to think about how knowledge-power relations operate when children are the researched. Hart's (1992) ladder challenges us to ask: Could we design research in which the knowledge-power relations are directed more strongly by children? Can children initiate and direct research? What would this look like? Is child initiated and directed research the only ethical way to engage children in research?

Fajerman's (2001, p. 8) adaptation of Arnstein's ladder adds further nuances to a consideration of the knowledge-power dynamics that operate when children participate in research projects. He identifies four different levels of child participation that we have adapted to the research context. Our adaptation of his work identifies four axes of research participation by children, each of which expresses a different set of knowledge-power dynamics. Those four axes of research participation are as follows:

Axis 1—Children are assigned to an adult-initiated project, but informed. Adults decide on the research project and adults volunteer children to participate in it. Research protocols focus on ensuring that children understand what is required of them in the research project, that they know who decided to involve them, and why. Adults respect the young people's views by seeking those views as a key part of the data gathering.

Axis 2—Adults initiate projects and share decisions with children. Adults have the initial research idea, but they involve children in every step of planning and implementing it. Children can volunteer to be involved or withdraw. Not only are children's views considered as research data, but also children are involved in making the decisions about how the research project will progress.

Axis 3—Children are consulted and informed. The project is designed and run by adults, but the children are consulted about the shape of the project in all stages. The children are helped to understand the process fully, and their opinions are taken seriously in how the research evolves.

Axis 4—Children initiate and direct research. Children have the initial idea about what they would like to research and decide how the project is to be carried out. Adults are available to the children but do not take charge.

Using this conceptualization of child participation, the knowledge-power relations between adults and children shift along an axis in which adult knowledge about research questions and process is privileged to an axis in which child knowledge about research questions and processes is privileged. Fajerman (2001) has challenged us to ask if including children's views as data in our research sufficiently honors children's rights in the research project. Holdsworth (2000) reiterates the challenge. He distinguished between the "voice" and "agency" of children who become involved in decisions about matters affecting them, stating:

> These are issues that are concerned, not with questions of whether young people have anything important to say, nor with the capacity of young people to speak up, but whether anyone is listening seriously. (Holdsworth, 2000, p. 253)

How seriously should qualitative researchers in early childhood listen to children in the conduct of their research? Is it possible to produce research that pushes at the knowledge-power relations between children and adults in ways that balance them increasingly toward children?

Researching Within a Child Rights Framework: Insights From an Australian Research Project

The research processes and case studies that we use in this chapter to explore the possibilities of taking a children's rights approach draw from a research project titled, *Preschool children's understandings of cultural and racial diversity*. It began in 2004, and it is funded by an Australian Research Council grant. The project is studying 60 preschool children from differing cultural and "racial" backgrounds to explore how they construct their cultural and "racial" understandings over a 24-month period.

The project seeks to answer four main questions:

1. What relationships exist between preschool children's understandings of cultural and "racial" diversity and their own gender, class, and ethnic identities?
2. What factors influence preschool children's cultural and "racial" understandings over time?
3. How can these relationships and understandings best be theorized?
4. What are the implications of what has been learned for early education curricula?

Drawing on feminist, poststructuralist, and postcolonial theories about identity formation in preschoolers (aged 3–5 years) and influenced by the calls for children's voice to inform our knowledge about them, we are studying how young children construct cultural and "racial" identities by talking with them about these issues. We are centering their voice in the research data (Axis 1 of our adaptation of Fajerman's [2001] levels of participation). However, we have also attempted to insert their voice into the research process in an effort to build more "child-friendly" research that responds to the challenges that the child participation movement (e.g., Fajerman, 2001; Hart, 1992) is bringing to us and that pushes us to other axes of child participation.

In this chapter we focus on three ways in which we have begun to do this in our research protocols. They are:

1. Allowing children to shape their research identities by choosing their psuedonyms
2. Centering children's choices during data collection by honoring their right to withdraw data
3. Centering children's efforts to direct research techniques by allowing their agenda to dominate interviews

In what follows, we illustrate how we have attempted more "child-friendly" research through these practices, and we raise questions about where this has left us as researchers. We began by attempting to give voice to children in and through the research process, and we are now attempting to focus on shifting the axis of knowledge/power in the research process toward children.

Efforts to Shift the Power/Knowledge Axis in the Research Process

Our research project was designed within ethical protocols approved by the university's Human Research Ethics Committee. To a large extent, these ethical protocols produced a research project that slipped and slid between two axes of knowledge/power relations between the adults and children. Adults (us as researchers) decided on the design of the research project, and the children's parents volunteered them for the project. Children's participation was conceptualized as "voice" in the data gathering of the project. However, as indicated above, at several points in the project we attempted to engage differently and bring the other axes of participation into sight.

Attempting Research Participation:
Axis 2—Children Shaping Research Identities

Whilst the research project *Children's constructions of racial and cultural diversity* was our idea, we did try to find spaces in which children could shape the research and thus we could begin to work across different axes of child participation in the research. One of the first opportunities to do this came when we explained to the children the role of pseudonyms in a research project.

Working within the first axis of participation (*children are informed within an adult initiated project*), children were informed about what a pseudonym was and why it was used in research. However, we also invited them to choose their pseudonym. This simple effort toward shifting the child participation axis in the research project brought us our first challenge. The challenge focused on the extent to which we could or should or would allow children to shape their identities in the research.

Pseudonyms: An Ethical Protection or Stripping Identity?

It was agreed as part of the ethics approval in the University of Melbourne's Human Ethics application that the children participating in the project would have pseudonyms. This is standard procedure to maintain children's right to confidentiality. It is also a widely applied ethical requirement for research more broadly. As Kumar states, "It is unethical to identify an individual respondent" (1996, p. 194).

Whilst adhering to this principle and recognizing that children can make decisions in their own right, we felt that the children also had a right to decide how they would be identified when research was reported. In each of the participating centers, the names children took generally derived from popular culture. For the girls, Barbie and her personas (e.g., Barbie Princess) were the most popular. For the boys, superheroes such as Spiderman and characters from children's shows such as *Bob the Builder* and *Buzz Lightyear of Star Command* predominated.

Whereas we may not have chosen these names for ourselves, they were not surprising choices, and their gendered nature was barely remarkable given what we know about young children's gendering in the early years (see Mac-Naughton, 2001d). However, one child's reaction to being asked to "rename" himself for the research was noteworthy.

Kylie (a member of the research team) was working with a group of twenty-three children in an inner urban long day care center. Twelve of the children were Vietnamese-Australian, and 9 were Chinese-Australian. The group included one Anglo-Australian child and one Greek-Australian child. After talking with the children about what a pseudonym was, Kylie asked the children to choose their pseudonym. As children told her the names they wanted, she wrote them down. The chosen names included Barbie, Fairy, Spiderman, and several animal names, including Tiger. However, when it was James's turn to tell Kylie his chosen pseudonym, he stood up and said:

James. No my name is James. That's my name.

Kylie assured James that he didn't have to choose a name just then and continued gathering names from the rest of the group. In thinking about James's strong desire to keep his name, Kylie reflected on the connections between his Chinese-Australian background, his "Western" name, and group acceptance.

She wondered if James's decision was culturally embedded in discourses of whiteness that produced an anglicized name as preferable to a Chinese name. Was Kylie asking James to give up a name that made him acceptable within the broader social context? Was his "Western" name necessary to his identity as an acceptable Australian? As Ang (2003) reminds us, "white/Western hegemony is not a random psychological aberration but the systematic consequence of a global historical development over the last 500 years" (p. 197). She further argues that "the hierarchical binary divide between white/non-white and Western/non-Western should be taken into account as a master-grid framing the potentialities of, and setting limits to, all subjectivities and struggles" (p. 199). Is it possible to believe that in contemporary Australia, any child could be free from the effects of the hierarchical binaries produced by white/Western hegemony in knowing themselves and making choices in their daily lives?

In a second research center, Karina (also a research team member) worked with one child who became anxious about the prospect of being "pseudonymed." His anxiety gains additional meaning if you place it beside a conversation that he had with Karina about his name. In this conversation, he spoke of how his full name connected him to his father and that his father chose his name. He felt that a change of name would somehow disconnect him from his family. His sense of identity is connected and constructed with his name as a tangible connection to this family and his father. This sense of identity and family connection may provide an important difference for him within a peer group of boys who shared similar white cultural backgrounds to each other and who often excluded him.

These two moments in the initial stages of the research project raised conflicting questions about the right of children to be in control of "naming" themselves, their cultural identities (MacNaughton, 2004), and their right to confidentiality in and through the research project. Does James have a choice not to have a pseudonym, when adults believe he should and must to secure his right to confidentiality? How does this adult-determined right born of adult responsibilities to ensure children are secure and protected connect with his right to his name? As Kylie reflected on her reaction to James's refusal to choose a pseudonym, she found it hard to disconnect it from knowledge-power relations in the research:

> Was my surprise at James not wanting to choose a name a result of being drawn back into a discourse where the child is a participant and has choices only within the paradigms and rules that I as an "expert" researcher set "in the best interests of the child"?

As a Chinese-Australian child, how much was James's name bound with his identity and his capacity to locate himself within his family, within the group of children at his center, and within the hierarchical binaries of white/non-white, Western/non-Western?

Pseudonyms: A Site Through Which Children Attempt to Shape Research

Our efforts at involving children in the research process by asking them to choose a pseudonym had varying effects. At times, it may have acted more as a point of disrespect than one of honoring children's rights. Children's names may connect them to discourses in particular ways that may speak of the struggles in belonging or acceptance. As DuGay, Evans, and Redman (2000) argue, discourse is central to identity construction:

> Distinguishing features of the [subject-of-language approach to identity] include the idea that identities are constituted through the reiterative power of discourse to produce that which it also names and regulates. (p. 2)

To take young children's right to self-name from them in the name of research confidentiality makes it difficult to move beyond a model of child participation in research that rests on adult control and toward a more child-friendly set of knowledge-power dynamics. As researchers, it is easy to position children as pliable subjects we can "empower" through our efforts to reshape research. However, the two children who refused to be "renamed" in our research project show that children can and do make concerted efforts to shape the research contexts and disrupt those knowledge/power relations that position adult worlds as privileged. These two children were aware and protective of interconnections and relationships outside the research site, and their names symbolized and reflected these. For these children, the practice of choosing pseudonyms was an experience in disconnection and a challenge to their identities. What does this mean for researchers? We generally honor an adult's choice to refuse a pseudonym. Should we honor a child's? By not honoring the child's right to refuse a pseudonym, we slide inevitably toward reestablishing the research as an adult-controlled and initiated project. How possible is it to avoid this?

Rethinking Choice in Research Participation:
Axis 1—Centering Children's Voice and Choice During Data Collection

In the initial stages of the project, children were asked to draw themselves and their friends in order for us to learn how they named and described "race." They were given colored and skin-toned pencils and asked to draw themselves and their friends. We asked the children to name the colors of skin, hair, eyes, and lips that they chose to use in their drawings. We audio-recorded these sessions and asked the children if we could take a photograph or scanned image of their drawings for the research. We had decided that another way to shift the child participation axis toward children was to ensure that they consented to our taking any data they generated; this included their drawings. On the assumption that not all children would be happy for us to remove their drawings for scanning, our fallback position was to use a digital camera to record their drawings, thus leaving them with their physical drawing. Yet again, their response to this effort by us to reshape knowledge/power relations brought challenges to us as researchers. We faced the question, how would we balance children's right to keep or withdraw data against our need/desire for their data?

Children's Data: Ours or Theirs?

Kylie was working with Tiger, a 3-year-old girl who talked about herself using her second language, English. Vietnamese was her first language. Initially Tiger did not want to interact with Kylie. When Kylie entered a play area, she moved from it but watched Kylie carefully from afar. Over a 3-week period Tiger appeared to become more comfortable with Kylie. She began to stand next to Kylie looking at and listening to what Kylie did. Kylie was excited when Tiger accepted her invitation to participate in the interview. Tiger spent 20 minutes drawing herself, looking in the mirror, and choosing colors to portray herself. Kylie was drawn into the excitement of collecting Tiger's data and had already begun imagining how her work might be used in the project *before* Tiger had finished. When Tiger completed her drawing the conversation unfolded in this way:

Kylie: Tiger, can I take your drawing with me to scan and take a copy of it, and then I will bring it back next week?

Tiger: No.

Kylie: I have brought my camera today. Can I take a photo of the drawing instead?

Tiger: No.

Tiger jumped up from the table and ran to her bag, which was in her locker in the bathroom. She put the drawing in her bag, and she then returned to play in the home corner.

Tiger's refusal to allow us to have her drawing raised important issues for us about the right of children to be in control of their research data and their right to refuse participation. Ethical engagement in researching with adults or children requires that we gain their permission to collect and use the information that they share with us as researchers. As Kumar (1996) emphasizes:

> In every discipline it is considered unethical to collect information without the knowledge of participants, their informed willingness, and expressed consent. (p. 192)

However, when working with young children, it has been traditional to rely on the informed consent of children's parents, rather than the children themselves. Young children especially are often not deemed "competent" to give consent, and/or their consent is not seen as necessary once parents or caregivers have consented on their behalf.

By attempting to frame our research from within a child rights perspective, we had grappled with reframing what informed consent might mean. For instance, can children give informed consent before they have spoken or acted? Children do not necessarily know what they are going to say or do or what the consequences of their actions might be (MacNaughton & Smith, 2005). Whilst we, as a research team, consistently asked children for permission to gather data from them, we always sought this permission prior to children knowing what data they might produce. For instance, we would ask questions such as: Would you like to draw a picture with me today? Do you want to come and talk with me now? I wanted to talk about friends and you as well, is this okay? and Can I record this?

The implications of seeking consent to take data prior to their production became apparent with Tiger. She had consented to join the research process and she agreed to join Kylie in drawing. Should this mean that she loses ownership of the data because she has consented to our recording them? Or, does she have the right to refuse access to any data she produces? We do not deny adults the right to withdraw data during the research process. What does this mean for data collection protocols and processes with children?

Tiger's decision to say "no" to Kylie helps us to further explore knowledge/power relations between the researched child and the adult researcher. It also raises questions about knowledge/power relations between the classed, gendered, and racialized researched child and adult research. In any form of transformative or rights-framed research, it is critical to consider how the researchers' own subjectivities and positionings may support or disrupt oppressive relationships that exist outside of the research site and how these may affect and structure the relationships within the research process and with participants.

There has been a long history of discussion within research literature that argues that class, "race"/cultural, and gender differences, oppression, and/or discrimination that structures the lives of individuals and communities outside the research site are often mirrored within the research site (St. Pierre & Pillow, 2001). These differences, oppression, and discrimination operate at multiple sites and across multiple dimensions at any given research moment. As researchers attempting to frame our research work with young children with a child rights perspective, we must work to recognize and disrupt these forces. As Agger (1998) discussed:

Feminists, like proponents of multiculturalism, argue that it is wrong to identify class as the only relevant dimension along which people are exploited. They argue that gender and race are structuring dimensions of inequality in their own right. Hence, multicultural theorists argue that class, race, and gender form a theoretical trinity that should guide all theorizing and research. (p. 101)

Within this research moment, Kylie recognized these tensions in her reflection, asking to what extent Tiger's reaction might be linked to her gender, race, and class. Taking the stance that class, race, and gender must guide all theorizing and research also raises further points for reflection on our research.

How may have Tiger's experiences of culture/class/gender affected how she saw the researcher? How may have Tiger's experiences of culture/gender/class constructed how she saw her participation in the research and what she was willing to consent to and participate in? How do the research team members' cultural/class/gender backgrounds influence how they see the research and the possibilities for relationships within the research? Asking these questions is part of doing transformative research (Maynard & Purvis, 1995), and to ignore them is to ignore what structures all dimensions of inequality in our lives and in the lives of young children.

Participation: A Site Through Which Children Attempt to Shape Research

As researchers, it is easy to position consent to participate as a single, simple, concrete, and practical process that involves asking children for permission to document their lives, then receiving this permission or not. We can overlook the need to consider the discursive positionings of the researched and the researcher and how these may influence research processes and make consent a complex process of negotiation between researcher and researched. Tiger's expressed desire to maintain control of her data causes us to reflect on the knowledge/power relations embedded in consent. How do we as researchers shift knowledge/power relationships so that child participation is pushed closer to the axis where children and adults share decisions about research involvement and processes? What does this mean for research and researchers? Would you honor a child's right to refuse you access to data after he or she has given you initial consent? How might our gender/class/"race"/culture positionings influence children and how and why they give and remove consent?

Rethinking Research Participation:
Axis 1— Centering Children's Right and Voice to Direct

During the initial one-on-one interviews with the children in the project, we wanted to talk with them about friendships. We asked them who they could and couldn't be friends with and why, who they desired and who was undesirable as a friend and why, and what made a good friend. We also wanted to talk with children about who they were and their family's cultural backgrounds. Children were asked if they wanted to join us for the interview and if they were aware of their right to refuse. During the interview, we attempted to gain the information we wanted whilst trying to allow children's concerns and interests to shape the interview. Clearly, we as researchers constructed the interviews. However, we did attempt during the interviews to shift the axis of child participation in small ways that lessened our adult direction and control of the interview. Again, this was not without its challenges.

Interviews: Adult or Child Agendas?

The initial interviews led Karina into her first lengthy conversation with Bob the Builder. Bob the Builder was a 3-year-old boy who spoke Italian and English. He was fascinated with the camera and voice recorder that Karina had introduced to the children prior to her first interviews with them.

Bob the Builder often spoke with the center staff of his unhappiness at being separated from his Mama and his Nonna and of his difficulties in establishing satisfying relationships with other children. As Karina had often observed him watching the other children from the sidelines of their play, she was excited by the prospect of talking with Bob the Builder about friendships and what they meant for him. He also often discussed his Nonna's life in Italy, drawing on both his Italian and English words. Karina thought that her interview with Bob the Builder would provide fascinating data about the difficulties involved in forging friendships between children from different ethnic and cultural backgrounds and about a young child's capacity to describe and understand his cultural background.

As the interview progressed, it became clear that what Karina had expected and hoped for was not to be. It also became clear that the questions we wanted to ask Bob the Builder were either problematic for him and/or of little interest to him. Bob the Builder was not interested in answering Karina's interview questions, and he actively avoided answering questions concerning his friendships at the center. For example:

Bob the Builder: ... I used to collect rubbish at the market.

And later in the interview:

Karina: Who would you like to be friends with here? Is there anyone you would like to be friends with and you're not?
Bob the Builder: Look at that there (pointing to an illustration of a flower on the cover of the pencil packet)

As the interview progressed Bob the Builder's interview agenda became totally focused on how he could learn to use the voice recorder as a tool to develop friendships within the group. The voice recorder was a highly desirable object in the group and Bob the Builder knew this. He had realized its potential as a pathway to building his longed-for friendships. The children would want to talk with him if he held the much-desired research voice recorder. Bob the Builder used the final part of his interview with Karina to insistently focus on this and how, if he was "pressing the button," he could approach and listen to other children:

Karina: What do you do with friends here?
Bob the Builder: Well, friends could press the recorders.

And later:

Bob the Builder: No. I want to (inaudible—points to the other children). You press the button, and I see what the kids say.

Whilst Bob the Builder avoided Karina's direct questions about friendships, his fascination with the voice recorder pushed the interview toward his friendship issues and illuminated his views about how to gain entry to the group. Karina's "interview" with Bob the Builder did not follow the linear rational model interview in which researcher asks the researched a question, notes the response, and then moves to the next question. To insist on this model with Bob the Builder would have silenced his interview agenda and ignored his right and capacity to direct the content and shape of a data collection moment in our project. By attempting to honor Bob the Builder's interview agenda, Karina entered a lengthy, changing, nonlinear, and uncertain conversation in which Bob the Builder used our research tools and research space as an opportunity to change a part of his daily life that was problematic and unfair.

Where does this leave our research questions—the questions we have been funded to answer? How could we account for our research findings if children reshaped every interview to ignore our questions? Researchers and children each have imperatives that drive their relationships with each other and that arise outside of the research relationship they create when they are faced with each other. It seems unthinkable to allow children to shape research agendas and processes at a time when funding for early childhood research is increasingly constricted and restricted by an increasingly narrow range of concerns about "what works" to improve child outcomes.

Yet, how can child outcomes be improved in early childhood programs if the research we conduct within them acts as a form of ethical violence toward children by ignoring, silencing, or redirecting their daily concerns and issues? For instance, what were the ethics of asking Bob the Builder hard questions about friendships and exclusion when we had little power and/or opportunity beyond the research interview to work with Bob the Builder and the other children to challenge and/or disrupt unfair group dynamics? Did Bob the Builder only agree to the interview because it gave him access to a much-sought-after piece of equipment in his center and to a much-desired space—the space of talking with Karina? To what extent did he realize that in entering that space he would expose himself to questions about friendships? Against these concerns, Karina's attempts to allow Bob the Builder to direct the interview showed him to be agentic and knowing, capable of resistance to and of reshaping the research agenda we had set for him. It showed him deeply engaged with the issues of his life and with strategies to improve outcomes for himself. To this extent, he disrupted the child research participation axis in which we had initially positioned him, and he attempted to reshape the knowledge/power relations between adult research and researched child. He did this to improve his peer group relationships.

Challenges and Possibilities for Building "Child Friendly" Research: Some Final Reflections

It is extremely difficult to imagine how research would work if we conceptualized children's participation in it along our fourth axis of child participation (*children initiate and direct research*). To create a research project with children that received funding and whose processes and findings were seen as valid and valuable to policy makers seems an impossible dream in the contemporary Australian educational research landscape. To imagine research partnerships with children in which they determined what child-friendly research looked like is likely to bring with it more questions than answers. Our small steps to enact such research produced pointers, possibilities, and challenges. In engaging with these challenges and sharing them through this chapter, our hope is to generate discussion about the almost impossible. Yet, to not engage with the almost impossible is to settle our research comfortably within axes of child participation that barely touch the inequitable knowledge/power relationships that are produced when adults are the researchers and children the researched. Our concern for research that is transformative rests on our concern for greater social justice in this world. For this reason, we have no choice but to try to imagine and enact the almost impossible.

References

Ackroyd J., & Pilkingham, A. (1999). Childhood and the construction of ethnic identities in a global age: A dramatic encounter. *Childhood*, 6(4): 443–454.

Agger, B. (1998). *Critical social theories. An introduction.* Boulder, CO: Westview Press.

Ang, I. (2003). I'm a feminist but … "Other" women and postnational feminism. In R. Lewis & S. Mills (Eds.), *Feminist postcolonial theory: A reader.* Edinburgh: Edinburgh University Press.

Arnstein, S. R. (1969). A ladder of citizen participation. *Journal of the American Planning Association,* 35(4), 216–224.

Bishop, R. (2005). Freeing ourselves from Neocolonial domination in research: A Kaupapa Māori approach to creating knowledge. In N. K. Denzin & Y. S. Lincoln (Eds.), *The Sage handbook of qualitative research* (3rd ed., pp. 109–138). Thousand Oaks, CA: Sage.

Burfoot, D. (2003). Children and young people's participation: Arguing for a better future. *Youth Studies Australia, 22*(3), 44–51.

Campbell, S., Buchannen, V. S., Jones, K., Saitta, S., Smith, K., & MacNaughton, G. (2001, July). *Re-creating intellectual work in early childhood: Stories from the academy and from the field.* Paper presented at the meeting of the Australian Early Childhood Association Biennial Conference, Excellence for Children, Sydney.

Candy, J., & Butterworth, D. (1998). Through children's eyes: The experience of migration to Australia. *Australian Journal of Early Childhood, 23*(3), 14–19.

Cannella, G. S. (1998). *Deconstructing early childhood education: Social justice and revolution.* New York: Peter Lang.

Christensen, P., & James, A. (Eds.). (2000). *Research with children.* London: Falmer Press.

Corrie, L., & Leito, N. (1999). The development of wellbeing: Young children's knowledge of their support networks and social competence. *Australian Journal of Early Childhood, 24*(3), 25–31.

CREATE Foundation. (2000a). Children and young people's participation in practice. Retrieved January 21, 2001, from http://www.community.nsw.gov.au/enact/ENACT.HTM

CREATE Foundation. (2000b). Consultation and participation models for children and young people in care. Retrieved September 1, 2004, from http://svc250.bne115v.serverweb.com/create_world/ctw2004/docs/con_part_models_report.doc

Dahlberg, G., Moss, P., & Pence, A. (1999). *Beyond quality in early childhood education and care: Postmodern perspectives.* London: Falmer Press.

Denzin, N. K. (2005). Emancipatory discourses and the ethics and politics of interpretation. In N. K. Denzin & Y. S. Lincoln (Eds.), *The Sage handbook of qualitative research* (3rd ed., pp. 933–958). Thousand Oaks, CA: Sage.

Denzin, N. K., & Lincoln, Y. S. (2005a). Preface. In N. K. Denzin & Y. S. Lincoln (Eds.), *The Sage handbook of qualitative research* (3rd ed., pp. ix–xix). Thousand Oaks, CA: Sage.

Denzin, N. K. & Lincoln, Y. S. (2005b). Introduction. The discipline and practice of qualitative research. In N. K. Denzin & Y. S. Lincoln (Eds.), *The Sage handbook of qualitative research* (3rd ed., pp. 1–32). Thousand Oaks, CA: Sage.

DuGay, P., Evans, J., & Redman, P. (2000). General introduction. In P. DuGay, J. Evans, & P. Redman (Eds.), *Identity: A reader* (pp. 1–5). London: Sage.

Fajerman, L. (2001). *Children are service users too: A guide to consulting children and young people.* Plymouth, England: Save the Children Publications.

Farrell, A. (Ed.). (2005). *Exploring ethical research with children.* Milton Keynes, England: Open University Press.

Fueur, M., Towne, L., & Shavelson, R. (2002). Scientific culture and educational research. *Educational Researcher 31*(8), 4–14.

Hart, R. (1992). *Children's participation: From tokenism to citizenship.* Florence, Italy: UNICEF International Child Development Centre.

Holdsworth, R. (2000). *Taking young people seriously means giving them serious things to do.* Paper presented at the Taking Children Seriously Workshop, July, University of Western Sydney, Macarthur.

Hughes, P. (2001). Paradigms, methods and knowledge. In G. MacNaughton, S. A. Rolfe, & I. Siraj-Blatchford (Eds.), *Doing early childhood research: International perspectives on theory and practice* (pp. 31–55). Crows Nest, NSW: Allen and Unwin.

Hughes, P., & Smith, K. (2005). *Human rights or citizens' rights? Children and public decision-making.* Paper presented at the Chinese Welfare Institute Conference, 28-30 October Shanghai, China.

Kaomea, J. (2003). Reading erasures and making the familiar strange: Defamiliarising methods of research in formerly colonised and historically oppressed communities. *Educational Researcher, 32*(2), 14–25.

Kumar, R. (1996). *Research methodology: A step-by-step guide for beginners.* Sydney: Longman.

Ladson-Billings, G., & Donnor, J. (2005). The moral activist role of critical race theory scholarship. In N. K. Denzin & Y. S. Lincoln (Eds.), *The Sage handbook of qualitative research* (3rd ed., pp. 279–302). Thousand Oaks, CA: Sage.

Lewis, A., & Lindsay, G. (Eds.). (2000). *Researching children's perspectives.* Milton Keynes, England: Open University Press.

MacNaughton, G. (2001a). "Blushes and birthday parties": Telling silences in young children's constructions of "race." *Journal for Australian Research in Early Childhood Education, 8*(1), 41–51.

MacNaughton, G. (2001b). Silences and subtexts in immigrant and non-immigrant's children's understandings of diversity. *Childhood Education, 78*(1), 30–36.

MacNaughton, G. (2001c). Dolls for equity: Foregrounding children's voices in learning respect and unlearning unfairness. *New Zealand Council for Educational Research Early Childhood Folio,* pp. 27–30.

MacNaughton, G. (2001d). *Rethinking gender in early childhood education.* Sydney: Allen and Unwin.

MacNaughton, G. (2003). Eclipsing voice in research with young children. *Australian Journal of Early Childhood, 28*(1), 36–43.

MacNaughton, G. (2004). The politics of logic in early childhood research: A case of the brain, hard facts and trees. *Australian Educational Researcher, 31*(3), 87–104.

MacNaughton, G., & Smith, K. (2005). Exploring ethics and difference: The choices and challenges of researching with children. In A. Farrell (Ed.), *Exploring ethical research with children* (pp. 112–123). England: Open University Press.

Martello, J. (1999). In their own words: Children's perceptions of learning to write. *Australian Journal of Early Childhood, 24*(3), 32–37.

Mason, J., & Urquhart, R. (2001). Developing a model for participation by children in research on decision making. *Children Australia, 26*(4), 16–21.

Maynard, M., & Purvis, J. (1995). *Researching women's lives from a feminist perspective.* London: Taylor & Francis.

Moreton-Robinson, A. (2004). Whiteness, epistemology and indigenous representation. In A. Moreton-Robinson (Ed.), *Whitening race: Essays in social and cultural criticism* (pp. 75–88). Canberra, Australia: Aboriginal Studies Press.

Office of the High Commissioner of Human Rights. (2005). General comment Number 7. Implementing child rights in early childhood. OHCHR.

O'Kane, C. (2000). The development of participatory techniques: Facilitating children's view about decisions which affect them. In P. Christensen & A. James (Eds.), *Research with children: Perspectives and practices.* London: Falmer Press.

Olesen, V. (2005). Early millennial feminist qualitative research: Challenges and contours. In N. K. Denzin & Y. S. Lincoln (Eds.), *The Sage handbook of qualitative research* (3rd ed., pp. 235–278). Thousand Oaks, CA: Sage.

Redman, P. (2000). Introduction. In P. DuGay, J. Evans, & P. Redman (Eds.), *Identity: A reader* (pp. 9–13). London: Sage.

Reimer, E. C. (2003). A scaffold for participation in agency work. *Children Australia, 28*(3), 30–37.

Roberts, H. (1981). *Doing feminist research.* London: Routledge.

Shephard, C., & Treseder, P. (2002). *Participation – spice it up! Practical tools for engaging children and young people in planning and consultations.* Cardiff, England: Sage.

Smith, K. (2003). *Reconceptualising observation in early childhood settings.* Unpublished doctoral dissertation, University of Melbourne.

St. Pierre, E., & Pillow, W. (Eds.). (2001). *Working the ruins: Feminist poststructural theory and methods in education.* London: Routledge.

Stanley, L., & Wise, S. (1983). *Breaking out.* London: Routledge.

Tuhiwai Smith, L. (2005). On tricky ground: Researching the native in the age of uncertainty. In N. K. Denzin & Y. S. Lincoln (Eds.), *The Sage handbook of qualitative research* (3rd ed., pp. 85–108). Thousand Oaks, CA: Sage.

UNICEF. (2004). *The Child Friendly Cities initiative.* Retrieved August 16, 2004, from http://www.childfriendlycities.org/about/the_initiative.html

11
Decolonizing Research in Cross-Cultural Contexts

BETH BLUE SWADENER

Arizona State University

KAGENDO MUTUA

University of Alabama

This chapter draws from the experiences of two researchers who have strug-gled with issues of working in postcolonial settings and have sought to better understand the possibilities for "decolonizing" research, specifically quali-tative research, in various cross-cultural contexts. The first author has done work in sub-Saharan Africa for the past 20 years, with focus on connecting early childhood policies and family experiences to larger neoliberal global-izing forces. The second author is Kenyan, does research in special education and disability studies, and has completed qualitative research in Kenya and the United States. Our chapter attempts to share some of the theory and writ-ing of indigenous scholars that we have found most helpful in situating decol-onizing research and includes personal narratives that describe our journeys and related concerns. We also highlight issues of power and voice in research with children and youth and ways in which qualitative studies of/with chil-dren and families can take a more anticolonial stance.

As researchers working with children and youth and their families in this era, it behooves all of us to continually engage with and resist the positivistic impulse that has strategically positioned itself in both research and practice today. During this era of high stakes testing and No Child Left Behind, in which the emphasis is on the quantification of outcomes of *all* children and of *all* educational endeavors, spaces for the articulation of the more subtle or "softer" outcomes of education have been diminished. Likewise, space for conducting and pursuing qualitative research endeavors is at risk for erasure by this positivistic impulse. More than any other time in recent history, the role of the university in the validation of what counts as research and the intersection of the use of the "rigorous" (read: positivist) methodologies and funding has become clearly more linear and unambiguous. Furthermore, the silencing of indigenous voices and epistemologies, which are quite often not positivistic in orientation, is also unabashed. Given these sociopolitical factors that are intersecting at the site of education and educational research, those doing qualitative research, and specifically researchers conducting qualitative research that has a direct bearing on children and youth and their families, must be mindful of the colonizing tendency of this impulse.

The project of decolonization has been viewed and interpreted variously, but in this chapter we highlight the ways in which decolonization is about the process of valuing, reclaiming, and foregrounding indigenous voices and epistemologies, with emphasis on doing research with children and youth in cross-cultural contexts. It is important to emphasize that for the purpose of this discussion "cross-cultural contexts" refer to conducting research in settings outside of the United States, as well as in nondominant cultural contexts within the U.S. (i.e., contexts in which the researcher would describe her/himself as an outsider). We suggest the broadening of the meaning of colonization to encompass the cultural imperialism of certain academic ventures that are meted out against indigenous cultures within a country, endeavors whose end result is a disturbance in the basic core of the indigenous culture. We seek to broaden the understanding of colonization beyond the geopolitical and sociohistorical experience of colonialism that often tends to limit and contain colonization within a specific time and space. We want to foreground the form of colonization that is sociocultural in nature, which often masks its political domination.

What is missed when colonization is limited only to its geopolitical and historical experience are the many similar experiences whose impacts on marginalized people the world over correspond to those produced at the site of geohistorical colonialism. We do not wish to appear to suggest a dichotomization of colonization as political or cultural because the two are intricately entwined, and both lead to outcomes for colonized Others that include cultural subjugation, limited access to position of subject in the narration of one's experiences, and the loss of the ability to chart one's life-course. Thus, we see decolonizing research resisting the lures and mires of postcolonial reason that position certain players within postcoloniality as more "valid" postcolonial researchers/scholars. Rather, within decolonizing projects, the possibilities of forging cross-cultural partnerships with, between, and among indigenous researchers and "allied others" (Rogers & Swadener, 1999) and working collaboratively on common goals that reflect anticolonial sensibilities in action are important facets of decolonization.

Issues in Decolonizing Research in Positivist Times

For a number of years, we have grappled with various issues entailed in decolonizing research, and our writings and presentations at conferences have reflected our evolving ideas on what decolonizing research is all about. As our thinking and theorizing has evolved on the subject, so has our increased appreciation of how much the prevailing political ethos plays into educational research. For instance, we, like several other scholars (see, e.g., Lather, 2004; Cannella & Lincoln, 2004; Ryan & Hood, 2004), recognize that within an era of growing neo-conservatism in the U.S., particularly as evidenced in the current forced adherence to neo-positivism in educational research, increased demand in education for standardization, documentation of outcomes, and the deployment of other accountability measures, spaces for the articulation or performance of decolonization and the use of other interpretative methodologies are at best radically reduced, if not altogether dismantled.

Within this prevailing political climate, as researchers working with children and their families as well as those further marginalized by disability, we grapple with how to represent their experiences in both valid and diverse ways that consider the heterogeneity inherent among children and families today. The push for ever-narrower methodological approaches (e.g., randomized assignment) that yield quantifiable data is problematic in a number of ways, as addressed in other sections of this volume. The current U.S. political climate not only dictates what is to count as valid research but also performs a positivistic litmus test to determine the fundability of a research project, at least from federal dollars. This privileging of particular methodologies is a colonizing move that makes assumptions about its ability to speak for all, on all subjects, and in all languages. Not only should such a sweeping political move be subjected to collective questioning, it should also require a sustained reflection on who/what is lost in its single-minded pursuit.

The universalization of ways of knowing and of the epistemologies that sustain those ways of knowing is an outcome of the current trend toward standardization of research methodologies. However, as stated earlier, there are no universals in knowledge that apply to all children and families. Instead, there are countless dynamic ways in which families define and constitute themselves today. Traditionally, positivist research has prescribed a static and fixed subject that, according to Serres with Latour (1995), spawned static systems of knowing and histories of being even though they claimed to describe a process of becoming. Indeed, a reversal to positivist notions of research and the re-centering of the scientific method threatens the progress made in research in terms of the articulation of the histories and experiences of indigenous/colonized groups whom traditional/positivist research has quite often denied agency.

Viewed within this larger sociopolitical context, decolonizing research offers counterhegemonic accounts of the experiences of groups that are quite often non-Western or variously labeled as indigenous, racial minorities, and disabled (read: colonized). Quite often, the epistemologies of such groups cannot be readily reflected or sustained by universalized measures of human experience (read: white or Euro-American experience). As researchers working with this dynamic population, which comprises children and families whose experiences and needs are many and diverse, we find ourselves needing to fight for survival within and against the colonizing tendencies of this neo-positivist trend.

Decolonizing Research: Putting Performance in Postcolonial Theory

In laying a theoretical foundation for decolonizing research, we draw on the works of postcolonial scholars including Eze (1997), Gandhi (1998), Mignolo (2000), Shohat (1992), Spivak (1993, 1999), and others to describe ways in which decolonizing research draws from and is based upon postcolonial theory and postcolonial studies. We argue that unlike postcolonial theory, decolonizing research goes beyond defining colonization solely in terms of its temporal and spatial dimensions (see, e.g., McLeod, 2000; Mihesuah, 2003), which often ignores the brutality of the material consequences of coloniality. Further, such a delimitation of coloniality implies that it is just a historical experience that is over and gone.

Decolonizing research argues for materialist and discursive connections within postcoloniality and lays open the technologies of colonization, including language (English language) as the medium of research representation (Skutnabb-Kangas, 2000), deployment of Western epistemologies (often in diametric opposition to indigenous epistemologies), deployment of methodological imperialism (as defined within the Western academy versus indigenous modes of inquiry, representation, and ways of knowing; L. T. Smith, 1999), and the determination of "valid" research questions (generated in the Western academy and "investigated" in indigenous contexts; Mutua & Swadener, 2004). Our aim in this section is to intersect qualitative research and postcolonial theory in ways that make possible the production of new spaces for recasting research in liberatory ways that foreground indigenous epistemologies and ways of knowing in the field. In particular, we aim at destabilizing the "center" of research and academic ways of knowing by reframing "the field" (Rogers & Swadener, 1999).

Increasingly, scholarship on decolonizing research emphasizes performativity. Not only is decolonizing research concerned with building a theoretical foundation for studies that claim to serve as decolonizing endeavors, but many researchers who advocate decolonizing methodologies (e.g., Kaomea, 2001; G. H. Smith, 2004; L. T. Smith, 1999; Warrior, 1995; Womack, 1999) are actively engaged performatively in decolonizing acts framed variously as activism, advocacy, or cultural reclamation. In terms of critical developments in the broad and often divergent area of "decolonizing research" and critical postcolonial paradigms in educational research, we would include indigenous "reclaiming" projects and research collectives in various cultural, national, and geopolitical contexts foregrounding indigenous researchers' concerns and voices. Indeed, in step with this expanding scholarship, growing numbers of conferences on indigenous scholarship, journals, and other venues are creating more openings for this dialogue. Such avenues are creating decolonizing spaces for the representation of indigenous epistemologies that are performative in style. They reflect indigenous expressions that go far beyond prevailing Western academic styles and venues for dissemination, including the centering of indigenous languages and modes of communication in song, oral storytelling, dance, poetry, and other cultural forms of expression.

Upon reviewing many publications considered to be exemplars of decolonizing research (Smith, 1999; Smith, 2005; Jankie 2004; Hamza, 2004; Cary and Mutua, 2005), as well as texts on research methods and methodology, it has become apparent that what makes research "decolonizing" or anticolonial is not an adherence to a specific research method or methodology. Of particular relevance to early childhood, according to Cannella and Viruru (2004) and others, is scholarship that questions the Western, patriarchal construction of gender, motherhood, and childhood, as well as much of the prevailing literature's framing of language and literacy. In other words, much of the early childhood literature has reified Anglo, middle-class values that may exclude nondominant and non-Western epistemologies and constructions of childhood, child rearing, heritage languages, and multiple interpretations of literacy. Soto and Swadener (2005) offer alternative strategies for interrogating research with children and youth and frame these issues in terms of power and voice as well as taking a decolonizing stance.

Decolonizing research does not constitute a single agreed-upon set of guidelines or methods, although several indigenous scholars have offered lists of minimal criteria to be met (e.g., Linda Tuhiwai Smith and Graham Hingangaroa Smith). Further, decolonizing research does not have a common definition. Indeed, having engaged with decolonizing research on a number of performative and theoretical levels as researchers, activists, and writers, we see the distinctive hallmarks of decolonizing research lying in the motives, concerns, and knowledge brought to the research process. We contend that decolonizing research is defined by certain themes and defining elements and concepts that arise when researchers engage in what they describe as decolonizing research versus research that studies coloniality or postcoloniality.

We would argue that decolonizing research is performative—it is enmeshed in activism. Maori researcher Graham Smith (e.g., 2004, 2005) has spoken and written in recent years against the use of the construct "decolonizing," arguing that it still foregrounds colonization, and other indigenous scholars have called for the use of "anticolonial" research as a more accurate descriptor of this endeavor. This example speaks to the issue of the performativity and continual interrogation of not only the process of research but also its outcomes. These recent moves in decolonizing illustrate ways in which scholars engaged in decolonizing research remain constantly mindful of the ways in which the process or outcomes of their research endeavors might reify hegemonic power structures, thereby creating marginality.

As an overarching schema, decolonizing research recognizes and works within the belief that non-Western knowledge forms are excluded from or marginalized in normative research paradigms, and therefore, non-Western/ indigenous voices and epistemologies are silenced and subjects lack agency within such representations. Further, decolonizing research recognizes as colonization the scripting and encrypting of a silent, inarticulate, and inconsequential research subject and how such encryptions legitimize oppression. Within this logic, decolonizing research is concerned not only with the non-Western research subject, but indeed with indigenous, racial minorities, and disabled subjects. Finally, decolonizing research as a performative act, individually and collectively, functions to highlight and advocate for the dismantling of both discursive and material oppression that is produced at the site of the encryption of the research subject as a "governable body" (Foucault, 1977).

Our Journeys Into Decolonizing Research

As we attempt to chart our journey to decolonizing research, we review the overall issues that are part of that collective journey, followed by examples of our individual narratives of how we have attempted to do decolonizing research with children and families in cross-cultural contexts. While we draw from postcolonial theory, we demonstrate the performativity that is inherent in decolonizing research and that more strongly connects theory with practice. We argue that in decolonizing research, a greater emphasis is placed on ways of "undoing", or minimally interrupting, the unidirectional power that flows from the researcher as the asker of the questions to the participants as the answerers of those questions, thereby locating the researcher at the apex in the knowledge production and the participants at the base as the passive respondents to research questions. Further, within our narratives, "the field" is deconstructed and reframed and a strong emphasis within its performativity is laid upon collaboration that blurs colonizing lines, including lines between researcher/researched, emic/etic, and academy/field. Within our personal narratives, we share the ways our work as qualitative researchers in early childhood and special education has caused us to confront issues of colonization and the ways in which we have tried to trouble the typical power relations of research.

Over the years at professional meetings, in informal spoken communications, and in our writing (e.g., Mutua & Swadener, 2004; Soto & Swadener, 2005; Swadener & Mutua, in press), one role that our work has played has been to raise questions regarding the dynamics, complexities, and contradictory nature of "decolonizing research." Issues raised have included questioning of whose agenda it is to decolonize research; who holds the power to name and how such power reifies existing power relations; who and how "scholarship" is legitimized; ways educational research creates "data plantations"; tensions between "indigenous insiders" versus etic researchers; exclusive availability of tools for decolonization only to indigenous researchers and whether this can be a shared process; reductive, binary categories (e.g., "developed" versus "developing," "First World" versus "Third World," "Western" versus "non-Western") and the dichotomization and polarization of discourses thereby reinscribing patterns of exploitation and privilege; subtle dynamics of "Third World" intellectuals working within the "First World" academy; role of funders in the de/colonization of research and the articulation of "valid" research questions; and how the discourse on decolonizing research might be colonized or appropriated. Given the complexities of the questions we have raised over the years, we have become more aware of our changing subject positions (as "indigenous"/"foreigner"/"insider"/"outsider") and the issues those changing subject positions bring to bear on the research process. Linda Smith (1999) also analyzes the contested/resisted roles of "native intellectuals" in postcolonial contexts.

> Currently the role of the "native" intellectual has been reformulated not in relation to nationalist or liberatory discourses but in relation to the "postcolonial" intellectual. Many intellectuals who position themselves as "postcolonial," move across the boundaries of indigenous and metropolitan, institution and community, politics and scholarship. Their place in the academy is still highly problematic. (p. 71)

Smith's criticisms of the "postcolonial" intellectual are important in drawing a distinction between postcolonial research and research that is decolonizing. Writing about postcoloniality, Leela Gandhi (1998) states that postcolonial works do not represent a unified unit, but rather what she refers to as a "cacophony of subaltern voices." While there is disparateness in postcolonial theorizing and postcolonial reason, it is hard to deny that the temporal and lived experience of geopolitical colonialism is filled with subaltern voices that are now allowing themselves and/or being allowed to speak. So it is not a bad thing that this is happening because these voices bring to bear issues and perspectives that were not considered, much less valued, in colonial research. On the other hand, decolonizing research is at least in part about resisting colonization in terms of its affirmation of indigenous epistemologies, the reclamation and affirmation of indigenous languages, and observance in the research process of indigenous customs.

Our work, which extends beyond research within indigenous contexts, recognizes that colonization in representation is more than a spatial-temporal experience. That colonization as a way of representing, producing/inscribing, and consuming the Other through the silencing and denial of agency extends beyond what are often constructed as the geo-spatial and historical experience of colonization. Hence, our work recognizes the same mechanisms and colonizing ways in certain research that studies, produces, and silences specific groups (e.g., persons with disabilities or children) through the ways it constructs and consumes knowledge and experiences about such groups. Therefore, in our work we recognize that decolonizing research extends to conducting research with groups, not exclusively in contexts where the geopolitical experience of colonization happened, but indeed among groups where colonizing research approaches are deployed. For example, we have written elsewhere about urban schools as "data plantations" and have noted the lack of power that children and persons with disabilities have as research "subjects."

In the remainder of this section, we each discuss our journeys as researchers and how we came to work with decolonizing discourses and collaborative methodologies. Our narratives highlight ways in which our experiences, while different, led us to a similar rethinking about the power of representation in texts that script, ascribe, and reify identities. Our narratives also highlight our theoretical and professional journeys within the U.S. academy from the standpoint of polarized identities such as "insider/outsider," "indigenous/foreigner," "citizen/alien," and our struggles with and resistance to those ascriptive identities. We use the narratives of our lived experiences to contextualize who we are or who we are constructed to be both in the U.S. academy and in contexts where we conduct our research, spaces that are not indeterminate or unsubscribed (Spivak, 1993). Further, we hope to uncover the texts and discourses that have scripted our identities. Of particular importance to this volume, we also focus on ways in which our work with children and families has confronted a number of colonizing patterns.

Beth. As a European American woman of lower middle class background and benefiting from an array of unearned privileges, I have actively interrogated ways in which my work may be reproducing colonial, exploitive, or oppressive patterns and relationships. My commitment has been strengthened by my work in "unlearning oppression" and participation in multi-racial alliances since the early 1980s, as well as by my activism in social justice movements from the early 1970s through the present. I have been doing research in sub-Saharan Africa since the mid-1980s, and have worked in high poverty, urban school, and preschool settings in the U.S. for the past 16 years.

Prior to using the language of decolonization, I spoke (and wrote) more about "authentic collaboration" or "partnership research," and attempted, in my collaborative work with classroom teachers and African colleagues, to foreground the voice and worldviews of such collaborators. I have also raised concerns about urban schools serving as "data plantations" that serve the researcher and exploit those in urban communities and schools, without sustained relationships being built or reciprocal possibilities explored.

My qualitative studies in early education began with a year-long ethnography of two culturally and linguistically diverse, fully inclusive child-care settings. I studied peer interactions across various "differences" as well as both the planned and informal curriculum. I was an immersed participant observer and had strong relationships with the children and teachers, particularly given the sustained time (lengthy, twice a week visits for 9 months) I spent in both settings. While I learned a great deal about the subtle dynamics of varying approaches to inclusionary practices, gender patterns in play and ways in which girls resisted certain gender role restrictions, I left that study feeling that I would like to work on a more equal footing with the teachers, in whose classrooms I "performed" research.

After a move to another university, my interests led directly to a 3-year collaborative video ethnography of a Friends Primary School, in which the teachers (a progressive group concerned with better facilitating children's social problem-solving and implementing a social justice curriculum) and I formulated research questions and I collected in-depth qualitative data informed by extensive videotaping in all classrooms and on the playground. The teachers wanted to produce a videotape that they could use for sharing their approach with other educators, so this was a culminating "product" of our collaborative work. Although I have published very little on this study, it provided an excellent foundation upon which to become more aware of the roles and limitation of collaborative research between university scholars and teachers engaging in participatory research.

Building on such a commitment to greater collaboration in my research, I then moved to a far more urban setting, where my work focused for over a decade on urban schooling issues, anti-bias curriculum, and strengthening alliances with diverse families and communities in teacher education and professional development. I completed another collaborative study, this time with Monica Miller Marsh, a kindergarten teacher in Cleveland, who did master's thesis research on her experiences of implementing many of the activities and approaches advocated in Derman-Sparks's (1989) *Anti-bias Curriculum*. While I did not videotape, I spent many hours in her classroom taking notes, informally interviewing children and parents, and discussing Monica's journal entries and reflections. This time, when we disseminated findings, Monica was first author or single author, and she completed a Ph.D. and has remained active in early childhood research. While neither of these longer-term qualitative studies could be described as "decolonizing" research, they did raise issues of power, voice, authorship, and audience.

My collaborative research with Kenyan colleagues in the mid-1990s was the first time I attempted to apply a discourse of decolonizing research and specifically engage in conversations with research colleagues on what it might mean to name ways in which various aspects of our work might be less colonizing. Doing cross-cultural or cross-national work in neo-colonial settings presents many ethical and methodological dilemmas, particularly when there is a conscious attempt to de-colonize the research (Gandhi, 1998; L. T. Smith, 1999). I had been somewhat critical of much of the postcolonial theory I had read, yet I was deeply influenced in the early 1980s by reading Harrison's *Decolonizing Anthropology*. When I first began to write about decolonizing research in the mid-1990s, I emphasized authentic collaboration in which colleagues in the setting of study are as fully involved as is possible, functional, and desirable to them. At that time, Kenyan colleagues and I generated guidelines for decolonizing research involving "insider" and "outsider" partners, which we asserted involved (at minimum) the following (Swadener, Kabiru, & Njenga, 2000): collaboration on all phases of the study; sustained time in a culture; studying the language(s) and cultures to the degree possible and developing the ability to code-switch and understand indigenous "ways of knowing" and communicating; co-authorship of all papers and publications resulting from the collaborative work; compensation of local collaborators, translators, and research partners for their time; and making findings available in relevant ways to local shareholders, including finding funding to distribute publications in home country of local community. I have also emphasized the importance for "outsiders" of participating in the community in ongoing (non-missionary) ways, including supporting organizations and individuals doing "anti-colonial" work, and, finally, interrogating privilege and the "myths of meritocracy," while strengthening alliances.

In more recent years, I have been interrogating and "troubling" my comfortable, rule-governed formulas for decolonizing research across differentiated power relationships, wherever they may be found. I have confronted the likelihood that decolonizing research is a messy, complex, and perhaps impossible endeavor—yet have affirmed that attempting to decolonize one's work is a project worth pursuing, in solidarity with local colleagues and movements. My sense is that decolonization transcends individual action and requires working with collectives or alliances that concern themselves with decolonizing projects. I will admit that in my most self-critical moments, I have considered focusing only on anti-racist, social justice scholarship in my own community. This distancing from international projects has never lasted long. I return nearly every year to Kenya, and my visits are more about relationships and community volunteer projects than about my research agenda.

I have also been concerned with colonizing discourses and decolonizing possibilities in my primary disciplines of early childhood education and policy studies (Soto & Swadener, 2002, 2005) and have been influenced by the work of Kaomea (2003), who utilizes postcolonial and indigenous methodologies to complicate culturally based curriculum issues in early childhood contexts, and Cannella and Viruru (2004), who advocate the terminology of "younger human beings" in order to resist social constructions of childhood that reflect patterns of power and patriarchy that pervade our field. My examination, with Lourdes Diaz Soto, of issues of power and voice in research with children has included an in-depth analysis of ways in which early childhood theory, research, and practices with children embody colonizing patterns. Soto's work, and mine in recent years, has focused on issues navigated by bilingual children (e.g., Rolstad, Swadener, & Nakagawa, 2004; Soto, 2002; Soto

& Swadener, 2005) and counterhegemonic practices in an era of antibilingual education policies in the U.S. I have also been concerned about minimizing colonizing aspects of early childhood dual language (Spanish immersion in preschool and kindergarten) research, in the context of work that I have been part of for the past 4 years (e.g., Rolstad, Swadener, & Nakagawa, 2004).

Kagendo. My journey into decolonizing research had been rather unconscious until I started working and writing with Beth. I will begin this narrative by sharing snippets of personal experiences that worked first at an unconscious level to spur me to think and engage openly with what decolonizing might look like and the possibilities it spelled.

If I were to name an originary moment of transformation from a passive postcolonial to a critical one (the active one was yet to be born), it would have to be in 1996 in San Francisco attending the American Anthropological Association (AAA) annual meeting, where Beth and I were giving a paper. I recall feeling distinctly uncomfortable in my "postcolonial skin" while listening to a session in which the presenters—all American and all white—were presenting the findings of their multi-year study in East Africa (Tanzania, to be exact). I recall the distance (almost surreal in a way) with which they described "those women" of their studies (who bore neither names nor any identifier that could cast them in ways that they could be viewed as real women with real everyday struggles). The palpable distance between the researcher and the researched in my mind psychologically and physically located the researcher above (literally) the researched, placing the researchers at a lofty vantage point where they had an unfettered view of all their *subjects*, but yet remained distanced and uncontaminated by them. Those "women of the study" were passive; as participants they bore no subjectivity, and the researchers were clearly unconscious of the ways in which they objectified those nameless women who were identified by the unusual activities that they participated in and the strength with which they bore their burdens. The descriptions seemingly invite "those of us in the West" to gawk at these creatures who, though laying claim to being human/women, were clearly not human/women. I sat there, uncomfortable, thinking: "Any of those women could be my mother."

That's when I took my subconscious vow against distanced objectification and brazen, unapologetic consumption of the Other, and against writing about people's lives in ways that denied them the chance to be active participants in the construction of their identities and of issues that are of import to them. My work, therefore, as a decolonizing scholar/researcher (minimally as a scholar fighting for decolonization), shaped by a colonial and postcolonial experience, attempts to highlight the presence/disturbance of a number of discourses that produce ascriptive identities that are disabled, colonized, voiceless, powerless, nameless, and presumed known and therefore dismissible by readers. Believing that people's lives (no matter who they might be) are far too complex and complicated to be captured in familiar epithets, I attempt not to tell the "usual stories" that "we already know" about them, but to uncover the complicated ways people live their everyday lives in spaces that are almost always already inscribed.

It took me a number of years studying and living in the U.S. to come to the realization that many of the experiences that I came to find objectionable in my everyday interactions with certain people, who variously constructed me first and foremost as alien/foreigner/African, were directly linked to the notion that I was an already "known" abject subject (Erevelles, in press): African, woman, Black. I came to realize that early cultural anthropological studies, cultural exposés of Africa broadcast as television shows of the National Geographic Explorer, the Discovery Channel, and a number of other texts, had encrypted my identity long before I learned to appreciate what it all meant, much less find ways to subversively resist its encryption in empowering and decolonizing ways. Up until the moment of my advent into the U.S., I had not described myself nor been described in so many heavily coded terms, if those terms were used (and I know some of them were), during my growing up and school years in Kenya. I never really interrogated their nuanced meanings. Part of that may be due to the invisibility of their oppressive tendencies in Kenya. Another part may be because they were not as heavily laden in oppressive nuances as they are in the United States of America; another part may be my lack of political savvy. Therefore, it was a loss of naïveté that I experienced when I finally began to appreciate the depth of their nuanced sense as well as the historicized, racialized, and genderized oppression that they carried. As I have done elsewhere (Cary & Mutua, 2005), I share snippets of my decolonizing journey to highlight the presence/disturbance of a number of discourses that have shaped my colonial and postcolonial lives (not that I can separate these political spaces—nor would I want to).

In this narrative, the scripting of my identity as always already "known" alien, residing in the U.S. at the exhaustible pleasure of the U.S. Bureau of Citizenship and Immigration (formerly Department of Immigration and Naturalization Service), comes with unearned liberties and permissions granted to certain people (quite often strangers) to ask all kinds of prying personal questions: "Do they have plumbing where you are from?" "How many brothers and sisters do you have/are you from a *really* big family?" When I answer that I have four sisters and two brothers, I can see the inquirer put a checkmark on the list of "facts" already and always known about me! "Has anyone else in your family gone to school/received a college education?" When I answer yes, all have college degrees and have traveled in many other parts of the world, I can see an asterisk against that disturbed "fact" that is creating some dissonance on the checklist! Typically at this point, the inquirer might switch to a compliment: "You speak English very well!" and often they add how much they just love to listen to my accent, which then accords them the liberty to ask me to speak for no reason at all, other than entertainment!

The consistent inquiry/interrogation to which I am often subjected appears to be premised on nothing other than my alien/postcolonial status. The often unstated, yet expected, demand to explain my presence (and intentions) in the U.S. is the question that stays in permanent default mode. I am required, for no other reason than being alien/postcolonial, to explain what I am doing in the U.S. I find the hypocrisy engendered in the collective amnesia of non-Native Americans, who all have an immigrant history but make the proximity of my advent into the U.S.A. be of consequence, to be morbidly interesting. I bring with me cultural differences that make difficult the lives of those who have to deal with me or the lives of those who arrived here before me. So, in the U.S., the issue of cultural difference has been constructed as a problem of the alien. For instance, it is my problem that people cannot pronounce my name, so it behooves me to make it easier on everyone by taking on an American name or producing a nickname.

As a professional in special education, specifically, severe disabilities, a field that is laden with labels, I began to notice and be troubled by the ways in which cognitive, physical, and sensory differences among people are coded and positions assigned based upon the ascriptive identities. Those labels are often negative, silencing, and disempowering. Using semiotics as a theoretical standpoint that allowed me to delve into the signs and symbols of disability and the meanings and relationships experienced as everyday life by persons with disabilities, I first began to grapple with how identities are created and what assumptions are made about people who bear certain ascriptive identities. Working with Beth, I became exposed to a different way of thinking about and engaging with these issues that lent new thinking about my own identity (real and/or ascribed) and that of the youth with disabilities with whom I worked. I started to see ways in which colonization and its products are more than a geopolitical historical experience that is limited in terms of both spatiality and temporality. Rather, I began to appreciate that the processes and outcomes of coloniality are manifest in multiple ways in which "knowledge" makes possible the production and consumption of Others.

Furthermore, certain hegemonic power arrangements assure the silence of certain Others in the process of knowledge production that encrypts Othering identities. My work, therefore, as a decolonizing scholar/researcher shaped by a colonial and postcolonial experience attempts to highlight the presence/disturbance of a number of discourses that produce ascriptive identities that are disabled, colonized, voiceless, powerless, nameless, and hence presumed known and therefore dismissible.

Decolonizing Research With Children and Families

A growing number of researchers in early childhood have written about decolonizing research done with and about children, families, and diverse communities. Internationally, particularly in Europe and North America, this literature has focused on immigrants, religious "minorities," and other socially excluded groups (e.g., lone or single mothers). It has also included calls for more power-sharing between those who have been the objects of study and the often dominant-culture researchers. Others (e.g., Soto & Swadener, 2005) have called for the use of a range of visual, interpretive, and performative research methodologies that maximize children's voices and concerns. As in any reconceptualist endeavor, it is far easier to write and speak about decolonizing possibilities than to enact them in our work. Reconceptualizing Research, Theory and Practice in Early Childhood conferences have had decolonizing research as a theme for meetings held in Hawaii and New Zealand and an increasing number of papers have focused on this topic. Presentations from Norwegian, Australian, New Zealand, and U.S. early childhood researchers have addressed different framings of decolonizing methodologies and postcolonial theories, as part of their deconstructions of the larger field and their own work.

While much has been written about the need to continually engage with the process of researching and of representing the Other, delimitations of Otherness, while expansive in reach, have not, however, been applied explicitly and consistently to children with disabilities and their families, especially those whose disabilities are classified as severe/profound intellectual disabilities. Therefore, a lot of existing research on this population has tended to be silent on how best to represent such children and their families. Consequently, much of what is known today in research about children with severe cognitive disabilities and their families derives from positivist research. This paucity of methodological approaches that acknowledge, validate, and accord subjectivity and agency to children with severe intellectual disabilities and their families has created a chasm in the theorizing of disability as Other and how the process of representing may indeed embody colonizing tendencies in the knowledge production about disability.

Recent work (Erevelles & Mutua, 2005; Mutua, 2006) involving interviewing adolescents with significant intellectual disabilities brought to bear major ethical research dilemmas that impacted not only how the interviews were structured but also how data were to be analyzed. The studies used open-ended, in-depth interview questions (Taylor & Bogdan, 1984) that covered a variety of topics, including perceptions about the utility of transition programs in steering the adolescent toward desired post school/adult outcomes, friends in school and community, leisure/recreation activities in school and community, plans for the future relating to independent living, community participation, and employment. However, during the very first interview completed with a participant given the pseudonym Dakota and her mother, it became clear that there was an ethical issue that had to be confronted and dealt with immediately. Dakota was a 20-year-old woman who had Down's syndrome and was classified as having severe-profound mental retardation. As with all the participants in the studies, due to IRB requirements, the interviewing had to be conducted in the presence of a parent. In this particular study, Dakota (and subsequent participants) would be asked a question and then her mother would be asked to respond to the same question, thereby providing the opportunity to hear the response on each of the questions from both their perspectives. Toward the end of the first interview, Dakota had grown very quiet as her mother delved into private detailed explanations and descriptions of Dakota's personal life. It was evident that there was a need to restructure the interviews. The restructuring involved interviewing the adolescent in the presence of the parent, with the parent's role limited to one of helping with clarifying, reframing, or substantiating questions and/or responses. A second interview with the parent alone would then follow, so that the son or daughter would not have to sit through a conversation entailing private details.

A second research issue related to the brevity of responses. None of the responses of any of the adolescent participants could be described as being representative of the "rich description" that is usually touted as good qualitative data. On the other hand, the participants' monosyllabic responses and sentence fragments were much more voluble than initially conceived. The interviews demonstrated that it was in the silences, the hesitations, the determined yet subtle insistences that spoke louder than complete and eloquently put together sentences that are considered essential in good research (Devault, 1990). This observation relates to literature spanning Women's Studies, Asian Studies, and Disability Studies, which has focused on silences, body language, and semiotic markers that go beyond privileging spoken words (e.g., Rogers & Swadener, 2001).

Consequently, the data could not be analyzed using traditional qualitative strategies such as the constant comparative method (Glaser & Strauss, 1967) and the formulation of thematic codes. Rather, each interview's transcript was carefully read several times looking for patterns, repetitions, planned digressions, and our own white noise in an effort to make meaning of what was said and what was left unsaid. Additionally, we focused on using existing theoretical categories derived from transition research and on foregrounding participants' re/constitution of selfhood in their own words—an intervention that forced us to reconsider our own commitments to the normative discourses of adolescence and of the value and nature of the spoken word that constitutes interview data. From this example, in addition to the reframing of the "field" (Rogers & Swadener, 1999), decolonizing research is also about decentering privilege. For all its liberatory ways, qualitative research, particularly inteview-based studies, may privilege the ability to speak—particularly in ways that capture themes of the research.

Individuals with significant deficits in intellectual function are not known for their eloquence, much less coherence or descriptiveness in their speech. However, they do have much to say that may require our rethinking of ways of listening and hearing. By deciding that those voices are important enough to be heard and that what others say on their behalf is not a sufficient index of what they would say for themselves, we are beginning to decolonize the research process. Likewise, those doing research in special education might benefit from the work of early childhood qualitative scholars who have long grappled with ways of observing and interacting with young children who have not yet developed sophisticated language. These are not merely methodological issues, but issues with which those committed to decolonizing research must grapple.

Among the recent issues raised regarding the potential of decolonizing methodologies are concerns about the risks of such methodologies being appropriated, indeed re-colonized, and at times reduced to slogans and superficial versions of the intended project. We will link some of these concerns to the impacts of neo-positivism and an "identity politics" backlash on interpretive research and discuss the growing challenges to performing decolonizing or anti-colonial research.

We share both the concerns and sense of possibility that Gandhi (1998) and others have articulated regarding the lack of unified voice in postcolonial and critical research, which at times makes our work vulnerable to criticism due to divergent, even competing, voices. Hence, such methodologies can be more easily dismissed, which may lead to backlash for these genres. We argue that this phenomenon is reflected in many global movements, including the rise of global anticapitalism, which reflects a complex network of indigenous and localized movements. In other words, despite the lack of unity of message or approach that undergirds these methodologies, the voices are too numerous and strong to silence. To repeat the words of Gandhi (1998), indigenous researchers and critical postcolonial scholars are part of the "cacophony of subaltern voices."

Further, a growing number of Native American scholars have written powerfully about resistance to the Western academy and have called for indigenizing the academy (e.g., Mihesuah & Wilson, 2004) and "literary separatism" (e.g., Womack, 1999), foregrounding indigenous narratives and traditions. Others have focused on critiquing and reframing historical texts (e.g., Cook-Lynn, 2001; Miller, 2003) and contesting dominant religious, epistemological, and scientific theories (e.g., Deloria, 1995, 2003; Douglas & Armstrong, 1998). The divergent nature of the issues that are important to the decolonizing project further speaks to the diverse nature of the issues upon which possibilities for decolonization hinge.

It should be noted that such "subaltern" voices speak hundreds of languages and communicate in song, oral storytelling, dance, poetry, and rituals. Such voices use performative styles, reflecting an array of indigenous epistemologies that go far beyond prevailing Western academic styles and venues for dissemination. Moreover, the voice of the subaltern/colonized subject is also one that utters sentence fragments, uses telegraphic speech (single words or nongrammatical phrases), and says much without words, resisting external definitions of what is of worth and often reflecting relational versus individualistic constructions of human beings and other creatures. This came up recently at one of our campuses as we planned for our second Indigenous Issues and Voices in Educational Research conference. As we worked on the call for proposals, we realized that the meeting needed to emphasize more performative expressions versus traditional scholarly papers. For example, we needed to plan for song, relevant cultural dance, poetry, storytelling, and other alternative "forms" of expression related to education, assessment, and identity issues in education and educational research. Increasingly, indigenous scholars are serving as their own gatekeepers—for example, recent critical literacy scholarship that asserts that only indigenous authors do literary critique of indigenous texts (e.g., Warrior, 1995). Decolonizing or anti-colonial scholars also must grapple with the issue of which language(s) in which to publish their work (e.g., Hamza, 2004). Currently, one of the issues in a number of disciplines related to language policy (e.g., applied linguistics, bilingual education, ESL, language and literacy) concerns *heritage languages*. As discussed in a previous section of this chapter, the hegemony of English and other "globalized" languages threatens indigenous languages and the language rights of those who speak such "endangered" languages or feel pressured to write in English when many indigenous concepts do not accurately translate—if they translate at all—into English or other European languages. A recent issue of the *Modern Language Journal*, for example, raises a number of questions about heritage languages and language policy, including "what counts as a heritage language?" and what are issues of heritage language associated with policy, research foci, programs, curricula, and pedagogies? (Byrnes, 2005, p. 583).

Concluding Thoughts

In this chapter, we have attempted to provide an overview of research that positions itself as working against colonization and reflecting indigenous or nondominant epistemologies and traditions. We have argued that, while there are no formulaic universals of "decolonizing" research methodologies, there are compelling examples of systematic approaches, including narrative and performative genres, most of which include activist agendas working toward social justice, sovereignty, self-determination, and emancipatory goals. Major contributions to this growing literature have come from Maori and indigenous North American scholars, as well as from all continents. We have also argued that decolonizing research goes beyond a postcolonial analysis to a more socially engaged, collaborative alliance model that reconstructs the very purposes of research and epistemologies that inform it, as well as the need to continually examine the representational gaps in current research, thereby rethinking normative constructions of the research subject and the privileging of ability (vs. disability). In evoking a performative metaphor, we recognize the many forms of knowing, communication, and being in a complex and persistently oppressive world.

In setting the context, we began this chapter by describing what projects of decolonizing research might entail and the questions that decolonization engages. Not wishing to imply or inscribe any static forms in decolonization vis-à-vis research methods or methodologies, we shared illustrations from our stories as players working to decolonize research as a way to demonstrate the fluidity of decolonizing research, while at the same time highlighting what we perceive to be some defining features of decolonizing performances. In so doing, we drew from critical personal narratives reflecting our collaborative work, beginning with highlights from our own discussions and deconstructions of our attempts to "decolonize" research, making reference to indigenous narratives and reflecting on the possibilities and limitations of performing decolonizing methodologies (Mutua & Swadener, 2004). Drawing upon the work of Ngugi, wa Thiong'o (1986), Spivak (1999), McCarthy (1998), Bhabha (1994), and others, we explored several themes related to decolonization, briefly deconstructed notions of "insider" and "outsider," and, with Linda Tuhiwai Smith (1999), Graham Hingangaroa Smith (2005), and others, we troubled overdetermined notions of the "native" or "postcolonial intellectual." Finally, we focused on performance theories in various research-focused decolonization projects and made connections to early childhood and qualitative inquiry.

We also argued that particular culturally framed genres of research and methodology are necessary and should reflect indigenous epistemologies, languages, and expressive forms in relevant ways. L. T. Smith (1999, p. 143) states that, "Methodology is important because it frames the questions being asked, determines the set of instruments and methods to be employed and shapes the analysis." Her distinction between methodology as "a theory of how research does or should proceed" and a method "as a technique for or way of proceeding gathering evidence is one that is increasingly used in both indigenous and feminist research contexts" (G. H. Smith, 2002). While this chapter draws heavily from the work of Maori scholars, particularly Linda Smith and Graham Smith, we recognize that much of their work focuses on issues specific to their geopolitical, national, and indigenous contexts. Recognizing the complexities of any anti-colonial project and the need for specific, local enactments that often draw ideas from larger global struggles, we draw inspiration but not universal formulas from this powerful body of work.

We write as long-time colleagues, friends, and collaborative researchers, sharing a commitment to naming colonial and imperialist patterns in research and contexts of our work and daily lives. We struggle with understanding the subtle ways that colonization manifests in our respective (and shared) fields of early childhood education, special education, and policy studies. We do not limit our analyses of colonization and so-called postcolonial issues to geopolitical contexts. We, with a growing number of researchers (e.g., Cannella & Viruru, 2004; Kaomea, 2003, 2005), recognize the colonization inherent in constructions of categories of people (e.g., children, persons with disabilities, English language learners, indigenous scholars) and have worked to understand these often oppressive and typically limiting constructions to interrupt and reframe them in our work. We approach research, then, from an antioppressive and decolonizing stance, while realizing the [im]possibilities and complexities of a truly decolonizing endeavor.

References

Bhabha, H. K. (1994). *The location of culture*. London: Routledge.

Byrnes, H. (2005). Perspectives. *The Modern Language Journal, 89*(iv), p. 582–585.

Cannella, G. S., & Lincoln, Y. S. (2004). Epilogue: Claiming a critical public social science—Reconceptualizing and redeploying research. *Qualitative Inquiry, 10,* 298–309.

Cannella, G. S., & Viruru, R. (2004). *Childhood and postcolonization*. New York: Routledge and Falmer Press.

Cary, L., & Mutua, K. (2005). *Postcolonial narratives: Discourse and epistemological spaces.* Unpublished manuscript.

Cook-Lynn, E. (2001). *Anti-Indianism in modern America: A voice from Tatekeya's earth*. Urbana: University of Illinois Press.

Deloria, V., Jr. (1995). *Red earth, white lies: Native Americans and the myth of scientific fact.* Golden CO: Fulcrum.

Deloria, V., Jr. (2003). *God is red: A Native view of religions* (3rd ed.). Golden, CO: Fulcrum.

Denzin, N. K. (2005, May). The First International Congress of Qualitative Inquiry, University of Illinois, Urbana-Champaign.

Derman-Sparks, L. (1989). Anti-bias curriculum in early childhood. Washington, DC: National Association for the Education of Young Children.

Devault, M. (1990). Talking and listening from women's standpoint: Feminist strategies for interviewing and analyzing. *Social Problems, 17*(1), 94–119.

Douglas, J. C., & Armstrong, J. C. (1998). *The Native creative process*. Penticton, B.C., Canada: Theytus Books.

Erevelles, N. (in press). Understanding curriculum as normalizing text: Disability Studies meets Curriculum Theory. *Journal of Curriculum Studies.*

Erevelles, N., & Mutua, N. K. (2005). "I am a woman now!" Rewriting cartographies of girlhood from the critical standpoint of disability. In P. Bettis & N. Adams, *Geographies of girlhood: Identity in-between*. Hillsdale, NJ: Erlbaum.

Eze, E. C. (Ed.). (1997). *Postcolonial African philosophy: A critical reader*. Oxford, England: Blackwell.

Foucault, M. (1977). *Discipline and punish: The birth of the prison*. New York: Vintage Books.

Gandhi, L. (1998). *Postcolonial theory: A critical introduction*. New York: Columbia University Press.

Glaser, B.G., & Strauss, A. (1967). *Discovery of grounded theory: Strategies for qualitative research.* Hawthorne, NY: Aldine.

Hamza, H. M. (2004). Decolonizing research on gender disparity in education in Niger: Complexities of language, culture and homecoming. In K. Mutua & B. B. Swadener (Eds.), *Decolonizing research in cross-cultural contexts: Critical personal narratives* (pp. 123–134). Albany: State University of New York Press.

Jankie, D. (2004). "Tell me who you are?" Problematizing the construction and positionalities of "insider/outsider" of a "Native" ethnographer in a postcolonial context. In K. Mutua & B. B. Swadener (Eds.), *Decolonizing research in cross-cultural contexts: Critical personal narratives* (pp. 87–105). Albany: State University of New York Press.

Kaomea, J. (2001). Dilemmas of an indigenous academic: A Native Hawaiian story. *Contemporary Issues in Early Childhood, 2*(1), 67–82.

Kaomea, J. (2003). Reading erasures and making the familiar strange: Defamiliarizing methods for research in formerly colonized and historically oppressed communities. *Educational Researcher, 32*(2), 14–25.

Kaomea, J. (2005). Reflections on an "always already" failing Native Hawaiian mother: Deconstructing colonial discourses on indigenous childrearing and early childhood education. *Hulili: Multidisiplinary Research on Hawaiian Well-Being, 2*(1), 67–85.

Lather, P. (2004). This is your father's paradigm: Government intrusion and the case of qualitative research in education. *Qualitative Inquiry, 10,* 15–34.

McCarthy, C. (1998). *The uses of culture: Education and the limits of ethnic affiliation.* New York: Routledge.

McLeod, J. (2000). *Beginning postcolonialism.* Manchester, England: Manchester University Press.

Mignolo, W. D. (2000). *Local histories/global designs: Coloniality, subaltern knowledges, and border thinking.* Princeton, NJ: Princeton University Press.

Mihesuah, D.A. (Ed.). (2003). *American Indian women: Decolonization, empowerment, activism.* Lincoln: University of Nebraska Press.

Mihesuah, D. A., & Wilson, A. C. (2004). *Indigenizing the academy.* Lincoln: University of Nebraska Press.

Miller, S. A. (2003). *Coacoochee's bones: A Seminole saga.* Lawrence: University Press of Kansas.

Mutua, K. (2006, April). *Being and becoming: The construction of gendered identities by adolescents with intellectual disabilities.* Paper presented at the annual meeting of the American Educational Research Association, San Francisco.

Mutua, K., & Swadener, B. B. (Eds.). (2004). *Decolonizing research in cross-cultural contexts: Critical personal narratives.* Albany: State University of New York Press.

Ngugi, wa Thiong'o. (1986). *Decolonizing the Mind: The Politics of Language in African Literature.* London: James Currey.

Rogers, L. J., & Swadener, B. B. (1999). Reflections on the future work on anthropology and education: Reframing the field. *Anthropology and Education Quarterly, 30*(4), 436–440.

Rogers, L. J., & Swadener, B. B. (2001). *Semiotics and dis/ability: Interrogating categories of difference.* Albany: State University of New York Press.

Rolstad, K., Swadener, B. B., & Nakagawa, K. (2004, April). *"Verde — sometimes we call it green": Construal of language difference and power in a Preschool Dual Immersion Program.* Paper presented at the annual meeting of the Educational Research Association, San Diego.

Ryan, K. E., & Hood, L. K. (2004). Guarding the castle and opening the gates. *Qualitative Inquiry, 10,* 79-95.

Serres, M., with Latour, B. (1995). *Conversations on science, culture and time.* Ann Arbor: University of Michigan Press.

Shohat, E. (1992). Notes on the "post-colonial." *Social Text, 31/32,* 99–112.

Skutnabb-Kangas, T. (2000). *Linguistic genocide in education — or worldwide diversity and human rights?* Mahwah, NJ: Erlbaum.

Smith, G. H. (Ed.). (2002). *Guardianship, custody and access: Maori perspectives and experiences.* Auckland, New Zealand: Ministry of Justice, Government Publications. Access: http://www.justice.govt.n/pubs/custody-access-maori/chapter-4.html

Smith, G. H. (2004, April). Keynote Address. Distinguished Scholars Colloquia – Indigenous Perspectives on Educational Research and Schooling in Global Contexts, Tempe, AZ.

Smith, G. H. (2005). *Why the University of Auckland?* Access: http://www.eo.auckland.ac.nz/maori/why_auckland

Smith, L.T. (1999). *Decolonizing methodologies: Research and indigenous peoples.* London: Zed Books.

Soto, L. D. (Ed.). (2002). *Making a difference in the lives of bilingual/bicultural children.* New York: Peter Lang.

Soto, L. D., & Swadener, B. B. (2002). Toward a liberatory early childhood theory, research, and praxis: Decolonizing a field. *Contemporary Issues in Early Childhood, 3,* 38–66.

Soto, L.D., & Swadener, B. B. (Eds.). (2005). *Power and voice in research with children.* New York: Peter Lang.

Spivak, G. C. (1993). *Outside the teaching machine.* New York: Routledge.

Spivak, G. C. (1999). *A critique of postcolonial reason: Toward a history of the vanishing present.* Cambridge, MA: Harvard University Press.

Swadener, B.B., Kabiru, M., & Njenga, A. (2000). *Does the village still raise the child?: A collaborative study of changing childrearing and early childhood education in Kenya.* Albany: State University of New York Press.

Swadener, B. B., & Mutua, K. (in press). Decolonizing performances: Deconstructing the global postcolonial. In N. K. Denzin, Y. S. Lincoln, & L.T. Smith (Eds.), *Handbook of critical, indigenous inquiry.* Thousand Oaks, CA: Sage.

Taylor, S., & Bogdan, R. (1984). *Introduction to qualitative research methods: The search for meanings.* New York: Wiley.

Warrior, R. A. (1995). *Tribal secrets: Recovering American Indian intellectual traditions.* Minneapolis: University of Minnesota Press.

Womack, C. S. (1999). *Red on red: Native American literary separatism.* Minneapolis: University of Minnesota Press.

12

Who Chooses What Research Methodology?

JEANETTE RHEDDING-JONES

Oslo University College

Introduction

This is a chapter about qualitative methods, but I find this term problematic. As I have been publishing and teaching about methodologies, I see "methods" as quite restricting, often with positivist overtones. Instead of methods, I prefer to talk about research strategies within methodologies. The chapter is about methodological decision making, especially as it connects to graduate studies in higher education. In some parts of the world, graduate studies are called postgraduate studies; similarly methods, methodologies, and research strategies differ not only within research cultures but across nations and languages.

I am hoping that I can give readers, including both advanced students and novice researchers, a tool for looking closely at how researchers make decisions about their work. In practice, this means how their epistemological and ontological assumptions play out as qualitative research is conceptualized, planned, and done. In writing this chapter, I am attempting to produce an analysis of how decisions are made, with examples and comments from some master's and doctoral students in early childhood education in Norway.

I invited students to answer a set of questions on email, and gave them the option of being identified by name. They each agreed to have their identities revealed, and they all have written in English. As I am supervising and mentoring their work as beginning or continuing researchers, there is a politics here that I shall now make overt. Always in higher education, as elsewhere, there are power effects. One of the effects of me being a supervisor is that "my" students will often choose to take up the kinds of methodologies and theories about which I write and teach. This is not so surprising because most students select their supervisors based on shared interests and approaches. Further, when it comes to examinations of the thesis and dissertation, and later publishing, it makes sense to be connected to the research cultures of your supervisor. These connections include who you choose to have in your reference list, who you decide to hear at conferences, and whose research you want your own to follow. So my students are working with particular methodologies and resisting others, partly because of my influence.

How then can a chapter such as this help a reader who is not personally working with me and who has no connections to Norway? The first point is to choose a supervisor whose research will inform yours, and who has a preference (or at least some sympathy) for the kind of project you will attempt, and for the ways you will conduct your research. In methodological terms, this is about how you will position yourself regarding social science inquiry. Will your research be mostly hermeneutic and phenomenological—with you as the researcher finding and interpreting meaning in your research data? Will it mostly be critical—with you as the researcher investigating, critiquing, and reconceptualizing? Will it be mostly poststructural—with you as the researcher deconstructing from sites, events, and documents? The three operative verbs, which describe how research functions and which relate to methodology, are *interpreting, critiquing,* and *deconstructing.* Each of these links to three approaches to social science: the interpretive, the critical, and the poststructural. In choosing one or a combination of these, a researcher makes decisions that will determine how she or he will conduct interviews, write research journals, record what is seen and heard, and select particular texts for analysis.

Fortunately, the supervisor or graduate teacher is not the only resource master's or doctoral students have. Your research is influenced by whom you read. The people whose publications you study will let you see what the possibilities are, visualize how the future of research may be better than it has been, and imagine how what you will do will fit into bigger research pictures than you thought possible. Yet many beginner researchers and some continuing researchers neglect methodology as a critical issue in their reference lists. When you are keen to research a particular topic, and you are new to reading at such a high level of theory, it is easy to forget to ask yourself, "Yes, but how will I *do* this? How will I go about *being* the researcher? How will I conduct the project?" To give yourself a strong methodological focus, I suggest you ask, as you read other people's published research, "How did this person get the research data? What data did this person apparently collect or construct? What sort of a researcher was this person at the time of being in the field, and at the point of selecting what to analyze or deconstruct? Was this researcher wanting to mostly interpret things, mostly be critical with a view to making changes to power relations, or mostly open up other worlds of ideas and other possibilities for difference?" From these questions, you can then read a published text to determine to what extent a researcher has been into phenomenology, critical theory, or postmodernism/poststructuralism.

I am presenting the doing of research as a personal matter. That is because it is always a person who does the research, and that person imagines particular people the research will speak to and particular people from whom the research comes. In early childhood education, we have our own personal and professional blurrings of experience, knowledge, and competence. How these will impact upon our research, (i.e., what the research is and how the research is done) are key matters. This chapter points to a return to the personal, as not only a postmodern insertion into academia but also a useful and ethical way of making research and professional practice come together. I am therefore suggesting that beginning researchers seriously think about who they are and how their ontologies or ways of being might make research a richer and more connected practice. For early childhood education research internationally, it is most important that we make research links to our work with and for *children*, and that we take into our research those qualities we have learned to value because of our non-research experiences.

Methodologies and Methods

To write this chapter by making reference to particular researchers choosing particular methodologies and research strategies, I asked the following questions of several of "my" students:

- What research methodologies do you as an early childhood education researcher choose to work with for your project?
- Why do you choose these methodologies?
- How do your methodologies link to the critical issues of your project?
- How does this link to your epistemologies or approaches to social science inquiry?

Bente Lande Lingstad, who describes herself as "a 40-year-old woman, a pre-school teacher who has worked in pre-school kindergartens for 17 years," says:

For my master's research project I have collected pre-school teachers' narratives as life histories, or a part of their life histories. The pre-school teachers have written these for the project, so my research methodology or method is to study their writing, as life history. I chose life histories because I want the pre-school teachers to speak for themselves, and I want their voices to be heard. Also I wanted to work with a new way of doing research, by then taking up genealogy and discourse analysis related to this. A critical issue in my project, that is emerging from the research data or the narratives, is social class. My chosen methodology lets this be seen and heard. I am working with poststructural ideas and practices as a useful approach to this particular social science of mine. This lets me work in ways that earlier would not have been possible for early childhood researchers. For example, with poststructural research I can blur the personal with the professional. Also I choose to not focus on children but on the people who work with them, as a way of breaking down the binary division between children and adults.

Here Bente answers the four questions in the order they were asked. She wants to do this particular project in this particular way because of who she is and what her work and life experiences have been. She knows that it is possible to work methodologically with narratives and life histories, and to insert the voices of the teachers into her research. In choosing to do research like this, she selects a methodology she believes will empower the speakers and allow her to develop theories of social class. In doing so, she resists what has been a normalized practice in early childhood education, that is, focusing on children rather than adults. In her last sentence, she shows that she understands how poststructural theory breaks down binaries and crosses over borders. Further, she says that she is aiming to work with genealogy and with discourse analysis—two terms she could only have picked up through her reading, her discussions on campus, and her master's coursework.

Working at another level of research is *Ann Merete Otterstad*, who has 10 years' experience teaching in higher education for early childhood settings and in conducting research and development. Before that, she had 5 years' experience as the leader of a pre-school day care center, and 11 years before that as a pre-school teacher. She has recently worked for a year as a teacher with bilingual and multilingual 6-year-olds from ethnically diverse backgrounds. She is now in the third year of her doctoral project. Some of this autobiographical information can be read as linking to what she says:

> I have chosen co-operative conversations as methodology, with the aim of doing decolonizing research with the "other." In the case of my research this regards pre-school teachers with ethnically diverse experiences. So I am working intensively over eighteen months with three pre-school teachers who are now master's students themselves, or have recently completed their master's studies, and who have non-Norwegian backgrounds. So they are all bilingual or multilingual.

Methodologically, Ann Merete is resisting working with normalized interviews, and she has limited the number of people in her project to 3. When she says she has been working intensively with these three teachers for a year and a half, it appears that this is a kind of action research, focusing on change and critical concepts regarding those who are multilingual. She elaborates on this further:

> I have chosen this methodology, of co-operative conversations, because I am concerned about doing research within the multicultural field. A problem is my positioning as representing the cultural majority. The people I do research with are often defined as belonging to the minority. This makes for inequality in power relations. I am therefore working methodologically by transcribing our conversations and giving them back to the people involved to re-read, as a departure for our next conversation. The second phase is to ask the pre-school teachers to point to

some narratives in the text they find of special interest and listen to their reasons for this. Following this the research methodologically opens up for the other's reading and "interpretations." In the third phase we do readings together, choosing interesting concepts from the transcribed texts, and we deconstruct with an aim of critical analysis. I see now that this co-operative methodology might be linked to a form of action research. I had not in the beginning of my project decided how to include "the other" in the research processes, but by trying out and having discussions with the participants during the various phases or processes we constructed the way together.

Following this chapter's earlier analysis of social science inquiry approaches as interpretive, critical, and/or poststructural, it appears that Ann Merete has made several decisions. She will not resist interpreting, though she will write it with inverted commas to show that she sees it as problematic and that she is not following phenomenological theory. She is not overtly critical of Norwegian monocultural practices, mainly because she is too busy trying to reconceptualize them. She is, however, critical of her own positioning in working with these three teachers, and this is why she has designed her methodology along these lines. In terms of the poststructural, she is working on a co-operative methodology, which is far from the notion of the researcher as "the expert"—as in positivist and much interpretive research. Here the structure she is resisting is the dichotomy of the researcher and the researched. At the same time, she acknowledges the dilemma of her positioning. In the next quote, she says how her methodology links to critical approaches to inquiry:

> The critical aspects of my research project are connected to political issues, and we are discussing matters such as power, minority/majority, silence, privilege, and voices. These connect to representation, positionings, and communication. I want to make changes here, and tell stories that are not told within the existing multicultural field as connected to professionalism as pre-school education in Norway.

It seems to me that Ann Merete is putting together her earlier professional experiences, in particular regarding "the multicultural," as she produces her methodological innovations. At the doctoral level, she has the time to do this. Politically, though, she could be risking failing her thesis if she has examiners who lack understanding or knowledge of the new methodologies she is devising. For this reason, it is crucial that she argues strongly for the methodology she takes up, and that she documents her methodological choices very well in relation to what is recently published in highly regarded sources. Such is the politics of higher education and getting a doctorate. As a conclusion, Ann Merete writes:

I have been reading critical theory with a focus on sociology ever since I took my master's degree, thirteen years ago. During this time I have been working in various ways with issues and theories regarding multiculturalism. Over the last five years I have been inspired by poststructuralist approaches which have now become an important focus for how I understand and read knowledge and power positions. So new theories/approaches are informing my understandings, critiques, and deconstructings. These not only place me in particular positions as a researcher; they give me alternative and critical ways of understanding the multicultural field, and finding out if understanding is actually possible.

In presenting these two students who selected and constructed their particular methodologies for particular reasons and within particular contexts, I hope I am showing some of the complexity of methodological decision making. In part, your methodology is circumstantial, after you pick a critical issue to do the research about. The circumstances, as I have said, include who your supervisor is and who you have read. All of this also happens at a particular time and in a particular place. Although I am writing about Norway in 2006, I hope that this analysis is useful to early childhood researchers in other nations. The work that any graduate student produces should be influenced by what is published internationally and also by the relevant nation's research practices, values, and requirements. For nations that see themselves as central to international movements, this may be problematic. For Norway, which aspires to keep its own language in academic contexts, there is a politics here that larger nations will not have. Methodologically, a Norwegian may borrow, adapt, and take up practices read about from elsewhere. Yet some nations simply may not see themselves as being international at all, having only their own nationhood in mind. Hence they can ignore what happens and what gets published elsewhere. For English speakers, this conveniently gets explained away because most of them speak only one language. Yet, to enrich our methodological options, we should ask: What might researchers of non-English-speaking nations offer international research that is not otherwise there (Rhedding-Jones, 2005a)?

In my case, the fact that I am a Norwegian-speaking Australian might be problematic. Because of my access to international research cultures, I may be colonizing my Norwegian students and getting them to take up what I see as the latest methodologies. In doing so, I am perhaps not in a position to see what it is they might be constructing on their own. As I have suggested, the politics of getting higher degrees passed by the local examiners could be methodologically problematic. My advice is: speak up if you are not of the majority, and defend your own positioning as a researcher and your own integrity because of your experience. This advice applies not only to nationality but to all forms of difference. It is very easy to have your research shaped by methodological norms, or have it distorted by normalized discourses because you are afraid of the consequences of doing research in "different" ways.

Case Study, Action Research, and Ethnography

In my teaching and publishing I have been arguing that research strategies, earlier called methods, are the ways that researchers conduct their research within methodologies. Hence, interviews or extended conversations later constructed as research data, audio and video recording, and collections of documents for analysis or deconstruction are the strategies (Rhedding-Jones, 2003a, 2005b). As strategies, they differ in research practice according to which approach to social science is driving the project. So, if you are interviewing within the poststructural, you might be blurring the roles of researcher and researched. If you are interviewing within a critical approach, you will be acutely conscious of the power dimensions in the interview situation. If your approach is interpretive, you might make a large number of video recordings of your interviews and then do detailed analysis to discover what was going on. All three approaches can in fact be utilized in the same project or in different parts of it, depending on what your research questions are and what it is you want to uncover.

What I am presenting as a researcher's choices are three levels of analysis. The first, and the one you need to think about before you make decisions about what you will actually *do*, regards your selected approach to social science inquiry: an interpretive approach, a critical approach, and/or a poststructural approach. Historically, these evolved in that order, as qualitative and postpositivist approaches; and each connects to different sets of theories of knowledge. The second level of analyzing your ways of conducting your research is to decide what kind of methodology you will take up. As I see things, most research in the social sciences is either a form of *case study* (where particular cases or issues or institutions are studied from the past or the present); a form of *action research* (where the researcher works through actions with groups of people to innovate and study change); or a form of *ethnography* (where the researcher is like an anthropologist immersed in a particular culture, but not trying to change it).

In early childhood education, a researcher is working with case study, or several case studies, when she or he researches, for example, particular kindergartens, particular examples of play (Rhedding-Jones, 2003b), or particular documents that inform pedagogical practice (Rhedding-Jones, 2002). An early childhood education researcher is working with action research when she or he works collaboratively with other people for change, for example, to introduce and retain more men or more people of immigrant background to the profession. Such a project will be documented and theorized with the participants so that the research experience is useful to all involved. Ethnographic early childhood education research would have to be conducted over a longer time, with the researcher being in the research field as part of its culture. For teacher-caregivers who are becoming researchers, this is quite easy, as your own experience makes you identify and empathize with other people such as parents, teachers, caregivers, directors, and assistants.

The third level of analysis regards the research strategies within the methodologies. At this level, an interview, some notes in a research journal, and some video extracts will fit into a case study, action research, or ethnography in different ways. I shall try to clarify this with some more examples and comments from the Norwegian graduate students who take up case study, action research, and ethnography, and their related data collection strategies. Again, I shall also present these individuals' self-descriptions, as I think these help inform our notions of why particular people are choosing particular *methodologies* and their related *research strategies*. First is another master's student, *Bente Ulla*, who says she is female, in her early thirties, with 11 years of practice in preschool day care centers as a fully qualified pedagogical leader.

> I have chosen a hybrid combination of methods and strategies in my project. I am not doing traditional empirical work, but a combination of deconstructing public documents, archives, and memories. I have chosen these methodologies/methods because they bring in different voices, and give me an opportunity to do different readings of discourses. Also I will be showing my readers something of my own subjectivity as a researcher. This links to the critical issue of my project which is care. I am writing about and researching care in early childhood education, and I link this to critical issues of power, gender, and multiculturalism. All this links to my epistemologies and approaches to social science inquiry because I take up a deconstructive epistemology, within a feminist poststructural approach.

Here is someone who is particularly concerned with being a woman—she names herself first of all as female, and she attached the adjective "feminist" to the poststructural. Further, she wants to investigate what has traditionally been women's prerogative: the care of the very young. To do this project, she will not work with children. In fact, she will not work empirically with people at all. She will work only with texts, including public documents, archives, and written down memories. In this extract, she does not say how she will work with memories, but I know from talking with her that the memories are her own. This then is, in part, an autobiographical project. If I have to categorize it, I would say it is a case study of care. She will study care by researching her own memories along with the found documents and archives. As a case study, this appears to be a study of the past. Yet Bente Ulla will go beyond the past to make statements and to theorize subjectivity and care. As a case study of care, her work will link to critical issues of power, gender, and multiculturalism. It will also link to poststructural approaches through the deconstructions Bente Ulla will make of her research data.

Karin Fajersson is currently applying to begin her doctoral studies. Her master's degree, completed 5 years ago, was a critical multicultural analysis of the national curriculum frameworks document for primary schools. This could be called a case study of monocultural constructs, using as its data the text and cultural context of the frameworks document. Since completing her master's dissertation, Karin has been teaching, lecturing, researching, and publishing. Of her plans to now begin a doctorate, and the preliminary research she has been doing toward this, she says:

> One of the methods I have chosen to work with as a strategy is focus groups. I use video and audio recorders and make accurate transcriptions of the conversation. The participants in the focusgroups produce data that I can read in different ways.

Because my question was not about classifying research as action research, ethnography, or case study, Karin is not naming these. Instead, she describes her research strategies, which we can perhaps see as linking to a particular methodology. Sometimes when people begin a project, they do not need to think about all the methodological choices I have outlined. These methodological understandings will come later as greater knowledge of methodology is built up. All projects follow different processes, and researchers find their own epistemological links as they go. There are many things to think about, including the theories, the methodologies, the themes or issues, and the positionings of the researcher. At this point of planning and preliminary recordings of conversations, Karin says she has chosen her methods because:

> The participants can respond to each other as well as to me as the researcher. The participation in the group represents opportunities for discussions and reflections. As a researcher I choose the theme for the focus groups, and I can come up with questions and comments during the time we spend together.

It may be that as Karin gets further into this project she will develop a form of action research. At the moment, she is open; and she knows she wants to do the project with her undergraduate students who are to become teachers. Linking her ways of researching to the critical issues of her project, she says:

> There is more than one way to talk about and understand an issue. My project is linked to teachers talking and reflecting upon everyday practices. Different discourses offer different possibilities for children. When teachers or others discuss issues in a focusgroup they use different discursive resources. Different discourses are used, legitimated, or

contested. My position as a researcher is mainly to listen, but I can also be part of the conversation by asking questions.

Again, I have the feeling that action research will develop over time, as this group decides what the critical issues are and then what innovations to practice they will take up. As an action research project, this will take a critical approach, and Karin's role as listener will be important for its development. Also, because Karin writes about discourses, it seems that she has knowledge of critical theories and the effects of power. Bearing this out she says:

> My choice of focus groups as a method is linked to my epistemological position. The discursive or linguistic turn in social science is critical. I want to focus on pragmatics, the uses of language, understood broadly. So my choices of methodology and strategies are grounded in social constructionism, and this will open up for deconstruction. Further, I am inspired by both critical and poststructural approaches.

Readers by now may be thinking that there are similar threads among each of the quoted graduate students. I have acknowledged that they are all working with me. More importantly, they are working with each other, in various ways. All are based in Oslo, and we share conversations in the corridors, over occasional dinners, in emails, at seminars, and sometimes we attend international conferences together. As a small research culture, we are informing each other's thinking, research actions, and academic writing. The master's students have studied coursework together; the doctoral students have taught together. The point is that the methodological choices happen within a context of some form of local research culture.

Next is *Nina Rossholt,* a sociologist who has been researching and teaching in early childhood education for several years. Her particular focus has been "the body," and she has done much empirical work with young children. She is well published in Norwegian, and she has recently begun doctoral studies. Of her work, Nina says:

> I use different methods, such as interview, observations, narratives, talks and making photos together with children aged 1–3. I am mainly working with action research at this moment, and so I have used narratives and stories about practices, as I want changes in the preschools. I am working against stereotypical ways of naming or doing research. I like the concept of the liberating gaze, *frigjørende blikk.* From my perspective we have to trouble the body by studying gaze, movements, ways of knowing. Then we see how we put borders between ourselves and others. I am saying that power and desire are linked together as embodied ways of being a subject. And I am working empirically with young children to research these things. I use the so-called interviews, observations,

narratives, talks and children's photography as it seems best at the time, in a particular situation. I work intuitively, by relating to the children.

Here Nina's challenge is to describe how some children at the age of 1–3 relate to each other bodily. She tells me that she will also attempt to show how a researcher may write about this not only in terms of common-sense stories but in terms of how people make sense of events. As Nina is studying how knowledge is bodily constituted through different discourses, this is a poststructural approach to social science. At the same time, she could be dealing with particular phenomena she will interpret. As methodology, this seems to be placed between being a case study about body, action research where practical change is wanted, and ethnography where the researcher has entered the world of the very young. It remains to be seen whether Nina will keep all these epistemological doors open, or whether she will narrow down her choices in the 4 years she has to complete her doctorate.

In one way, this chapter is about who chooses to do case studies, action research, or ethnography, and who applies the related research strategies of recording, representing, listening, looking, selecting, analyzing, and deconstructing within a wider framework of approaches to social science inquiry. In another way, the chapter presents critical possibilities, phenomenological possibilities, and/or poststructural possibilities, each with different textual practices and each discursively producing interpretations, analyses, critiques, and deconstructions. How all of this might fit with the practices of higher education's awarding of master's degrees and doctorates is the critical edge of the chapter. As the national language and research culture here is Norwegian, some matters regarding the internationalization of early childhood education are raised. These matters, and the politics of selecting or constructing research methodologies given international choices, link to postcolonial theory. Who here is colonizing whom? Is the progress of new methodologies and their practical strategies just another imposition? Must we all become poststructuralists, like earlier generations of researchers had to divorce positivism and wean themselves off too much quantitativism? I think the answers to these questions lie in complex research ethics that are closely linked to the professions of education and care.

Conceptualizing, Planning, and Doing

I see research work as personal and professional in combination. This allows each of us to take up different ways of doing research at different times and in different places. I am not now the researcher I was (Rhedding-Jones, 2001); I aim to always move on to something else. That something else is not only methodological; it is also theoretical and practical. For me, conceptualizing, planning, and doing means assessing your personal and professional situation and gauging your likely effectiveness.

To put this into more academic language, this section deals with how epistemological and ontological assumptions play out as qualitative research is conceptualized, planned, and done. I see ontology as the ways of being of the researcher and of the subjects/people of the research (Rhedding-Jones, 2005b). Epistemology is about the connections between methodology (and all that that implies) and theories. It is a blurring of theories, research practices, and philosophy. How you do this blurring and how you make these connect is up to you. There is a great deal of autonomy possible in graduate research; or there should be. If you are having problems doing your conceptualizing, your planning, or your "doing," then ask yourself if you need to immerse yourself more than you have in particular research cultures. Choose these carefully, as none of us do this work in isolation—what we do and say is because of others. Of course, you don't need actual bodies around you, though these are nice. You can locate yourself through texts, as a reader of other people's writing. You need to become highly skilled as a reader, so that your own writing and your research actions are grounded in what you read. It is the well-published writers who will give you the support you need, and show you how the seemingly impossible can be done. Here are two highly ambitious master's students attempting what no one around them has yet managed. Following this chapter's pattern of small bio-notes first, here is what *Eline Grelland* says:

> I am a professional counsellor in grief support to children aged 0–8 and their families; and a final year master of early childhood education and care graduate student. As my research methodology I will use bricolage, with a variety of methods investigating a range of documents and children's books, children's drawings, and written and oral stories/narratives from preschool teachers, about a child's way of expressing the loss of a parent or sibling. I have chosen bricolage to embrace the complexity of the lived daily life of bereaved preschool children. My use of bricolage, and cooperating with the preschool teachers, is a resistance to what I see as the dominating patriarchal-therapeutic understandings of children in grief within the field of psychology and crisis. I believe we need to understand how children choose to do (or to not do) their expressions of grief in daily life, in the context of the kindergarten: with other children, with adults, or alone. The search for a way of embracing complexity led me to bricolage; and the search for a way of unveiling the patriarchal usage of psychology led me to the feminist poststructural. Using a feminist poststructural epistemology also opens up a possibility of undoing the knowledge so many perceive as a definite truth. I am thus building knowledge in a totally different way.

Eline has obviously done much reading, independently. Also, she has much professional experience as a grief counsellor. All of this will come together in what she produces as her dissertation, with her thesis coming from her deconstructions of patriarchal uses of psychology. In deciding on bricolage, Eline has selected a methodology that goes beyond case study, action research, and ethnography. Perhaps what she does will put these three together in new ways. She will have to be careful, though, that she is not just using a trendy new word. Bricolage used without postmodern understandings could just be the same old mixed methods of the past. In this extract, she does not have the space to defend her use of bricolage, but she will have to do this in her dissertation. Eline will have to argue for it and then show how its methodological use is justified.

Marcela Bustos, who is Spanish-speaking with a family history from Chile, surprised us all by deciding not to research critical multiculturalism or bilingualism. She speaks eloquently about these matters and is known for her activism. Instead, she will focus her master's research on heterosexual normativity. As a heterosexual researcher, she will bring her knowledge of difference to a research field that needs it. So here is a novice researcher who puts her political act of topic selection together with what the kindergartens here are currently lacking: a concept of what they are doing to normalize a particular sexual orientation amongst the children. Marcela says (in her third language):

> I want to work with deconstruction. I want to deconstruct data that I have chosen and that I collect. I want to ask questions I believe are important to ask. But I can not tell the truth about what I write about, I can not do the correct interpretation, I can not write about a universal truth that I find if I work hard enough, if I am clever enough. Because I do not believe that there is a universal truth out there to *avsløre* (I do not remember the English word). Deconstruction and poststructuralism give me the possibilities to what I want to do. I can do readings that do not exclude other readings, but that focus on the issues I find important to point to in contemporary early childhood education in Norway. My critical issue is heteronormativity. I do not mean that this is the only or the most important issue in early childhood, but there are important questions that need to be asked. By doing deconstructions and using poststructural epistemology, I can do my readings, without locking out other readings. What I will read are the picture story books currently in use in the kindergartens. I will also critically read the Norwegian government's policy documents and the new curriculum frameworks documents about early childhood education. I don't want to do empirical work looking as an observer at the children and their teacher-caregivers. And I don't want to put words into people's mouths by interviewing them and making them say things they think I want to hear. It will be enough to just point to what the texts do, I think.

Here Marcela rejects many of the methodological concepts she has worked with recently (Otterstad & Bustos, 2005), including her knowledge of decolonizing methodologies. Instead, she focuses on just what is needed to do this particular project about gay rights and early childhood. The case here is the location and nonlocation of gay discourses, and the textual practices of normalizing heterosexual families, childcare, and early education. To do this project, Marcela will not go into queer theory, as this is not a doctorate, and she has only a year or so to do this work. Instead, she will make political a difference in an area she sees as problematic. So this is critical theory as a social science approach. Methodologically, this will not become action research, though someone else might take this up in future years, and start where Marcela's work will end. Perhaps Marcela herself will do a doctorate about this later.

In part, the selection of a methodology is calculation; in part, it is art. Whatever the choice, there are always at least two parts to the work: deciding how to get the data and deciding what to do with the data once they are collected. What I did with my own doctorate was work ethnographically for 4 years with a small group of children, their teacher, and their families. Then I did deconstructions of my research journal, the children's writings and drawings, and the audio and video recordings I had (Rhedding-Jones, 1995, 1996, 2000). The project took me 5 years as an enrolled student, though I spent a year before enrollment chatting with my prospective supervisors and reading what they suggested. By the time I actually began the candidacy, I was ready to go out to work ethnographically with the children. What you do as a methodologist, then, depends on what it is you are interested in finding out. I was questioning personal positionings and gender, and in the process examined spoken and written language. This eventually became a thesis about discourses, subjectivity, and psychoanalytic theories.

Summary

This chapter presents research methodologies as dynamic and political ways of doing research. It exemplifies the methodological practices of seven graduate students and their supervisor/mentor in Norway. Research is seen as constructed within local research cultures in relation to international epistemological and ontological shifts. In early childhood education research, these are effects of the relations between adults and children, between sites, events, and texts, between discourses of normalization and its resistance, and between institutions and new practices. To study the actual process of selecting research strategies within methodologies and approaches to social science inquiry, the chapter analyzes, discusses, and deconstructs what the students say their methodologies are. These methodologies are loosely classified as some kind of case study, action research, or ethnography. Sometimes the methodologies may be put together in innovative ways, and sometimes new methodologies emerge. Within methodologies are the research strategies of getting and constructing research data, and then working and playing with these data as analyses, interpretations, and deconstructions. As research strategies, researchers do interviews, make recordings, and select texts for analysis in different ways because of their selected methodologies. These methodologies fit within different approaches to social science inquiry. Post-positivist approaches are the interpretive, the critical, and the deconstructive. These link to hermeneutics and phenomenology; to critical theories such as feminism, social class, and the anti-colonial; and to postmodern writings and poststructural theories. Thus, contemporary methodologies are located between approaches and research strategies. As such, early childhood methodologies link to critical issues in practices with, about, and for children and to new theoretical constructions and new genres of writing for the field. Methodological decision making, especially for graduate students, is about being aware of these possibilities, connections, and implications.

References

Otterstad, A.-M., & Bustos, M. (2005, October). *Questioning decolonizing research methodology* (pp. 16–20). Plenary paper presented at the 13th Conference of Reconceptualizing Early Childhood Education, Madison, WI.

Rhedding-Jones, J. (1995). What do you do after you've met poststructuralism? Research possibilities regarding feminism, ethnography and literacy. *International Journal of Curriculum Studies, 27*(5), 479–500.

Rhedding-Jones, J. (1996). Researching early schooling: Poststructural practices and academic writing in an ethnography. *British Journal of Sociology of Education, 17*(1), 21–37.

Rhedding-Jones, J. (2000). The other girls: Culture, psychoanalytic theories and writing. *International Journal of Qualitative Studies in Education, 13*(3), 263–279.

Rhedding-Jones, J. (2001). Shifting ethnicities: "Native informants" and other theories from/for early childhood education. *Contemporary Issues in Early Childhood, 2*(2), 135–156.

Rhedding-Jones, J. (2002). An undoing of documents and texts: Towards a critical multiculturalism in early childhood education. *Contemporary Issues in Early Childhood, 3*(1), 90–116.

Rhedding-Jones, J. (2003a). Feminist methodologies and research for early childhood literacies. In N. Hall, J. Larson, & J. Marsh (Eds.), *Handbook of early childhood literacy* (pp. 400–410). London: Sage.

Rhedding-Jones, J. (2003b). Questioning play and work, early childhood and pedagogy. In D. Lytle (Ed.), *Play and educational theory and practice* (pp. 243–254). Westport, CT: Praeger.

Rhedding-Jones, J. (2005a). Decentering Anglo-American power in early childhood education: Learning and culture and "child development" in higher education coursework. *Journal of Curriculum Theorizing, 21*(3), 133–155.

Rhedding-Jones, J. (2005b). *What is research? Methodological practices and new approaches.* Oslo, Norway: Universitetsforlaget.

13
Assessing the Quality of Early Childhood Qualitative Research

J. AMOS HATCH

University of Tennessee

It has been said that there are as many kinds of qualitative research as there are qualitative researchers. While each qualitative study will have its own unique design, data collection methods, and analysis procedures, my view is that it is important and helpful to have criteria available by which to assess the quality of qualitative studies. In *Doing Qualitative Research in Education Settings* (Hatch, 2002), I concluded each chapter with a set of questions designed to help researchers gauge their progress along each step of planning, implementing, and writing up their qualitative work. The questions at the end of the concluding chapter were a composite of the preceding chapters' questions, and they represent a list that may help researchers evaluate their own work, guide consumers of research as they assess the work of others, and assist those responsible for critiquing the work of qualitative researchers (e.g., doctoral committee members, journal editors, proposal reviewers) in making more informed decisions.

This chapter is organized around a synthesis of the questions that conclude my 2002 book; but, the focus here is specifically on qualitative research done in early childhood settings. The idea is to give qualitative researchers interested in studying social phenomena related to young children tools for thinking about what makes a solid piece of qualitative inquiry. Other scholars from a variety of disciplines have addressed issues related to standards in qualitative research (e.g., Creswell, 1998; Leedy, 1997; Lincoln, 1995), and their insights can be useful. What I hope this chapter provides that is not found elsewhere is a set of direct, answerable questions that constitute a framework for assessing early childhood qualitative research adequacy.

As will become evident as the chapter unfolds, answers to each question will look different for different studies. The premise is not that there is one and only one "correct" answer to each question. Different metaphysical assumptions will lead to different research questions and different data collection, analysis, and reporting procedures. So, I expect that answers will be different. The constant is that each qualitative researcher should be able to generate a defensible answer to each of the questions below. As I lay out a rationale for the importance of each question for early childhood qualitative researchers, I will describe elements of possible answers given the range of paradigmatic and methodological choices available to contemporary researchers.

Has the Researcher Located Himself or Herself in Relation to Particular Qualitative Paradigms?

I am one who believes that Kuhn's (1970) original notion of scientific paradigms is still one of the most powerful conceptual tools for understanding research of any ilk. I encourage the novice early childhood qualitative researchers with whom I work to start their research journeys with a careful introspective look at what they believe about the nature of reality (their ontological assumptions) and what can be known (their epistemological assumptions). Their answers to these metaphysical questions help them to see where their thinking about how the world is ordered (or not) and how researchers can generate knowledge fits within different research paradigms. For me, the unpacking of these assumptions is an essential first step that points qualitative researchers in a direction that can be taken with confidence. Beginning a research journey without examining paradigmatic assumptions (as when researchers start with research questions) often leads to research that is logically inconsistent at best.

Kuhn (1970) argued that the history of science can be traced through an examination of how research paradigms have risen to the status of "normal science" then fallen from favor and been replaced by competing paradigms. To be considered a paradigm, Kuhn believed a school of thought must have generated firm answers to the following questions: What are the fundamental entities of which the world is composed? How do these interact with each other and the senses? What questions can legitimately be asked about such entities and what techniques employed in seeking solutions? Based on these criteria, I have generated descriptions of four qualitative research paradigms: postpositivist, constructivist, critical/feminist, and poststructuralist (Hatch, 2002). I see each of these as legitimate research paradigms, and I believe that locating themselves within the assumptive boundaries of one of these systems of thought is an essential first step for all qualitative researchers. Further, I am arguing that paradigmatic positionings ought to be made more explicit in reports of qualitative research. Four qualitative paradigms are briefly outlined below.

Postpositivists believe that although an objective reality exists, it can never be fully apprehended. Therefore, the outcomes of inquiry ought to be close approximations of reality. Postpositivist researchers see themselves as data collection instruments, and they seek to improve the validity and reliability of their work through rigorous data collection and low inference data analysis procedures. Knowledge forms produced from postpositivist studies include descriptions, patterns, generalizations, and grounded theory.

Constructivists assume a world in which universal, fixed realities are unknowable. The qualitative work done within this paradigm seeks to uncover multiple realities as they are experienced by individual participants. Researchers spend considerable amounts of time observing and/or interviewing participants in order to capture the understandings that participants use to make sense of their constructed realities. Knowledge products are often case studies or rich narratives that use participants' voices and rich contextual descriptions that allow readers to place themselves in the shoes of the participants.

Critical/feminists see a material world that is made up of historically situated social structures that have a real impact on the lives of individuals who operate within those structures. Critical researchers are interested in exposing social conditions that limit the life chances of individuals based on social class and race; feminist qualitative researchers typically study the oppressive social circumstances experienced by women and girls. Knowledge for critical/feminists is always value mediated, so the philosophies and values of the researcher are taken to be "integral rather than antithetical" (Carr, 1995, p. 97) to the research process. These scholars produce critiques designed to expose the inequalities that keep the powerful in control and limit the opportunities of those who are oppressed.

Poststructuralists take the view that order is created in the minds of individuals in an effort to give meaning to events that have "no intrinsic or immanent relations" (Freeman, 1993, p. 95). Theirs is a kind of anti-paradigm in that the tools of poststructuralist thought can be used to deconstruct the very notion of paradigms. Qualitative researchers doing poststructuralist work often focus on producing multi-vocal texts that acknowledge the local, temporary, and partial nature of the stories being told. Poststructuralist researchers accept the differences among lives as lived, lives as experienced, and lives as told; and they self-consciously acknowledge that they create lives when they generate lives as written (Hatch & Wisniewski, 1995).

When I read qualitative research in my role as instructor, reviewer, or consumer, I want to know the paradigmatic assumptions upon which the work is based. I have had occasion to write literature reviews in which it was my task to synthesize early childhood qualitative research. Most recently, a colleague and I (Hatch & Barclay-McLaughlin, 2006) wrote a chapter for the *Handbook of Research on the Education of Young Children* in which we organized our review according to the paradigms described above. I can testify from that experience that more often than not, early childhood researchers are not explicit about identifying the research paradigms that ground their work. Sometimes paradigmatic assumptions are evident in the language of the report, but when that is not the case and explicit ontological and epistemological expositions are not included, I count that as a serious flaw.

Has the Researcher Selected Appropriate Qualitative Research Approaches, Given His or Her Paradigm Choices?

Deciding what to call their work is an important issue for early childhood qualitative researchers. Again, my experience has taught me that many qualitative researchers do not do a good job of identifying or describing the research approaches they utilize in their studies. It's fine with me if researchers resist the idea of adopting someone else's formula for doing a particular type of study; and I'm okay with the idea that approaches that have been described in the literature should be adapted to fit each individual project. But, I am bothered when qualitative research reports include little or no description of how the study being reported relates to well-established approaches in the field; and I am dismayed when researchers claim to be doing ethnography, grounded theory, or any other type of qualitative study while providing scant evidence that they understand the basis for such a claim.

One of the major reasons for starting with an examination of paradigmatic assumptions is to ensure that decisions about research approaches are logically consistent. While most approaches are flexible enough to be adapted for use within any of the qualitative paradigms (e.g., interview studies), some are bound by their defining elements to one paradigm and no other (e.g., grounded theory is strictly a postpositivist approach). Space will not allow a complete description of the many approaches that have been detailed in the qualitative literature. More complete descriptions are found in almost any introductory qualitative research text (e.g., Creswell, 1998; Bogdan & Biklen, 1992; Schram, 2006). What follows is an outline of some prominent approaches, citations to original sources, and my judgments about how these relate to the four paradigms described above (adapted from Hatch, 2002).

Ethnography is a particular kind of qualitative research that seeks to describe culture or parts of culture from the point of view of cultural insiders (Spradley, 1979; Wolcott, 1988). Ethnography was developed by anthropologists who spend extended periods of time doing fieldwork within cultural groups. Fieldwork usually involves observation, interviewing, and artifact collection. Classic anthropological ethnographies were framed within the postpositivist paradigm. Some scholars call their work critical ethnography, feminist ethnography, or poststructuralist ethnography. When such labels are applied, the adjectives signal the paradigm, while "ethnography" usually refers to the writers' intent to represent cultural knowledge in some form.

Participant Observation Studies also place researchers in social settings, but unlike ethnographers, they do not have the broad purpose of capturing the cultural knowledge that insiders use to make sense of those settings. Direct observations recorded in fieldnotes are the primary data collection tools in this type of study. Researchers often enter the field with specific interests (e.g., what is the nature of teacher–parent relationships?) and/or specific questions (e.g., how do these kindergartners understand reading instruction?) that concentrate their studies in ways that ethnographers do not. Participant observation fieldwork involves data collection strategies that can be utilized within any of the qualitative research paradigms.

Interview Studies feature special kinds of informant interview strategies as their principal data collection method. Qualitative interviewers create a special kind of speech event during which they ask open-ended questions, encourage informants to explain their unique perspectives on the issues at hand, and listen intently for special language and other clues that reveal informants' meaning structures (Mishler, 1986; Seidman, 1998). Focus group interviewing is a specialized type of data collection approach that involves interviewing sets of individuals who have shared characteristics or common experiences (see Krueger, 1994; Morgan, 1997). Qualitative interview and focus group studies can be undertaken from within any of the paradigms outlined.

Historical Studies or historiographies involve the collection and analysis of data for the purpose of reconstructing events or combinations of events that happened in the past. Primary data sources include oral or written testimony, original documents, photographs, diaries, journals, drawings, mementos, or other original artifacts. Secondary sources are elements created by others that relate to the event or events in question, such as textbooks, journal articles, newspaper accounts, public records, and other information about individuals or groups (Berg, 1998; Salkind, 1991). It is the job of the historiographer to examine potential sources of data for authenticity and accuracy, to make interpretations based on multiple data sources, and to weave these into a "meaningful set of explanations" (Berg, 1998, p. 202). Qualitative educational historians operate within several research paradigms.

Grounded Theory Studies are designed to collect and analyze qualitative data in rigorous, systematic, and disciplined ways. The original book, *The Discovery of Grounded Theory* (Glaser & Strauss, 1967), and elaborations that have followed (e.g., Strauss, 1987; Strauss & Corbin, 1998) detail procedures for generating theories that are inductively derived from careful examination of the data (i.e., *grounded* in the data). Vital to these procedures is the notion of constant comparison, through which researchers engage in detailed analytic processes that require repeated confirmations of potential explanatory patterns discovered in the data. Grounded theory is the archetype postpositivist method.

Naturalistic inquiry is a specific kind of research that is described best in the work of Lincoln and Guba (1985). In contrast to conventional positivist research, Lincoln and Guba offer design elements that include (a) determining a focus for the inquiry; (b) determining the fit of paradigm to focus; (c) determining the fit of the inquiry paradigm to the substantive theory selected to guide the inquiry; (d) determining where and from whom data will be collected; (e) determining successive phases of the inquiry; (f) determining instrumentation; (g) planning data collection and recording modes; (h) planning data analysis procedures; (i) planning the logistics; and (j) planning for trustworthiness (pp. 226–247). Naturalistic inquiry is firmly rooted in the constructivist research paradigm.

Narrative Studies focus on gathering and interpreting the stories that people use to describe their lives. Different types of narrative studies include life histories, life story research, biography, personal experience methods, oral history, and narrative inquiry (see Hatch & Wisniewski, 1995; Yow, 1994). All are based on the notion that humans make sense of their lives through story. Clandinin and Connelly (1994) identify the following methods for generating the data of narrative studies: oral history; annals and chronicles; family stories; photographs, memory boxes, and other personal/family artifacts; research interviews; journals; autobiographical writing; letters; conversations; and fieldnotes and other stories from the field. Narrative work fits most comfortably within the paradigmatic boundaries of constructivist and critical/feminist thinking, although it is possible to apply postpositivist analytic techniques to narrative data (see Polkinghorne, 1995). Some poststructuralist narrative researchers are calling for "different ways of representing the other and ourselves … (such as) creating impressionist tales, dramas, fictions, and poetic representations of lives" (Sparkes, as quoted in Hatch & Wisniewski, 1995, p. 121).

Phenomenological Studies usually combine both interpretive/hermeneutic methods and descriptive/phenomenological methods for the purpose of examining the lived experiences or lifeworlds of people being studied. In Van Manen's (1990) words, "Phenomenology describes how one orients to lived experience, hermeneutics describes how one interprets the 'texts' of life" (p. 4). Phenomenological researchers seek to reveal the essence of human experience by asking, "What is the nature of this phenomenon?" The methods they use to gather experiential descriptions from others include (a) protocol writing (asking individuals to write their experiences down); (b) interviewing (gathering experiential narrative material through conversation); (c) observing (collecting anecdotes of experience through close observation); (d) studying experiential descriptions in literature and art (examining poetry, novels, stories, plays, biographies, works of art, and the phenomenological literature for insight into the nature of the phenomena under investigation); and (e) examining diaries, journals, and logs (searching for meaning in writings individuals have done for themselves; adapted from Van Manen, 1990, pp. 62–76). Hermeneutic phenomenology is a constructivist approach.

Case Studies are a special kind of qualitative work that investigates a contextualized contemporary (as opposed to historical) phenomenon within specified boundaries (Merriam, 1988; Yin, 1994). Merriam (1988) offers examples of such bounded phenomena in education: "a program, an event, a person, a process, an institution, or a social group" (p. 13). Data collection and analysis procedures parallel those of other qualitative approaches. It is their focus on "bounded systems" (Smith, 1979) that makes qualitative case studies different. While most qualitative case studies are postpositivist in nature, there is nothing inherent in a bounded system approach that precludes the application of constructivist, critical/feminist, or poststructuralist principles.

In order to make sound judgments about the quality of early childhood qualitative research, it is important for authors to let readers know the qualitative approaches that are being applied. Again, the intent is not to circumscribe flexibility or inhibit creativity, only to get researchers to openly reveal what it is they are doing and why. In addition, it is an attempt to decrease the chances that inexperienced qualitative researchers will call their work by a particular name (e.g., naturalistic inquiry or narrative)when it fails to meet the defining criteria of that particular approach.

Has the Researcher Described His or Her Methodological and Substantive Theory Bases?

Describing a methodological theory base is directly related to but not the same as identifying a research approach. Describing a substantive theory base is related to but not the same as writing a review of the literature. When I teach qualitative research methods to aspiring early childhood researchers (and others), I insist that they produce written articulations of the theoretical foundations that scaffold both their intended qualitative research methods and their substantive areas of inquiry. Denzin's (1978) declaration concerning the interrelationships among theories, interests, and methods still works for me:

> Research methods are of little use until they are seen in the light of theoretical perspectives. Substantive specialty is of little use or interest until it is firmly embedded within a theoretical framework and grounded upon sound research strategies. (pp. 3–4)

Methodological theory is that which is used to describe and explain the research approaches to be applied—the methods of the study. If the first two questions above have been addressed, the explication of methodological theory should be a matter of synthesizing the researcher's paradigmatic assumptions within a discussion of the theoretical roots of the qualitative approach he or she is adopting or adapting. I ask students to do a careful study of the methodological approaches they are considering and to examine as many research reports as possible that apply those approaches. A description of methodological theory is the place for qualitative researchers (novice or otherwise) to spell out what they mean when they identify their work as a critical ethnography, a postpositivist case study, a focus group study within the constructivist paradigm, a poststructuralist historiography, or whatever. Doing this in writing gives invaluable direction to researchers and important background to their readers.

Substantive theory is that which is used to describe and explain the phenomena to be investigated—the substance of the study. There is some disagreement about the exact place of substantive theory in qualitative studies. Some qualitative scholars say a careful exploration of extant theory should not be undertaken prior to data collection and analysis (e.g., Glaser & Strauss, 1967), while others recommend extensive familiarity with existing theory prior to entering the field (e.g., Yin, 1994). Virtually all agree that findings cannot be understood except in relation to what is already "known" in the field, and good scholarship undertaken within any paradigm using any research approach should make clear connections to theoretical perspectives that have been used to describe and explain past inquiry in any subject area. For me, a description of substantive theory is not equivalent to a review of the literature. Such a description might usefully be included in a literature review, but the focus here is on theory. Again, I have my advanced students read everything pertinent to their areas of substantive interest, searching out explanations of theoretical bases and finding examples of important empirical work.

As the Denzin quote above suggests, connections among theories and methods need to be explored and justified. This is not to say that substantive theoretical orientations that have only been applied in quantitative studies should never be explored by qualitative researchers. For example, theories explaining young children's social development might inform analyses and interpretations of a qualitative study of social interactions in preschool. Still, care needs to be taken, no matter the source of the substantive theory, to be clear about its usefulness for understanding and explaining findings that are generated qualitatively. One of the distinguishing characteristics of good qualitative research is its inductive nature (Hatch, 2002), so substantive theory should never be used to set up qualitative research projects that are driven by pre-established categories designed to test pre-determined hypotheses. Articulating relationships between methodological and substantive theories is good practice that leads to the development of good research questions.

Has the Researcher Articulated a Set of Research Questions That Make Sense Given His or Her Methodological and Substantive Theories?

Research questions are a key element in any kind of study, and these should be easy to find in any written report of research. Research questions are critical to qualitative research design because they are the only component that ties directly to all of the other components of design (Maxwell, 1996). Identifying appropriate research questions is important to early childhood qualitative research because well-constructed research questions give direction to the study, limit the scope of the investigation, and provide a device for evaluating progress and satisfactory completion. Research questions are often refined and sometimes changed during the course of qualitative studies, but without them, studies can lack direction, focus, or the means to evaluate their worth.

A solid set of research questions (it might be a set of one) gives direction to a study by carving out a piece of territory for exploration. Applying different approaches within different paradigms will lead to questions that are different in form and substance. By way of example, the following represents a list of possible questions that might be asked by different early childhood researchers studying social phenomena in a Head Start center:

- A postpositivist doing an ethnography might ask: What do participants in this center know that allows them to operate within this setting?
- A constructivist doing a phenomenological study might ask: What is the nature of teacher–parent relationships in this center?
- A critical/feminist researcher doing a participation observation study might ask: What conditions in this setting serve to reproduce the unequal power relations that characterize society?
- A poststructuralist doing a narrative study might ask: What are participants' stories of working in a Head Start center during the implementation of standards-based accountability reforms?

I like the general model of asking one overarching research question (like those in the examples), then, if needed, asking sub-questions that spell out subsets of information within the larger question. A qualitative study that a graduate school colleague and I conducted in a summer school program for primary-aged children who had "failed" serves as an example. Our overarching research question was "What is the nature of reading instruction in a remedial summer program?" The question signaled the basic intent of the study, established some boundaries on its breadth, and was answerable given our constructivist participant observation design. Our sub-questions were "What do teachers do to help children who have been identified as having difficulties learning to read?" and "What kinds of activities and experiences do teachers provide for these children?" (Hatch & Bondy, 1984, p. 29). Our research questions helped us focus on what teachers did and had students doing during reading time. Our questions were open-ended, few in number, and stated in straightforward language. I recommend these qualities to all researchers. Closed-ended questions are better suited for quantitative studies, too many questions can lead to a scattered approach to data collection and analysis, and complex language or jargon often leads to confusion and misinterpretation.

Although it is common for research questions to change during a qualitative project, having them in place at the outset is essential to the design and implementation process. When I meet with students at various stages of their research, I encourage them to constantly refer back to their research questions. New researchers almost always feel overwhelmed at the start of data collection. Referring back to research questions puts a frame of reference on what to look for. Data analysis is even more debilitating for most students.

Qualitative data are usually voluminous, and research questions give initial structure to the inherently messy data analysis process. Later, students frequently don't know when to stop their analysis. Asking if research questions have been answered provides one way to judge if enough data processing has been done.

Deciding on research questions is not easy. It will help a great deal if researchers have gone through the process of identifying methodological and substantive theory bases. Researchers who skip these steps run the risk of adopting questions that do not fit with their basic assumptions or are not answerable given the kind of research they want to do. The questions selected should build logically from the researcher's theoretical orientation and substantive interests. When they do not, it is a powerful signal that the research may not have been carefully planned and executed.

Has the Researcher Described the Research Context and Provided a Rationale for Why the Context was Selected?

In *Studying Children in Context*, Graue and Walsh (1998) define context as "a culturally and historically situated place and time, a specific here and now" (p. 9). The title of their book foregrounds the important place of context in early childhood qualitative research. I agree with Graue and Walsh that one of the hallmarks of good qualitative work is that it is contextualized in ways that are ignored or neglected in most quantitative studies. Reports of early childhood research done within any of the qualitative paradigms have meaning only in specific culturally and historically situated places and times. Findings from qualitative work can take many forms, but unless readers can situate those findings in relation to well-described contexts, findings will have little meaning and questionable utility.

For qualitative researchers, descriptions of context always include the physical setting in which social phenomena under examination occurred, a set of participants and their relationships to one another, and the activities in which participants are engaged (Hatch, 1995). Providing such descriptions can be a challenge because contexts are complex and dynamic. They move and change as time passes, participants move in and out, and activities are enacted. Dealing with this kind of complexity is one of the features that make qualitative work "real" in relation to the static settings assumed in most quantitative studies.

In some qualitative reports, including a section called "contexts" that situates the study in time and place is an easy and efficient way to provide readers with a way to contextualize findings. This will be the case for many ethnographies, participant observation studies, historical studies, grounded theory studies, naturalistic inquiries, and case studies. In other reports, context descriptions will often be more subtly embedded in the narratives of the report, as in many interview, phenomenological, and narrative studies. In reports of the latter variety, contexts are more likely to be revealed in data processed through the perceptions of participants (e.g., phenomenological interviews with child care providers can be conducted without ever setting foot in a center or home). In any case, it is incumbent on qualitative researchers to provide readers with enough information about context that findings can be meaningfully interpreted.

However context descriptions are framed, it should be evident to readers that the contexts of the study are appropriate for answering the research questions of the study. Again, in some reports, this fit will be self-evident as findings unfold; but in others, it will be necessary to include an explicit rationale statement that explains to readers why contexts were selected. By providing this kind of information, qualitative researchers are not attempting to generate arguments for traditional forms of validity or generalizability (see Bogdan & Biklin, 1992; Lincoln & Guba, 1985). They are trying to provide enough insight into the conditions surrounding the research for readers to make their own decisions about the connections between what is being reported and contexts with which readers are familiar.

Has the Researcher Described Research Participants, Explained Criteria for Selecting Them, and Justified Their Level of Involvement?

As noted above, participants are key elements in any research context. Participants are the ultimate gatekeepers in qualitative studies. In many ways, they control researchers' access to the data of the study. They are so central to qualitative studies that special care needs to be taken to be sure that readers are given clear descriptions of research participants, why they were selected, and how they took part in the study.

As an element of context, it will be difficult for consumers of qualitative research to make sense of research findings unless researchers supply them with descriptive information that allows consumers to frame the findings in relation to certain kinds of participants. For example, a study of young children's understanding of violence will be interpreted differently when participants are preschoolers from the poorest sections of Baghdad as opposed to third graders from elite private schools in New York City. In some kinds of qualitative studies, the numbers of participants are small. That means that data collected from and about these participants will be more intensely focused and contribute more to the final products of the research than data from studies with large numbers of participants (Hatch, 2002). It follows that because of their increased impact on findings, participants in studies with small numbers must be described with great care.

In any qualitative early childhood study, the criteria used for participant selection should be included in final reports. These criteria, of course, will be directly tied to paradigmatic assumptions, methodological approaches, substantive interests, research questions, and decisions about contexts. A recent doctoral graduate of mine is a postpositivist researcher who did an interview study of Hong Kong kindergarten teachers' perspectives on teaching children with disabilities. The participant selection criteria for her dissertation study were described as follows:

> Each (teacher) was working as a general education teacher in the integrated early childhood programs of Hong Kong at the time of the study. All of the interviewed teachers' nationality was Hong Kong Chinese. Informants could be novice or experienced integrated teachers. All eight informants taught kindergarten classes that included children with disabilities. (Cheuk, 2005, p. 62)

It's easy to see that her participant selection criteria would have been quite different if, for example, she had been a critical/feminist researcher interested in doing a historical study of shifts in early childhood education policy during Hong Kong's transition to political independence during the 1990s.

Patton (1990, pp. 169–186) presented a list of "purposeful sampling strategies" for qualitative researchers. Although the list has a strongly postpositivist bent, many of my students have found it useful for thinking about their own participant selection processes. I have abstracted Patton's strategies below and added an early childhood qualitative research possibility to each:

- *Extreme or deviant case samples* include individuals who demonstrate highly unusual manifestations of the phenomenon of interest (e.g., a case study of children who have been expelled from preschool programs for violent acts).
- *Intensity samples* are made up of individuals who manifest the phenomenon intensely but not extremely (e.g., a participant observation study of first grade students identified as "hyperactive").
- *Maximum variation samples* seek to include individuals with different perspectives on the same phenomenon (e.g., a focus group study of stakeholder perspectives on full-day kindergarten).
- *Homogeneous samples* are made up of individuals with similar characteristics or experiences (e.g., a narrative study of young, white, middle-class, female teachers who work in urban early childhood settings).
- *Typical case samples* include individuals who represent what is considered typical (e.g., a case study of young children nominated by kindergarten teachers as "ready for first grade").
- *Stratified purposeful samples* are those that include individuals selected to represent particular subgroups of interest (e.g., a historical study of the implementation of inclusion in a primary school that includes interviews with teachers, administrators, and parents).
- *Critical case samples* include individuals who represent dramatic examples of or are of critical importance to the phenomenon of inter-

est (e.g., an interview study of directors of highly successful Head Start programs).

- *Snowball or chain samples* are created when one informant identifies the next as someone who would make a good participant (e.g., a phenomenological study that follows a chain of teachers who identify each other as individuals who know about infant-toddler teaching).
- *Criterion samples* are made up of individuals who fit particular predetermined criteria (e.g., a narrative study of early childhood teachers who have earned National Board Certification).
- *Theory-based or operational construct samples* include individuals who manifest a theoretical construct of interest (e.g., a naturalistic inquiry in a preschool classroom identified as "developmentally appropriate").
- *Confirming and disconfirming samples* are made up of individuals who can shed light on tentative findings that researchers have put together (e.g., a focus group study of teacher education students to confirm or disconfirm interpretations from a study of an early childhood internship program).
- *Opportunistic samples* develop fortuitously during the course of data collection, leading researchers to new informants (e.g., a grounded theory study of parents of children with autism in which an informant tells the researcher she is a member of a special child support group).
- *Politically important case samples* are those that strategically include or eliminate individuals who represent certain political positions (e.g., a phenomenological study of primary teachers who have openly refused to implement a state-mandated diversity curriculum).
- *Convenience samples* select individuals because they are easy to access (e.g., an ethnographic study of the researcher's own kindergarten class).
- *Combination or mixed purposeful samples* are combinations of the sampling strategies above (e.g., an interview study of supervisors, principals, and teachers responsible for public preschools in districts selected to represent rural, sub-urban, or urban categories across a state).

To satisfy the intent of this criterion, I do not think it is necessary for researchers to identify a specific sampling strategy from this or any list. I do think it's important to let readers of qualitative research know how and why participants were selected. A framework such as the one presented here can provide a useful tool for thinking about and describing participant selection processes.

Different research designs created within different qualitative paradigms lead to different levels of involvement for research participants. As a general rule, postpositivists see participants as key informants on whom they rely in order to gain insider perspectives on the social phenomena of interest. The optimum relationship in most postpositivist work is for researchers to have established enough rapport so that informants can teach researchers how they make sense of their social worlds (Berg, 1998).

Constructivists are more likely to join participants in a collaborative research effort. Many constructivist researchers partner with their participants in co-constructing their findings. This can range from giving participants opportunities to review data and/or interpretations to including them as full partners in the research process, sometimes making them co-authors on papers, articles, and books.

Critical/feminists are likely to join their participants in special relationships that provide opportunities for consciousness-raising, critique, and even resistance. Transformation is part of the ethos of this kind of work, so trusting relationships between researchers and participants are necessary if recognizing and throwing off oppression are part and parcel of the research enterprise. Poststructuralists' relations with participants are less easy to gauge than in the other qualitative paradigms. As a rule of thumb, I see no particular level of involvement that I would ascribe to poststructuralist qualitative research.

The level of involvement between researchers and their participants has direct bearing on qualitative studies of any variety. Therefore, it is important that reports of qualitative research, no matter what the paradigm, include information that lets the reader in on researcher-participant relationships. As above, the form in which this information is delivered (in a special section, woven into the fabric of the research story, or otherwise) is not important, so long as the reader is not left to guess who the participants were, why they were chosen, and what they contributed to the study.

Has the Researcher Described All of the Data Collected as Part of the Study, Making It Clear How, When, and Why the Data Were Collected?

The kind of inquiry this chapter is about can be characterized as empirical but not statistical. For me, if it's qualitative *research*, it has to be data-based, and data have to have been systematically gathered and analyzed. Unless authors are able to describe their data collection (and analysis) processes in detail, I worry that their work may be something other than research—not necessarily inferior, but still not empirical research. In order to assess the quality of any qualitative research project, it is necessary for readers to have a good idea of what the author counted as data and how those data were collected.

Data can take many forms in qualitative studies. The primary data collection modes continue to be observing, interviewing, and gathering unobtrusive data. Other frequently utilized forms of data include video recordings, participant journals, and focus group records. Brief discussions of the primary data forms are provided below, along with specific suggestions about what should be included in descriptions of each.

Observation as a data collection tool in early childhood qualitative research means that researchers are present in social settings and taking careful field notes that will be converted into research protocols. Field notes are a shorthand version of what people say and do in the social setting being examined. While in the setting, researchers record events and conversations in as much detail as they can, then, as soon as possible after the observation, they convert their field notes into full-blown research protocols. These protocols are the "filled-in" versions of researcher field notes (Bernard, 1994), and they are most usefully typed into word processing programs in preparation for data analysis. Reports of research that include observations as a data source should tell the reader when observations began and ended, how frequently they occurred, the duration of observations, and in what contexts. An example might read as follows:

> Observations were conducted once per week in each of three kindergarten classrooms beginning the first week of January and concluding the last week of May. Each observation lasted from ninety to one hundred twenty minutes, and observations were divided equally among different parts of the kindergarten day so that data were gathered that captured all of the regular activities of the kindergartens being studied.

Interviews can supply the primary or only data in some qualitative studies, or they can be used as supplements to studies that emphasize other data collection strategies. I classify qualitative interviews into three basic types: informal (unstructured conversations that take place in the research scene); formal (planned conversations set up for the purpose of data collection); and standardized (special formal interviews in which researcher questions are presented in the same order and form to a number of different informants; Hatch, 2002). Informal interviews are only used in studies that involve other data collection strategies, usually observation. Formal interviews (often called "in-depth" or "semi-structured" interviews) are the type most frequently used in qualitative studies. They are guided by researcher questions but take on a life of their own as researchers listen, prompt, and ask follow-up questions that develop from the interview interaction. Standardized interviews fit most comfortably within the assumptions of the postpositivist paradigm.

Informal interviews are most often recorded in hand-written notes, and then typed up after leaving the research scene. Formal interviews and most standardized interviews are recorded on audio tape and then transcribed verbatim into research protocols. Beyond the critical importance of describing interview participants (see above), reports of studies that include interview data should tell readers what types of interviews were used, how many were conducted, how long they typically lasted, and under what circumstances they were completed. For example:

Formal interviews were conducted with each early childhood intern at the beginning, middle, and end of the internship year. Interviews averaged one hour in length, and all were conducted in the privacy of the center conference room. Interview tapes were transcribed immediately, and participants were given the opportunity to review and edit transcripts.

Unobtrusive data are gathered without the direct involvement of participants. They are unobtrusive because their collection does not interfere with the ongoing events of the research setting under investigation. Kinds of unobtrusive data include the following (along with an early childhood example): artifacts (objects that participants use in their everyday activity, such as worksheets in third grade); traces (the unintended residue of human activity, such as wear marks on the carpet in a preschool classroom); documents (official written communication, such as a state kindergarten curriculum guide); personal communications (unofficial written communication, such as a Head Start teacher's diary); records (special kinds of documents for keeping track of important information, such as primary children's cumulative folders); and photographs (pictures taken by individuals or collected by institutions, such as family photo albums). Similar kinds of data strategically can be collected by or for researchers (e.g., participant journals or photographs), but they are unobtrusive only if they would have been collected whether research was happening or not. Unobtrusive data will most likely be supplementary to other data in qualitative research projects. Qualitative reports should tell the reader exactly what unobtrusive data were collected and why. For example:

> Unobtrusive data were collected throughout the study. These data were used to triangulate observation and interview data related to reading instruction. Sources included state and district curriculum materials, textbooks, district and school memos, teacher-made materials, samples of children's work, notes to parents, report cards, attendance records, and children's cumulative files.

The same pattern holds no matter what forms research data take. In order to make a fair assessment of any qualitative study, readers need to know what data were collected, how, when, and why. When data are poorly described, appear to be "thin" (i.e., lacking in depth or breadth), or seem ill-suited to the research questions of the study, serious concerns about the quality of the research ought to be raised.

Has the Researcher Explained and Justified Data Analysis Procedures Used in the Study, Making It Clear How and When Data Were Analyzed?

I review eight or ten manuscripts a year for a variety of journals. More often than not, the answer to the question that frames this section is "No." I'm not sure why qualitative researchers, including those writing up early childhood studies, tend to brush over describing their data analysis procedures. I frequently see statements such as, "Data were read and re-read in a search for themes"; or "Data were analyzed inductively"; or "Grounded theory was used to analyze data." If these statements were topic sentences for complex descriptions that told exactly what the researcher did, that would be fine. But, when these are the only clues to how data analysis was handled, they are not sufficient.

A major issue in qualitative research revolves around the tension between structure and flexibility. Qualitative researchers are justifiably proud of their resistance to following formulaic approaches as they design, implement, and report their research. Except for some postpositivists, most qualitative researchers see prescribed systems for data analysis as constraining and counter to their notions of what makes their kind of research different from positivist, quantitative research. I agree with the sentiments of such arguments; but that doesn't mean that I think it is okay for qualitative researchers to present findings without explaining and justifying exactly how those findings are related to the data of their studies. I am one who believes that having a structure from which to adapt and modify is a good way to think about qualitative data analysis. I have provided step-by-step descriptions of five data analysis models that are made to be adapted (Hatch, 2002), and I will present one of those models as an example below. But, I am perfectly happy when researchers create their own procedures, so long as it's clear to readers how data analysis was accomplished in the studies they are reporting.

What follows is a list of steps I include in a data analysis model that I recommend for processing data collected in critical/feminist qualitative studies. It is presented as an example of a "structure" that can be flexibly adapted to fit the needs of a variety of qualitative studies in early childhood.

1. Read the data for a sense of the whole and review entries previously recorded in research journals and/or bracketed in protocols.
2. Write a self-reflexive statement explicating your ideological positionings and identifying ideological issues you see in the context under investigation.
3. Read the data, marking places where issues related to your ideological concerns are evident.
4. Study marked places in the data, then write generalizations that represent potential relationships between your ideological concerns and the data.
5. Re-read the entire dataset and code the data based on your generalizations.
6. Decide if your generalizations are supported by the data and write a draft summary.

7. Negotiate meanings with participants, addressing issues of consciousness raising, emancipation, and resistance.
8. Write a revised summary and identify excerpts that support generalizations. (Hatch, 2002, p. 192)

Novice qualitative researchers frequently have no idea where to start when it comes time to analyze their data. Again, except in some postpositivist research such as that guided by the work of Glaser and Strauss (1967), Miles and Hubermann (1994), or Spradley (1980), little or no guidance for how to actually do data analysis is provided in the literature. Doctoral students with whom I work and others who have adapted my models find them useful starting places for designing their own data analyses. My advice is always to study each element of the model, thinking about why it has been included. If an element does not make sense for your study, drop it, change it, and/or add another step to accomplish the aims of your analysis.

Whether applying prescribed data analysis strategies, adapting models from the literature, or utilizing data analysis procedures of your own design, it is imperative to include clear descriptions of data analysis in reports of qualitative research. Included in such descriptions should be information about when analysis was done (i.e., at the conclusion of data collection, periodically during the data collection process, or recursively throughout data collection). Data analysis procedures are "justified" when they fit logically within the paradigm that frames the study, generate answers to the study's research questions, and make sense given the methods and data of the study. Such information is vital to making informed judgments about the quality of the research being reported.

Has the Researcher Written His or Her Report Using a Narrative Form That Communicates Findings Clearly?

Form and function are tightly bound in early childhood qualitative research reports. Although findings will take different shapes in different kinds of studies, all qualitative reports will include narrative elements that distinguish them from the detached, "objective" stance taken in most positivist research reports. For example, most qualitative reports will be written in first-person, active voice, locating researchers in the text in the same ways they are present in every part of their studies. In addition, the voices of participants in the form of excerpts from research data will almost always be heard as qualitative findings are reported. Further, most qualitative research reports will include sufficient contextual detail that readers can judge for themselves the meaningfulness of the findings for situations they know about.

Given these general characteristics, the forms that qualitative reports take vary widely, and the ultimate test of how well alternative forms work is determined by their function—that is, how well they communicate to their audiences. I find Van Maanen's (1988) description of various narrative models to be a useful framework for thinking about different forms that qualitative early childhood findings might take. I have abstracted Van Maanen's description as follows:

- *Confessional tales* are first-person accounts that acknowledge the researcher's presence throughout the research process and report the researcher's interpretations of what's important in the setting.
- *Impressionist tales* use literary devices to produce evocative stories that take the reader inside what happened, while readers are generally left to form their own interpretations of what it means.
- *Critical tales* often use a Marxist or feminist framework to describe the effects of social structures on the diminished life chances of disadvantaged groups.
- *Formal tales* are used by specialists within the qualitative field such as ethnomethodologists and sociolinguists whose principal aim is to document the application of particular theoretical perspectives to the analysis of specific events.
- *Literary tales* rely directly on nonfiction writing techniques and combine a journalistic concern for what is noteworthy with the drama associated with good novels.
- *Jointly told tales* include both researcher and participant voices in a dialogic or polyphonic format designed to bridge gaps between meaning systems (pp. 45–138).

It's easy to see connections between the qualitative research paradigms introduced above and the different "tales" in Van Maanen's framework. Again, while hard and fast rules are seldom appropriate, some paradigmatic choices logically lead to some forms of reporting and not others. For example, it's hard to imagine that a postpositivist would present his or her findings in the form of a jointly told tale or that a constructivist would be attracted to writing formal tales. I believe the form that findings take ought to follow naturally from the data analyses of the study (see Hatch, 2002). Different kinds of analyses generate different looking findings, and the shape of those findings will dictate the application of a form that looks like one of Van Maanen's tales, takes on elements of a combination of such forms, or generates its own unique form.

Good qualitative research reports include evidence that findings are supported by the data of the study. No matter what the paradigmatic assumptions or research methods, readers should leave qualitative reports with a clear sense that findings were databased. This is usually accomplished by including direct evidence in the form of observation, interview, or unobtrusive data excerpts. In some studies, data will be displayed, but less directly, as in impressionist or literary tales in which authors craft stories that imbed research data in the text. In any case, data must drive qualitative findings, and readers must have confidence that findings are justified based on sufficient data exposition in qualitative research reports.

In any kind of research reporting, it is important to make connections between findings and relevant theory and previous research. This is as true for qualitative as for quantitative reports. Most dissertation committees demand a full section to address these connections, but sometimes these elements get short shrift in article-length qualitative reports. The importance of revealing methodological and substantive theory bases is argued above. It follows that an explanation concerning how those theoretical perspectives relate to the findings of the study is also important. These explanations can be framed as a separate section, woven into findings, or included in a discussion section; but connections to theory and previous research should be part of solid early childhood qualitative reports.

Has the Researcher Presented Findings That Flow Logically From His or Her Paradigmatic Assumptions, Methodological Orientation, Research Questions, Data, and Analysis?

Different paradigmatic assumptions lead to different research questions, different data collection and analysis procedures, and different looking findings. This last question speaks to the overall logic of the study being assessed. If the previous nine questions have been answered satisfactorily, then the spirit of this question will have been met. When there are gaps in the logic or when one element in the research does not follow from another, the value of the project as a whole becomes suspect.

Because of their reliance on narrative description to carry the message, qualitative early childhood researchers have a special burden as writers. When they are able to infuse elements of good literature (e.g., authenticity, credibility, continuity, plausibility, verisimilitude) in their writing, their reports are improved (see Hatch & Wisniewski, 1995). But, creating research reports that also qualify as good literature is too high a standard for most of us. What we can do is a better job of creating dissertations, books, and articles that demonstrate their own worth. By applying criteria like those imbedded in the questions above, early childhood qualitative scholars can look their readers in the eye and say this is a high quality piece of empirical research.

References

Berg, B. L. (1998). *Qualitative research methods for the social sciences.* Boston: Allyn & Bacon.

Bernard, H. R. (1994). *Research methods in anthropology: Qualitative and quantitative approaches.* Thousand Oaks, CA: Sage.

Bogdan, R. C., & Biklen, S. K. (1992). *Qualitative research for education: An introduction to theory and methods.* Boston: Allyn & Bacon.

Carr, W. (1995). *For education: Towards critical educational inquiry.* Buckingham, England: Open University Press.

Cheuk, W. Y. J. (2005). *A qualitative study of teachers' perceptions of integrated kindergarten programs in Hong Kong.* Doctoral dissertation, University of Tennessee, Knoxville.

Clandinin, D. J., & Connelly, F. M. (1994). Personal experience methods. In N. K. Denzin & Y. S. Lincoln (Eds.), *Handbook of qualitative research* (pp. 413–427). Thousand Oaks, CA: Sage.

Creswell, J. W. (1998). *Qualitative inquiry and research design: Choosing among the five traditions.* Thousand Oaks, CA: Sage.

Denzin, N. K. (1978). *The research act.* Chicago: Aldine.

Freeman, M. P. (1993). *Rewriting the self: History, memory, narrative.* New York: Routledge.

Glaser, B. G., & Strauss, A. L. (1967). *The discovery of grounded theory: Strategies for qualitative research.* Mill Valley, CA: Sociology Press.

Graue, M. E., & Walsh, D. J. (1998). *Studying children in context: Theories, methods, and ethics.* Thousand Oaks, CA: Sage.

Hatch, J. A. (1995). Studying childhood as a cultural invention: A rationale and framework. In J. A. Hatch (Ed.), *Qualitative research in early childhood settings* (pp. 117–133). Westport, CT: Praeger.

Hatch, J. A. (2002). *Doing qualitative research in education settings.* Albany: State University of New York Press.

Hatch, J. A., & Barclay-McLaughlin, G. (2006). Qualitative research: Paradigms and possibilities. In B. Spodek & O. Saracho (Eds.), *Handbook of research on the education of young children* (2nd ed., pp. 497–514). Mahwah, NJ: Erlbaum.

Hatch, J. A., & Bondy, E. (1984). A double dose of the same medicine: Implications from a naturalistic study of summer school reading instruction. *Urban Education, 19*, 29–38.

Hatch, J. A., & Wisniewski, R. (1995). Life history and narrative: Questions, issues, and exemplary works. In J. A. Hatch & R. Wisniewski (Eds.), *Life history and narrative* (pp. 113–136). London: Falmer Press.

Krueger, R. A. (1994). *Focus groups: A practical guide for applied research.* Thousand Oaks, CA: Sage.

Kuhn, T. S. (1970). *The structure of scientific revolutions.* Chicago: University of Chicago Press.

Leedy, P. D. (1997). *Practical research: Planning and design.* Upper Saddle River, NJ: Merrill.

Lincoln, Y. S. (1995). Emerging criteria for quality in qualitative and interpretive inquiry. *Qualitative Inquiry, 1*, 275–289.

Lincoln, Y. S., & Guba, E. G. (1985). *Naturalistic inquiry.* Beverly Hills, CA: Sage.

Maxwell, J. A. (1996). *Qualitative research design: An interactive approach.* Thousand Oaks, CA: Sage.

Merriam, S. B. (1988). *Case study research in education: A qualitative approach.* San Francisco: Jossey-Bass.

Miles, M. B., & Huberman, A. M. (1994). *Qualitative data analysis: A sourcebook of new methods.* Newbury Park, CA: Sage.

Mishler, E. G. (1986). *Research interviewing: Context and narrative.* Cambridge, MA: Harvard University Press.

Morgan, D. L. (1997). *Focus groups as qualitative research* (2nd ed.). Newbury Park, CA: Sage.

Patton, M. Q. (1990). *Qualitative research and evaluation methods.* Newbury Park, CA: Sage.

Polkinghorne, D. E. (1995). Narrative configuration and qualitative analysis. In J. A. Hatch & R. Wisniewski (Eds.), *Life history and narrative* (pp. 5–24). London: Falmer Press.

Salkind, N. J. (1991). *Exploring research.* New York: Macmillan.

Schram, T. H. (2006). *Conceptualizing and composing qualitative research* (2nd ed). Upper Saddle River, NJ: Pearson/Prentice Hall.

Seidman, I. (1998). *Interviewing as qualitative research: A guide for researchers in education and the social sciences.* New York: Teachers College Press.

Smith, L. M. (1979). An evolving logic of participant observation, educational ethnography, and other case studies. *Review of Research in Education, 6*, 316–377.

Spradley, J. P. (1979). *The ethnographic interview.* New York: Holt, Rinehart, & Winston.

Spradley, J. P. (1980). *Participant observation.* New York: Holt, Rinehart, & Winston.

Strauss, A. L. (1987). *Qualitative analysis for social scientists.* Cambridge, England: Cambridge University Press.

Strauss, A. L., & Corbin, J. (1998). *Basics of qualitative research: Grounded theory procedures and techniques.* Newbury Park, CA: Sage.

Van Maanen, J. (1988). *Tales of the field: On writing ethnography.* Chicago: University of Chicago Press.

Van Manen, M. (1990). *Researching lived experience: Human science for an action sensitive pedagogy.* Albany: State University of New York Press.

Wolcott, H. F. (1988). Ethnographic research in education. In R. M. Jaeger (Ed.), *Complimentary methods for research in education*. Washington, DC: American Educational Research Association.

Yin, R. K. (1994). *Case study research: Design and methods*. Thousand Oaks, CA: Sage.

Yow, V. R. (1994). *Recording oral history: A practical guide for social scientists*. Thousand Oaks, CA: Sage.

Contributors

Nesrin Bakir, Tony Byungho Lee, Ya-hui Chung, and **Kayoun Chung** are current or former graduate students in the College of Education at the University of Illinois at Urbana-Champaign, USA. As members of the digital video group that collaborated on their chapter, they have made extensive use of digital video in their field-based research.

Karina Davis is a Research Fellow within the Centre for Equity and Innovation in Early Childhood (CEIEC) in the Faculty of Education at the University of Melbourne, Australia. She works predominantly within the CEIEC on research projects that explore children's and/or adults' perceptions, understandings, and identities and how these intersect with cultural diversity. She employs qualitative research methodologies both within the research she is part of at the CEIEC and within her own research projects.

Lisa S. Goldstein is an Associate Professor of Curriculum and Instruction at the University of Texas at Austin, USA. She is the director of the early childhood teacher education program, teaches undergraduate and graduate classes focused on theory, curriculum, and teaching in early childhood education, and offers specialized coursework in qualitative research methodologies. Her research interests center around the teaching practices and decision making of preservice and practicing kindergarten and primary grade teachers in public school contexts.

Susan Grieshaber is a Professor at the Queensland University of Technology, Brisbane, Australia. She has continued to learn about research methods since completing her doctoral studies in 1993 and now teaches graduate courses in research methodology and early childhood education as well as working with teacher education students. Sue is the author of *Rethinking Parent and Child Conflict* (2004) and has co-edited *Embracing Identities in Early Childhood Education* (2001) and *Practical Transformations and Transformational Practices* (2005).

J. Amos Hatch is a Professor of Theory and Practice in Teacher Education at the University of Tennessee–Knoxville, USA. He teaches graduate courses in early childhood education and qualitative research and works with teacher education students preparing to teach in urban-multicultural settings. He has been doing and writing about early childhood qualitative research since the mid-1980s, and he served for five years as editor of *The International Journal of Qualitative Studies in Education.* This is his fourth book related to qualitative research.

Janice A. Jipson is a Professor of Interdisciplinary Studies in Curriculum at National Louis University, USA, where she teaches courses in qualitative and action research. She is one of the founders of the Reconceptualizing Early Childhood Education Special Interest Group and is editor of the early childhood series, *Rethinking Childhood Education.* She has written extensively about narrative- and arts-based research, including several books: *Daredevil Research: Re-creating Analytic Practice* with Nicholas Paley; *Resistance and Representation: Rethinking Early Childhood Education* with Richard Johnson; and *Questions of You and the Struggle of Collaborative Life,* also with Nicholas Paley.

Carrie Lobman is an Assistant Professor of Elementary and Early Childhood Education at Rutgers, the State University of New Jersey, USA. She teaches courses in elementary and early childhood education and research. Her research interests include play, a performatory and improvisational approach to human development, and early childhood teacher education and professional development.

Glenda MacNaughton directs the Centre for Equity and Innovation in Early Childhood (CEIEC), a University of Melbourne (Australia) research center. With CEIEC colleagues, she is currently researching how gender, class, and race construct young children's learning, human rights in the early childhood curriculum, and staff–parent relations in early childhood. Dr. MacNaughton has a long-standing interest in reconceptualist research in early childhood, and she has written extensively about the ethics and politics of researching in the field.

Kagendo Mutua is an Associate Professor of Special Education at the University of Alabama, USA. Her research revolves around cross-cultural studies of transition and secondary programming for adolescents with severe/multiple disabilities and their families in Kenya and the United States. Her work is published in several journals, including *Journal of Special Education, International Journal of Disability, Development and Education,* and *Educational Studies.* She has also co-edited a volume with Beth Blue Swadener, *Decolonizing Research in Cross-Cultural Contexts: Critical Personal Narratives,* and is a co-editor of a book series, *Research in Africa, Caribbean, and The Middle East.*

Elizabeth P. Quintero, an Associate Professor of Early Childhood at New York University (USA), teaches graduate courses in early childhood education, focusing on families and young children in multilingual, multicultural communities. She has published books and articles documenting child and family strengths through qualitative research, most recently, *Refugee and Immigrant Family Voices: Experience, and Education* (in press) and *Problem Posing With Multicultural Children's Literature: Developing Critical Early Childhood Curricula* (2004).

Stuart Reifel is a Professor of Curriculum Instruction and Educational Administration at The University of Texas at Austin, USA, where he is W. K. Kellogg Endowed Fellow. He is adviser for graduate studies in early childhood education. After five years teaching nursery school and kindergarten, he has studied early childhood play (often in collaboration with graduate students), edited *Play & Culture Studies* and *Advances in Early Education and Day Care*, and written on curricular and developmental meanings of play. He is former president of The Association for the Study of Play.

Jeanette Rhedding-Jones is a Professor in Early Childhood Education, Oslo University College, Norway. She teaches graduate courses in qualitative research methodologies, critical issues for practice, and theories of knowledge. In Norway, she is working with people who have professional experience with children aged one to six in preschool day care centers *(barnehager)*. She has been doing early childhood research since the early 1980s, and publishing internationally about it since 1991. Her recent book, *What Is Research? Methodological Practices and New Approaches,* was published in 2005.

Frances O'Connell Rust is a Professor of Teacher Education in the Department of Teaching and Learning at the New York University Steinhardt School of Education, USA. She was a contributing author to the National Academy of Education's *Preparing Teachers for a Changing World* (2005). She is the author of several articles and books on teacher education, most recently, *Taking Action Through Teacher Research* (2003), which she co-edited with Ellen Meyers. She is past president of the National Association of Early Childhood Teacher Educators (NAECTE), Executive Editor of *Teachers and Teaching—Theory and Practice,* and Associate Editor of *The Journal of Early Childhood Teacher Education.*

Sharon Ryan is an Associate Professor of Early Childhood Education at Rutgers, the State University of New Jersey, USA, where she teaches courses in qualitative methodology and early childhood curriculum. Dr Ryan's research interests include early childhood curriculum and policy, teacher education, and the potential of critical theories for rethinking early childhood research and practice.

Kylie Smith is a Research Fellow at the University of Melbourne's Centre for Equity and Innovation in Early Childhood and Director at the University of Melbourne's Swanston Street Children's Centre (Australia). She has been researching with practitioners, parents, children, and policy makers exploring how critical and postmodern theories can support change in the classroom to create curriculum, policy, and practice for social justice.

Beth Blue Swadener is a Professor of Early Childhood Education and Policy Studies at Arizona State University, USA. Her qualitative research focuses on social policy, professional development, dual language programs, and child and family issues in Africa. She has published seven books, including *Decolonizing Research in Cross-Cultural Context* and *Power and Voice in Research with Children* and numerous articles and chapters. She is also active in a number of social justice and child advocacy projects.

Daniel J. Walsh is a Professor of Early Childhood Education at the University of Illinois at Urbana-Champaign, USA. He teaches a two-course sequence in the undergraduate Early Childhood Program and graduate courses in early childhood education and research methodology. He has done extensive fieldwork in early schooling using digital video, most recently in kindergartens in Japan. He is presently involved in a cross-cultural study with colleagues in Japan and Germany on early childhood educators' beliefs about children's development.

Index